LOVE IN A TORN LAND

Also by Jean Sasson

The Rape of Kuwait
Princess: A True Story of Life Behind the Veil in Saudi Arabia
Daughters of Arabia
Desert Royal
Ester's Child
Mayada, Daughter of Iraq

For more information on Jean Sasson and her books, see her
website at
www.jeansasson.com

Love in a Torn Land

One woman's daring escape from Saddam's
poison gas attacks on the Kurdish people of Iraq

Jean Sasson

Doubleday

LONDON · TORONTO · SYDNEY · AUCKLAND · JOHANNESBURG

TRANSWORLD PUBLISHERS
61–63 Uxbridge Road, London W5 5SA
a division of The Random House Group Ltd
www.booksattransworld.co.uk

First published in Great Britain
in 2007 by Doubleday
a division of Transworld Publishers

This book is a work of non-fiction based on the life, experiences and recollections of
Joanna Al-Askari Hussain. In some limited cases names of people, places, dates, sequences or
the detail of events have been changed solely to protect the privacy of others. The author has
stated to the publishers that, except in such minor respects not affecting the substantial
accuracy of the work, the contents of this book are true.

A CIP catalogue record for this book
is available from the British Library.

ISBN 9780385611725 (cased)
9780385610872 (tpb)

Addresses for Random House Group Ltd companies outside the UK
can be found at: www.randomhouse.co.uk
The Random House Group Ltd Reg. No. 954009

The Random House Group Ltd makes every effort to ensure that the papers used in its
books are made from trees that have been legally sourced from well-managed and credibly
certified forests. Our paper procurement policy can be found at:
www.randomhouse.co.uk/paper.htm

4pt Bembo by
raphic Art Ltd

in Great Britain by
plc, Chatham, Kent

9 7 5 3 1

Jean Sasson's dedication:

To Roxanne

Joanna Al-Askari Hussain's dedication:

To my own courageous *peshmerga*, Sarbast,
and our two sons, Kosha and Dylan

To Auntie Aisha

To the brave wives of the *peshmerga*

When I was a child, I built a wall of hatred around me.
When I was asked, 'From what did you build this wall?'
I replied, 'From the stones of insults.'

Proverb, author unknown

Contents

Note from Jean Sasson

On my life's journey I have travelled to many corners of the world. During my travels, I have been privileged to meet and come to know many fascinating women, some of whom I've shared with the world through the pages of my books. During the writing of *Love in a Torn Land*, the true story of a Kurdish woman, once again I found myself in a unique position to explore an exotic culture while coming to know a true-life heroine, Joanna Al-Askari Hussain. I consider my journey with Joanna a great gift, which I now pass to my readers through the pages of this book.

Note from Joanna Al-Askari Hussain

I have described to Jean Sasson the details of my life, including what I saw and felt during the terrifying days and nights my husband and I were fleeing for our lives. We survived extreme physical danger, including chemical attacks and bombings. While everything in this book happened to me, it is important for the reader to remember that during the chaos of war I was occupied with surviving. I was not keeping a diary. In the event that the confusion of war and the fog of time have obscured my memory, I may have erred as to the exact timing and detail of certain events. But the reader can be confident that I lived through every incident described.

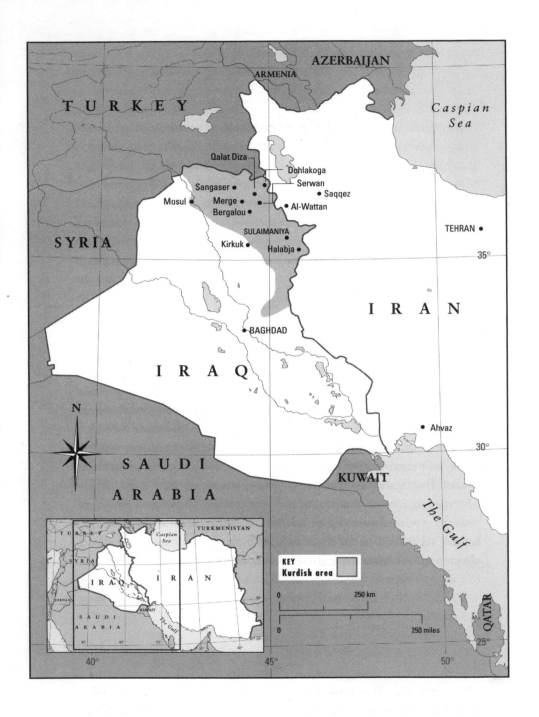

AZERBAIJAN

ARMENIA

TURKEY

Caspian Sea

Qalat Diza

Dohlakoga

Serwan

Sangaser

Saqqez

Mosul

Merge

Al-Wattan

Bergalou

SYRIA

SULAIMANIYA

TEHRAN

Kirkuk

Halabja

35°

IRAN

BAGHDAD

IRAQ

N

Ahvaz

30°

SAUDI

ARABIA

KUWAIT

The Gulf

KEY
Kurdish area

0   250 km

0   250 miles

QATAR

25°

40°   45°   50°

TURKEY   *Caspian Sea*   TURKMENISTAN

SYRIA

IRAQ   IRAN

JORDAN

SAUDI
ARABIA   KUWAIT   *The Gulf*

Prologue

Suddenly I was startled by the roar of an unexpected artillery bombardment. While we were always subject to attacks, our enemy was off their usual schedule. Generally we could set our watches by the afternoon and evening bombardments.

I felt a rush of confusion. I was too far from our house to run for safety, so I darted off the trail, crouching, waiting for an opportunity to dash home and take cover in a corner room.

Just then I noticed something strange. These artillery shells were different. Once airborne, they fell silently, but when they landed dirty white clouds puffed up from them. My mouth dry with anxiety, I continued watching the strange spectacle, not letting myself imagine the worst scenario.

Then another strange thing occurred: birds began falling out of the sky.

I instinctively cried out, 'It's raining birds!'

The combination of silent bombs and plunging birds stirred my disbelief. I whipped my head from side to side, searching all around me. The edge of the afternoon sky was dotted with flashes of colour as gaudy specks plummeted to earth: more birds. The poor creatures were fluttering helplessly, falling as heavily as stones – down, down, down to the ground.

I winced as I heard dreadful thumps all around me. I had always loved birds. I couldn't bear to see the pitiful sight.

If birds were dropping from the sky, I knew that I should move, and move fast, to the shelter. But I was frozen in place.

I searched the trail for my husband. I knew him well. If he knew that I was in danger, he would come to me. But perhaps he would think I was already in the shelter. Because of the suddenness of the danger, perhaps he would be forced to seek cover in the communal shelter in the centre of the village.

I bit my lower lip as I continued to look for my husband's brawny frame, feeling a rush of concern for his safety.

Just then a bird fell directly at my feet, the dull thud of its impact causing me to gasp. The creature was in great distress. Its tiny black beak scissored vigorously and then more slowly, as it pitifully sucked at the air.

I was smart enough to know that animals provide the first indication of a chemical attack. Was this the poisonous gas attack promised by Ali Al-Majid? With that chilling thought I threw caution to the wind, leaping to my feet and sprinting down the path home, fearing for my life.

Everything was a blur, but I caught sight of an untethered mule as it snapped and bucked into a frenzy. It hustled past me on the path, trotting so fast that it seemed to dance. Never had I seen a mule move that rapidly. I kept running, trying to avoid the splayed birds strewn in my path. Finally I dashed into the house, gasping for breath.

Safe!

Seconds later, my husband burst in through the door.

Mouth open, panting, I stared at him without speaking.

He yelled, 'Joanna, upon my honour, this is a chemical attack!'

Yes! I knew it! I now recognized the unpleasant odour I had heard about from survivors of previous chemical attacks: a smell like rotten apples, onions and garlic.

My husband moved quickly, reaching up to a shelf above the side door. 'Joanna, put this on!' He handed me a gas mask, then pulled a second mask on to his own face and tightened the small bands that fastened it around his head.

I held my breath while I fumbled with the strap.

In all the excitement, the simple task felt cumbersome.

While we had discussed the masks several times, with my husband urging me to familiarize myself with the apparatus, I had stupidly failed to do so. Finally he grabbed the mask from my hands and slipped it into place over my head and face.

Hand in hand, we ran to our earth shelter and crawled down into it as far back as possible.

Once settled, I realized that I had been holding my breath the whole way. I hungrily drew in a much needed mouthful of air but all I managed to do was strain my throat muscles. I could not capture a single breath.

Desperate, I yanked at the mask until it slid from my face and shouted, 'I can't breathe in this thing!' Finally I had his full attention. He wiggled towards me and, grabbing my mask from my hands, examined it.

I felt as if I was about to explode and I was forced to breathe in the foul gases. I felt as if my eyes had been set on fire. The pain was so intense that hot needles probing my eyeballs could not have hurt any more. I could not stand it another moment. I started rubbing my eyes with my hands, not caring that I had been warned never to rub my eyes during a chemical attack.

'The gas is in my eyes,' I screamed, as I began to choke on the poisoned air that was fogging the shelter.

The gases were settling low over the ground, filling the shallow dugout. My husband moved quickly, crawling out of the shelter and then pulling me out behind him. With my mask in one hand, he grabbed me with the other, pulling me back into the house.

I thought we should run up the mountains, for I distinctly remembered my husband telling me that one should seek low shelter during a conventional bombing attack and climb as high as possible during a chemical attack. But first I must have a working mask.

My throat was aching, my eyes were stinging. I crumpled to the floor and my husband knelt beside me. A clammy fog was clotting my senses and muddling my thinking.

Well, hello death, I thought to myself.

I Childhood

1

Little Peshmerga Girl

Baghdad
Saturday 8 July 1972

In a country where Kurds are hated, I am a Kurd.

Although I was born and grew up in Baghdad, my heart belonged to Sulaimaniya. Baghdad was the city of my Arab father and Sulaimaniya was the city of my Kurdish mother. Sulaimaniya is 331 kilometres north of Baghdad, in the area known as Kurdistan. For ten long months of every year, from September through to June, I plodded along in dusty Baghdad, dreaming of July and August, which I called the 'happy months', when I would leave behind the drab brown plains of Mesopotamia and journey with my mother and siblings to the colour-splashed mountains and valleys of Kurdistan.

I well remember one particular day in 1972 when I was ten. I was so excited about our forthcoming trip that I was called a pest by my mother and siblings, who were getting ready for our departure. I felt ignored. But when my dear uncle Aziz, who had lived with us for several years, noticed me standing listlessly in the kitchen, he led me into the back garden, where a flowering bougainvillea climbed our garden wall. To help the time pass faster he encouraged me to pick lemons and *naranjas*. We had a wide variety of fruit trees and berry bushes in our back garden, including oranges, apricots, plums, *naranjas* and dates. How fortunate I was to live in a land where luscious fruits grew like colourful jewels all around me. Of all the fruits, the *naranja*, an orange-like citrus fruit, was my favourite. When it was ripe we squeezed it and poured the juice into ice trays to freeze. My mother would serve frozen cubes of *naranja* in glasses filled with icy water and sugar, while family and visitors lounged on the veranda.

I loved such occasions. Acting as if I was grown up, I crossed my legs like a lady and sipped the delicious drink, loudly interjecting my opinions into the adult conversation. Because at ten I was the youngest child, and greatly loved, they pretended to take me seriously.

To my excitement, my older brother Ra'ad, who was eighteen years old and set to begin college in the autumn, appeared at the back door and called out, 'Joanna! Go and watch out for the taxi.'

Uncle Aziz nodded, holding out his hands for the fruit I had picked. I dashed through the kitchen, where Mother and Muna, my fourteen-year-old sister, were preparing a picnic of chicken sandwiches and date cookies to eat while we were on the road. I skipped through the house to the front porch, where I stood first on one foot and then on the other, impatient, willing the taxi to arrive so that we could leave for the bus station.

As I kept a watchful gaze on the boulevard, I wished that we owned a car so that we could travel to the north in style. The families of our Al-Askari cousins all owned expensive cars because they were rich. Unfortunately, we were poor. But, even if we had been wealthy, my father would not have been permitted a licence to drive a motorized vehicle because he was unable to hear the warning roars of the cars, buses and donkey carts that raced through the streets of Baghdad.

My father had been deaf since he was a young boy.

His only means of transportation was an old blue bicycle. I stared at his bicycle, parked against the garden fence. How I longed to jump on it and ride away! But I was not allowed on it, although my brothers were. Ra'ad balanced on the back while Sa'ad, Muna's twin, perched on the front. I was envious of my brothers; such a thing was not considered proper for a girl in Baghdad.

To take my mind off the injustices of my life, I forced myself to concentrate on the street in case the taxi came.

It was fun to watch all the activity. The kaleidoscope of a Baghdad morning was in full swing. Human figures shimmered like a mirage, with men hurrying to reach the neighbourhood café while harried housewives rushed to the market. Older boys were amusing themselves with marbles, calling out their negligible bets, while small boys shouted as they played hopscotch. There were few girls in public view because in those days respectable girls were expected to remain inside once the school year had finished.

I was thankful that my mother didn't make me help with the housework, because I hated chores. Although she maintained the cleanest house in all Baghdad, and my older siblings had specific duties, I was excused because I was the youngest.

'Salt! Salt!' The cry of the nomad camel driver drew my attention as he made his weekly pass through the neighbourhood. Many were the mornings I had heard his hoarse cries while I was still warm under the bed covers, so I stared at him with interest.

He kept up a steady bellow. 'Salt! Salt!'

Dressed in a frayed grey shirt and worn brown trousers, he was a dark-skinned, craggy-faced man with arched eyebrows. A knotted rope of red and blue wool was looped from his arm around the long neck of a small camel. I instantly loved that camel, with her blonde wavy coat and bowed lips curled into a smile, shuffling and rocking as if she was moving to the beat of a song. Her precious cargo was packed in rough cloth bags that swayed on either side. When her master tapped her on the rump with his stick, she belched a rumbling complaint and frothing saliva gathered at the corners of her open mouth.

'Salt! Salt!' the hawker yelled as he puffed on a cigarette that hung from the side of his mouth. He raised his eyes to meet mine, plucking the cigarette out of his mouth as a hopeful smile crossed his face. His eyes widened and his head bobbed with anticipation.

I shook my head and waved him off, aware that Mother still had an unopened bag of his salt in the kitchen.

He shrugged good-naturedly and turned away, shouting, 'Salt! Salt!'

My eyes were lured to a young peasant woman dressed in a billowy blouse, a colourful skirt and a carefully twisted turban with a large round tray balanced on top. White cloths were wrapped around her feet and ankles, for protection from the heat. I knew enough to know that she had come from the south, from an area of Iraq called the Marshes. Women from that region were known to be as beautiful as the landscape. She was peddling buffalo cream stored in round wooden containers on the tray on her head.

I watched as she ambled out of a side street, with a trail of mangy neighbourhood cats at her shuffling feet. The cats darted from side to side, miaowing expectantly at the scent of the fragrant cream. Despite her youth and beauty, she appeared weighed down with resigned despair.

I felt sorry for her and if I had had money in my pocket I would have purchased all the cream her buffalo could produce. I was pleased to see a customer approach, his outstretched palms indicating the quantity of cream he wanted to buy. The unsmiling girl unhooked a thin steel needle hanging from her waist, reached over her head and grasped one of the wooden containers. Then, using the needle as a tool, she sliced the congealed buffalo cream. The cats looked on hopefully, at the ready for any spills, but the girl was too skilled for such carelessness. After dropping a few coins into her waiting hand, the customer left with his precious purchase.

The cats around the cream pedlar's feet increased in number, but she didn't seem to notice them, or me, as she slunk past our front gate. Her life must be very hard for her to be so permanently gloomy. Her petulant lips made that clear. As she strolled away, I tried to imagine that young woman's life, so unlike my own, for I knew even at my young age that Iraq was populated by a huge variety of people with vastly differing lifestyles and beliefs.

After the First World War, and the defeat of the Ottoman Empire, the British and the French resolved that three geographic regions would be joined together to make up modern Iraq. The central part of Iraq was the largely limestone plateau where Baghdad is located. Although modern Baghdad is not considered a beautiful city, it had a unique and glorious past, boasting palaces, mosques, markets and gardens.

Iraq's second region was the Marshes, the wet lowland plain of the south. A marvellous variety of fish and birds and plant life was abundant there. An old Arabic text says that the distinctive landscape resulted from a devastating flood so powerful that mud houses melted back into mud while the land itself split into thousands of tiny islands. The survivors of the great flood lived in huts that were boats, called mash-houf huts, pieced together with reeds and bitumen.

Iraq's third region was the mountainous north, famed for its snow-clad mountains and lush forests. It was a place of beauty with scenic mountain ranges, waterfalls and orchards. Because of its cool temperatures, many holiday resorts had sprung up in that area. While Arab Iraqis simply referred to the region as northern Iraq, Kurds called the area by its true name, Kurdistan – our destination that day.

I searched the street once more for the taxi, and caught sight of a group of young neighbourhood bullies, a gang of four boys near my own age who always took great pleasure in ridiculing me for being a Kurd. When our eyes locked, they began to leap about on their bare feet and jeer, their laughter interspersed with hateful chants: 'House of the Kurds! Kurd girl!' One particularly spiteful boy laughed the loudest, shouting '*La! La!* Girl of the deaf-and-dumb!'

My eyes met his.

For a moment his words drove all the power and feeling out of me, but my passiveness lasted only as long as it took me to get off the porch. I shouted, 'Hey!' barely pausing long enough to gather several loose stones from under Mother's sweet-smelling *yass* bush, which I tossed as hard as I could. I had never reacted in such an aggressive manner before, but recently I had resolved to be more like my father, a bold man who always defended himself, even if it meant a physical fight.

Unaccustomed to a girl defending herself, the boys were so startled that they turned and ran.

I hit one of the boys on his arm. When he shrieked, the others fell over their feet to avoid the same fate. How stupid they looked! I laughed aloud, feeling enormous satisfaction as I watched the cowards run down the street. That they were running from a girl made it all the more sweet.

I had never felt so powerful. Never would they frighten me again. Never!

I was smart enough to realize that I must hide my deed, for my family would be horrified to know that a daughter had behaved in such a rough manner. I quickly rubbed the dirt off my palms. When I glanced up to make certain that my tormentors had not returned, the taxi had finally arrived.

'He's here!' I cried out, running towards the house. I opened the door and shouted as loudly as I could, 'The taxi driver is here! Come on!'

It was a mad dash, with everyone rushing and grabbing suitcases from the front porch to pack in the boot.

The skinny taxi driver jumped out and shouted loudly as he directed the loading of our luggage. Although Mother had taught me not to stare at people, I gawked at his brown face, so wrinkled and worn. His hands were gnarled and he nervously rubbed them on his ragged, threadbare trousers. He was a poor man, I realized. Most people in Baghdad were poor.

I glanced at Daddy, Uncle Aziz and my brothers. Despite the fact that we were poor, too, they were all attired in neat, clean clothes, free from tears or holes. I glanced down at my bright pink dress. For the most part, Arabs in Baghdad wore dull colours, generally black or dark blue, but not we Kurds: we relished vivid colours. My pretty pink dress was freshly washed and ironed and smelled new, even though it was not.

Mother knew how to keep everything perfect. She kept her home and family so clean and tidy that it was possible that our enemies didn't know we were poor; certainly we didn't look poor. Perhaps our tidiness intensified their hatred.

The men were having difficulty closing the boot.

I helpfully pointed out, 'This taxi is leaning to one side.'

The taxi driver saw what I saw and began yelling directions as he inspected the weight on the tyres. The tyres looked thin, even to my untrained eye, but I decided to keep that information to myself. Mother might insist on cancelling the taxi and calling another. I did not want our trip to be delayed another moment, as I had been eagerly anticipating it since we had last left Sulaimaniya, a year ago in August.

When the taxi driver thought everything was secure, he slid into the driver's seat, shouting, '*Yella, yella*, let's go.'

Mother and Muna joined me in the back seat. Uncle Aziz came round to my side and gently pushed me to the centre. Although he would accompany us to the station, it had been decided that he would not go with us to Kurdistan.

In 1962, the year I was born, while my uncle was a student in

Sulaimaniya he was arrested for being a Kurd. The torture he endured changed his life for ever. After that he was unable to cope with life in the north, and so he had moved to Baghdad to live with his older sister, my mother. Even years after his torture, there were occasions when something would trigger bizarre behaviour. He might refuse to speak or to come out of his room. He was incapable of attending college or holding down a job. But he was a greatly loved uncle, always willing to join in silly games with me. So he would remain behind in Baghdad without us, while we visited my grandmother Ameena, aunts and cousins in Sulaimaniya.

The taxi driver shouted loudly that he was in a hurry and we must go. Ra'ad and Sa'ad quickly got into the front seat next to him.

As the taxi pulled away from the kerb, I remembered that I had forgotten to say goodbye to my father. He rarely travelled to Kurdistan with us. He was not Kurdish himself, but even if he had been, he would have stayed behind in Baghdad to work, for there was never enough money for him to join his family on holiday. Poor Daddy.

As we drove away, I twisted around until I could see his face through the window of the taxi. His brown eyes were crinkling, his lips stretching into a smile.

I stared back at his kindly face until he reached down to pick something up from the ground. His scalp was exposed, his hair plastered down in some places and sticking out in others. He had obviously worked up a sweat during the loading of the taxi. Suddenly I had a queasy feeling in my stomach, a flutter of unexplained apprehension about my father's well-being. But I quickly pushed the feeling aside as we made our way into the thick of midday Baghdad traffic.

Unlike most cities, Baghdad did not grow from a small village but was designed according to a masterplan. That was in AD 762, when Caliph Abu Jafar Al-Mansour had the idea of creating a circular city with three distinct circular enclosures on the west bank of the River Tigris. Caliph Al-Mansour ruled from the innermost enclosure, the army was housed in the second enclosure and the citizens lived in the outermost enclosure. But modern Baghdad had spread well beyond these carefully laid out circles, losing what charm it might have had.

With only a few main roads, Baghdad was chaotic as well. Our driver nosed his taxi on to the thoroughfare, competing with hordes of people, donkey carts, cars and minibuses.

Colourful billboards advertised Western products. Others touted the advantages Iraqis were supposedly enjoying under the current government of the Baathist party, the political party that had come to power during yet another government coup four years before, in 1968. I had overheard my brother Ra'ad jokingly call the Baathists the 'come-back kids', because they had been in power once before, in 1963, but had been quickly deposed because of the disorder and malice demonstrated during their first attempt at governing. But now everyone said the Baathists were firmly entrenched.

Although I was too young to understand politics, I was aware of the destructive effects of the 1958 revolution, which had caused deaths in my family and my father to lose his business. More attentive than most children of my age, I was aware of optimistic whispers regarding Iraq's new government. I knew that the adults wanted only one thing: an end to the confusion and upheaval that occurred each time there was a change of government in Iraq. But on that sun-drenched July day, no one could have guessed the heartbreak and terror that the Baathist government would ultimately bring to all Iraqis.

In years past our family had travelled by train from Baghdad to Kirkuk and from there to Sulaimaniya by car. But that summer of 1972, Mother said we must save money, so we were to travel by bus. Soon we arrived at the Nahdha bus station in downtown Baghdad. More travel bedlam erupted as we piled out of the taxi and waited while Ra'ad, Sa'ad and Uncle Aziz unloaded and stacked our bags. A porter appeared and for a small tip eagerly helped transport the luggage. We walked hurriedly to the area of the station where the minibuses to Sulaimaniya were parked haphazardly, awaiting passengers.

Suddenly we were confronted by one of the bus drivers, an older balding man with a thick moustache, so long that it drooped down on either side to his chin. He was extremely friendly and encouraged us aboard his bus, claiming that he was such an experienced bus driver that he would cut an hour off the trip. Most importantly, he declared that children under the age of twelve could ride free. We gratefully boarded that bus because money was always short. I was very thin and small for my age, so there was no question that I was under age twelve. Muna was very petite and could have passed for twelve as well, but Mother refused to lie.

The well-worn bus creaked as we slowly pulled away from the station and once again we weaved through the busy streets. The bus lurched through the commercial area of Baghdad, where most of the city's ancient souks and factories with tall chimneys were located. We were soon on Highway 4, a modern road to Kirkuk, on our way north to Sulaimaniya, the city where Mother was born.

Although the bus could easily transport twenty-five people, only eleven were on board. Mother and Ra'ad conferred about that oddity and Ra'ad queried it with the driver, but he brushed off my brother's concerns with a wink.

'This gives us more room,' Muna whispered, with a hesitant smile on her face. She had a point.

My sister Muna was so timid and nervous that everyone in our family felt they must protect her. She and her twin, Sa'ad, were opposites in every way. Sa'ad was dark-skinned, physically strong and personally forceful. Muna, on the other hand, was porcelain pale, fragile and painfully docile. So opposite were they that many people accused us of mocking their intelligence when told that they were twins.

I was not there to witness the day when Muna and Sa'ad were born, but I had heard the tale of it more than once. In Mother's third pregnancy, no one suspected that she was expecting twins, not even her doctor. A few hours after she went into labour, a noticeably disinterested nurse appeared and presented my father with a hefty baby boy. While family members were delighted at the birth of a second son, everyone soon grew worried when Mother continued shrieking from behind a pair of closed doors. When her cries finally subsided, the same nurse, no longer indifferent but suddenly possessed with so much energy that she was wheezing from excitement, rushed from the delivery room and straight to my father with a second baby.

Everyone present gaped at the sight of the tiny bundle in the nurse's hands. The nurse declared the new baby a twin to Sa'ad, who was twice her size. No one could believe what she was saying. Several Kurdish relatives from up north accused her of playing a spiteful joke on our family because Mother was a Kurd.

But they were wrong. Muna was not a joke. My sister was real, although she was so small that she had to remain at the hospital for several weeks. Even when Muna was discharged, the doctor refused to guarantee her survival. Mother was told to swaddle her little body in strips of cotton for the first few months of her life to protect her translucent skin, which was so delicate that it bled when stroked. Swaddling was also necessary because there were no baby clothes in all Iraq to fit an infant much smaller than a doll.

I felt enormous affection for my sister, comprehending that I must shield her from the cruel world, despite the fact that I was younger by four years.

As soon as we had left the city, the passengers napped or gazed out of the windows, but having been born with an inquisitive temperament, I made it my business to inspect all the passengers.

Two Kurdish men were sitting quietly at the front of the bus. Their traditional costumes of turbans and distinctive baggy pants identified them as our own kind. I wondered if they were Kurdish freedom fighters, known as *peshmerga*, about whom I had heard such romantic stories. But of course, even if they were, they would have to conceal that fact, for to be a *peshmerga* in Iraq was to risk an automatic death sentence.

The younger of the two Kurds was a gigantic young man with the broad shoulders and thick arms of a weight-lifter. But his wide dreamy eyes and kindly mien belied his physical power. A fringe of black curly hair escaped from under his turban at the nape of his neck. The second man was older, small and wiry. I stared at his unusual sagging, creased eyelids. Nevertheless he looked jolly, glittering with life.

The other four passengers were a couple and their two small children. By their attire I knew they were Arab Iraqis. The husband was dressed in the *dishdasha*, a shirt-like, ankle-length white robe worn by many native Iraqi men. His wife was wearing a black cloak over a blue dress. The children were dressed in Western-style clothing and they stared in an unfriendly way at our Kurdish costumes.

Although Mother and I were the only two members of our family who routinely wore traditional Kurdish costumes, on that day we were all wearing our best Kurdish clothes. Ra'ad and Sa'ad looked dashing in their voluminous Kurdish blouses and wide trousers belted with sashes. Typical Kurdish caps, called *klaw*, were perched on their heads and they wore sandals known as *klash* on their feet. The three females in the family were decked out in brightly coloured Kurdish dresses. While I was in my favourite shade of deep pink, Muna was in bright blue and Mother in sunny yellow. Our girlish heads were bare, while Mother's black hair was covered with a dazzling golden scarf with clinking silver coins sewn to the edges.

To be friendly, Mother offered the Arab children some of our date cookies. But their parents reacted as though the cookies were poisoned. They yanked the hands of their children, curtly telling Mother, '*La! La!* No! No!'

My surprised mother fell back against her seat. I was shocked by their rudeness, despite the fact that I was old enough to understand a fact of life: most Iraqi Arabs hated Kurds.

Mother quickly recovered herself and offered her own children the treats.

I felt so insulted that I took enormous pleasure in munching the cookies, loudly announcing to everyone how delicious they were. I felt vindicated when I saw the Arab kids stare reproachfully at their parents.

The older of the two Kurdish men looked around, smiling, and offered boiled sweets to all the children. This time the two Arab kids moved their little hands rapidly. They each grabbed a sweet, removed the wrapping and popped it into their mouth with such speed that their parents couldn't stop them.

I laughed out loud at the parents' surprised faces, and the two men laughed with me, even the one who was so quiet that he had not spoken a word during the trip.

The journey would take nearly nine hours. We were the only passengers travelling all the way to Sulaimaniya. The family of Arabs, we learned, would be leaving the bus at a small Sunni village an hour or so out of Baghdad, and the oldest of the two Kurdish men said that they would disembark at a village outside Kirkuk.

The day was unbearably hot. A large fly buzzed around the bus, and I feebly swatted at it. Just as I drifted off into sleep, I was startled awake by the angry voice of the Arab bus driver, who had been so friendly before. I could only assume that the heat had brought on a bad temper.

'You! Kurds! Be quiet back there! Noisy kids give me a headache!' he shouted.

I felt affronted: we hadn't made a sound. I arched my neck proudly. I glanced at the Arab family. The husband and wife exchanged a look.

I dug my fingers into my palms, itching to react, yet knowing that with Mother and my siblings around I could do nothing. I looked hopefully at the two Kurdish men to see if they might defend us from this unprovoked attack, but their profiles showed that their stares were frozen, studying the landscapes we passed. They were obviously unwilling to get into an altercation with the driver.

I was disappointed, but I told myself that if they were indeed *peshmerga* in disguise, they must protect their cover.

Before leaving Baghdad we had been warned that life for Kurds in the north had become extremely difficult, even dangerous. The Kurds were always suspected of fostering dissent and civil unrest and draconian new laws had been passed by the government. If a Kurd was found with a pair of binoculars, he would be hanged. If a Kurd owned a typewriter without permission, he could be arrested and tried. Cameras had always been suspect and now a camera with a zoom lens could cost a Kurd his life. Kurds could be arrested on a whim. An Arab might report a Kurd for criticizing the regime, and even if the report was untrue, the Kurd would be automatically punished.

My mother and older siblings shifted uncomfortably in their seats, but because we were Kurds and the discourteous driver was an Arab, no one dared speak.

The trip had lost its shine for me.

We soon arrived at a modest cluster of brown-brick houses on the outskirts of Baghdad, where the Arab family got off the bus. They gathered their belongings, which consisted of two old carrying cases, and scurried past us without a glance. They were effusive in expressing gratitude to the bus driver.

My soul burned for revenge.

They lived in a modest neighbourhood, typical for poor Iraqi families, where the houses were one-storey concrete buildings the same colour as the sand. On the flat roofs were drying clothes and an assortment of rusted metal chairs.

I was pleased to see the unfriendly Arabs leave.

Shortly afterwards we made another quick stop at a small, dirty petrol station. As we neared Kurdistan, petrol would become scarce because as a collective punishment the government limited petrol supplies to Kurds. The driver would have to look for roadside stalls where young Kurdish boys sold petrol out of plastic jugs.

When the bus got back on the road, everyone dozed until lunchtime, when Mother and Muna woke us, passing us chicken salad sandwiches and Fanta orange drinks Mother had purchased at the petrol station. Both Kurdish men were grateful when Mother quietly insisted that they share our sandwiches. But the bus driver refused her offer of a sandwich. He acted as if the sandwiches were contaminated.

Soon after that the flat earth fell away from us and we passed over a metal suspension bridge that spanned a gorge. For the first time I could see the green beauty of a rising mountain range. We would soon be in Kurdistan, the one place on earth that always made me feel confident and happy. Even at that young age, I knew that I belonged there and not in Baghdad.

'I love Kurdistan!' I announced to no one in particular, winning smiles from the two Kurdish men.

The Arab driver produced a disgusted grunt but made no comment.

It was illegal to call northern Iraq by its proper name, Kurdistan. But I felt brave because it was unlikely that a young girl like me would be punished. Besides, I knew that soon we would be at Grandmother Ameena's house and this troubling trip would be behind us.

The bus driver became less bad-tempered once we were in the cool of the Kurdish mountains. To my surprise he turned on a tape recorder which filled the interior of the bus with rousing Kurdish folk songs and he urged us all to sing along. Everyone knew that it was illegal to sing Kurdish songs that invoked nationalistic feelings, yet on occasion Kurdish folk songs could be heard even on Baghdad radio. The older of the two Kurdish men pretended to sing along with the music. I forgave him for I knew he was doing so in order to keep the peace, but I certainly wasn't going to perform at the command of that rude man.

Within an hour the bus came to a stop and the two Kurds took their leave. Holding their hands over their hearts, they said farewell and scrambled happily from the bus. They walked rapidly in the direction of a settlement clinging to the side of the mountain, where the tops of the houses were so low and close to one another that I believed that if I tried, I could use them as stepping stones up the mountain.

The bus moved on. By then we had been on that hot bus for over six hours. Weariness was setting in. But then the vehicle made an unexpected turn off the main highway, and the bus driver announced that we were stopping.

Mother quickly shouted in Kurdish, 'What? Where are you going?'

Her question was ignored.

Ra'ad repeated Mother's words in Arabic, since she was not fluent in the Arabic language.

The driver wobbled his head and lamely announced, 'A pick-up. A regular. He needs a ride to Sulaimaniya.'

Ra'ad translated for Mother. Her lips turned down in a scowl. She was not pleased with the turn of events.

The road was unpaved, and dust flew from under the wheels and in through the open windows, causing everyone to cough. Ra'ad got out of his seat and moved towards Mother to confer about the troubling situation, but just then there was a shocking noise: a rattle of gunfire.

The driver slammed on the brakes and my forehead struck the seat back in front of me.

Ra'ad stumbled backwards but caught his footing. He fell back on the seat and gave an involuntary gasp.

I was frightened. I looked at Mother, who motioned, 'Come, Joanna.'

I rushed to her side and peered through the window. I spotted a group of armed men moving stealthily down a winding path. What was happening?

We heard shouts. 'Off! Off the bus!'

The bus driver was the first to disembark but we were quick to file out and follow him.

Ra'ad looked at Mother, whispering, 'Bandits.'

Bandits! Were we being robbed? My heart started beating hard and fast.

When we had got off the bus I saw five armed men. They looked at us angrily.

Many people in Iraq were living in hopeless poverty. Desperate bandits materialized in every part of society. Even Kurds could be guilty of highway robbery. But the men holding us at gunpoint were not Kurds. Arab bandits would never have pity for us, even if they knew that Father was a full-blooded Arab. In fact, such information would most likely make them hate us all the more.

One of the bandits started shouting at the driver. We quickly understood that the driver was in league with the bandits. It was his task to travel around Iraq and lure unsuspecting passengers on to his bus. Then he drove them to prearranged meeting places in secluded areas to be robbed.

But it was clear from the bandits' chatter that they were disappointed. They were expecting more passengers. Nevertheless, it was certain that these men were going to rob us. Suddenly I could think of nothing but my beautiful black doll, which Auntie Fatima had brought back from London for me. Auntie Fatima was my father's younger sister, a brilliant woman who held a high government position. None of us had ever seen such a doll. She was made of black porcelain, with a perfect face and long lashes. Her dress was light green silk. Best of all, she even had matching underpants. The doll was so precious and unique that Mother said she was a collectible and put her in a box, saving her, she said, for 'special occasions'. I had pleaded for days before Mother had agreed that I could take her to Kurdistan, to show her off to my Kurdish cousins. Would the bandits take her from me?

I glanced up at Mother and from her worried expression I knew that she was anxious about more important things than my doll. Mother was frightened for our safety. She pulled Muna's arm, moving her close to her side. Ever since she was a young girl, many people had praised Muna for her beauty: she had honey-blonde colouring, light skin and perfect features. Perhaps Mother was worried that these men would want Muna for a bride, even though she was still very young. She held one arm firmly around Muna, and I saw her throw a meaningful look at Ra'ad and Sa'ad, signifying that they were to remain calm.

The bandits might well have believed my brothers to be a threat and capable of fighting back, especially Ra'ad, my older brother. Although he was not yet an adult, he was over six feet tall, towering a full head above the bandits. There was no way for them to know that he was not a fighter and would much prefer to sit in a corner and study. On the other hand, Sa'ad could create a problem. He was a big boy, too, but he was hot-headed and hard-headed. Out of the corner of my eye I saw him flexing and tensing his muscles.

But the bandits were preoccupied. They were furious with the driver for delivering such a poor lot of passengers. The shortest bandit, who was obviously the leader, suddenly had enough of the driver's smart mouth and menaced him with his gun.

The cowardly driver spun around and then made for the high bushes edging the dirt road. Recklessly, the bandit sprayed the dirt road with bullets, terrifying everyone.

When the driver heard the gunfire and saw the bullets rising from the ground around his feet, he skidded to an abrupt stop, swirled around and shouted, 'Hey! Hey!' Making conciliatory signals to his bandit friends, he slunk back.

I was so shocked that I stood with my mouth open.

The leader cursed him with a threat.

The driver pointed to our luggage, eight crammed bags lashed to the top of the bus. 'Perhaps you will be satisfied with those.' He looked fiercely in our direction. 'Surely these Kurds will have something of value.'

My worst fears came true when the leader ordered two of his men to retrieve our luggage. They leaned their guns against the bus frame. One of the bandits then helped the other up on to the top before climbing up to join him and they began tossing our bags to the ground. Then they leapt down and opened the bags one by one, quickly searching for valuables.

I saw Mother holding her hand to her mouth. My brothers and sister looked stricken as well, as they watched our personal belongings being strewn on the ground.

Nothing pleased the men. They were so disgusted by our meagre belongings that they began to fling them aside.

The driver shrugged his shoulders. 'They're Kurds. What do you expect? Precious jewels?' He glared at us as if we were to blame for the displeasure of his partners and poor on purpose.

One of the men demanded of Mother, 'Where is your money?'

Mother fumbled with her bag and a few coins tumbled to the dirt. Mother never took cash to Kurdistan. Our family in Sulaimaniya always took care of all our needs.

At that moment my precious black doll was hurled to the ground. A cry escaped my lips and I rushed to pick her up, despite my mother's warning shout, 'Na, Joanna! Na!'

I examined the doll. She was still in one piece. Apart from a few scratches on her face and a little dirt on her clothing, she was as good as new.

The driver made an alarming movement in my direction, his hands outstretched, but I screamed, tucking the doll behind me.

The leader of the thieves briskly ordered, 'Leave her.'

I slowly backed away until I was out of sight behind Mother, peering out cautiously.

After selecting the best of our clothes and gifts we had purchased for our relatives, all six criminals piled in the bus, complaining loudly about our poverty. We were a waste of their time.

We were dismayed to see them preparing to drive away, leaving us on the side of the lonely road.

The driver sniffed at us one final time. 'Stupid Kurds!' he yelled, mocking us for being so trusting.

I stared at the departing bus, as its spinning wheels covered me in road dust. When it faded into the distance, I began to sob, for the pity of it all.

Mother was so relieved that her children had escaped unharmed that she appeared unperturbed that we were without transport, food or water in the middle of a dangerous mountain region where there might be wild animals.

Through my sobs, I studied the foliage surrounding us, fully expecting to see wolves, foxes and wild cats coming for us. And snakes. Surely that rugged landscape was crawling with poisonous snakes. Ever since a mischievous cousin in Kurdistan had chased me with a snake two summers before, I had been terrified of them.

My mother and siblings stared at our things strewn across the dirt road. The bandits had left our three most worn bags, so moving like robots we repacked the few items left behind.

'Perhaps there is a village near by,' Mother offered, breaking the stunned silence.

'The main road is not far away,' Ra'ad said softly, pointing in the direction we had come from.

Sa'ad was so angry that he could hardly speak. He grunted.

Muna, like me, began to weep.

Ra'ad and Sa'ad hoisted the three large bags on their shoulders and we formed a line, walking in the middle of the roadway, avoiding the sides where the hard ground was stony and overhung with tall grass and thistles. Convinced that there were poisonous snakes lurking on the side, I kept in the middle of the road, carrying my doll, with two people on either side of me.

Soon Muna stopped crying and sweetly volunteered to carry my doll, who was getting heavy.

The July sun was shining, so thirst quickly set in. My tongue was swollen and my lips parched. Our water supply had gone with the bus. There were plenty of mountain springs in Kurdistan, but no one volunteered to make their way through the thick undergrowth to locate one. I could think of nothing but the delicious grape juice Grandmother Ameena served at her home in Sulaimaniya, poured over the pure mountain ice that was cut and delivered daily all the way from the tallest mountain peaks. Nothing in the world tasted better than that icy grape juice.

The chicken sandwiches long forgotten, I was hungry as well. I longed for just one bite of Grandmother's freshly baked bread and cheese stuffed with herbs.

Just when my legs started to tremble and I felt that I could not go one step further, we heard the noise of an engine. A red tractor appeared over the top of the hill. A farmer was perched on the driver's seat. Quickly I recognized from his clothes that he was Kurdish.

The farmer appeared puzzled at the sight of us. He slowed without coming to a complete stop, idling his tractor engine. His eyebrows raised, he stared at us suspiciously.

'What are you people doing here?'

Ra'ad stepped forward to explain our situation.

The farmer's sceptical expression changed into sympathy. He questioned Ra'ad about our family background. It only took a few moments to discover a marvellous coincidence: this Kurdish farmer was the uncle of Hady, the man who had named me as a child and married Alia, my older sister.

The farmer jumped to the ground. 'Come. Let me help you. Get on the tractor and I'll take you to my home,' he kindly offered. 'You can spend the night as my guests.'

We were saved!

The farmer, Ra'ad and Sa'ad found places to stack our luggage and the farmer said, 'Everyone, find a safe seat.'

How diversely we settled on that tractor! I twisted into a circle to curl up next to Mother while Muna and Sa'ad sprawled on the tyre covers. Ra'ad volunteered to sit on the tractor engine. I knew my brother well. He wished to spare the rest of us from balancing on that hot place.

The farmer started the engine and we were off. Although the sun remained warm on our backs, there was a light wind on our faces as we rode splendidly away from that dangerous place.

When I turned to look at Ra'ad, I laughed aloud. He was leaning forward like a horseman about to win a race. Happy at last, I felt the breeze stirring my long hair and as I tilted my nose high in the Kurdish air, it smelled like freedom.

2

Hill of the Martyrs

Sulaimaniya, Kurdistan
July 1972

We gladly accepted the farmer's generous invitation to spend the night at his home. He lived in a tiny house in the shadow of a grove of tall trees. It made me think of a fairytale.

When the tractor pulled into the dirt drive, I saw faces peering from behind lavender-coloured lace curtains, the fabric billowing through glassless windows.

Hady's uncle confided that he was a fortunate man with a good wife and three obedient daughters. At his urging, his family coyly stepped on to the large front porch, beckoning us with welcoming gestures.

I was the first off the tractor, executing an impressive leap before walking quickly to the porch and through the front door. I noticed that the family had few visible possessions. As in all Kurdish homes, whether simple or grand, the rooms were garlanded with freshly cut flowers.

The family welcomed us as honoured guests, the farmer claiming, 'Guests bring good luck with them.'

His wife cheerily escorted us to the back porch, where she pointed out a bucket of fresh spring water, urging us to take a drink, wash and take a seat so that she could serve us food. She told us warmly, 'A visitor comes with ten blessings, eats one and leaves nine.'

She poured us each a glass of a delicious cold yogurt drink known as *dow*, before calling for her three timid daughters, who, to my delight, had already arranged large platters with freshly baked flat bread, white cheese and figs. Then we were urged to eat some *kubba*, a popular dish of mashed cracked wheat mixed with minced meat, onions and almonds.

While we ate, Ra'ad narrated the story of how we had been tricked into being robbed. The farmer was garrulous, peppering his conversation with Kurdish proverbs such as 'Don't worry. Many will show you the way, once your cart has overturned.' Trying to hide my giggles, I feigned choking, cupping my mouth with my hands, but Mother silenced me with a secret nudge.

The dear man insisted that we take the family's cotton mattresses on the front porch while his family slept in the garden under the juniper and willow trees. There was no finer host than Hady's uncle.

After a night's rest we woke up to a tasty breakfast of hot tea, boiled eggs, fresh yogurt and more fresh bread while the farmer arranged for a trusted cousin to transport us to Grandmother Ameena's house in Sulaimaniya.

The cousin's car looked worn and aged, but the engine was fine-tuned and we gathered an impressive speed as soon as we left the farmer's house.

I was so excited that the trip seemed much shorter than the two hours it took to cover the distance. The car climbed a hill and rounded a bend before barrelling down into a valley that was thick with the greenest grass and flowering slopes.

In a splendid blaze of colour, picturesque Sulaimaniya burst into view. Built by Suleiman Pasha the Great in 1780, the city stands 900 metres above sea level in an emerald, bowl-shaped valley nestled between two mountains.

Grandmother's grand old home was situated in a neighbourhood with large, open houses bordered by flourishing gardens and ancient shade trees. For me, Grandmother's home was the most beautiful house in the world. All the rooms opened into a garden courtyard with a large fountain in the centre. The roomy bedroom balconies above were shaded by the leaves of a thick grape vine.

Mother had had the good fortune to grow up in that house. She was born in 1928, the fourth daughter. Her father, Hassoon Aziz, was an Ottoman army officer from a well-known family, a mix of Turks and Arabs, while Grandmother Ameena's family was Kurdish. Grandfather had one son from a previous marriage but his marriage to Grandmother Ameena had only produced daughters so far. So when Mother was born, Grandfather Hassoon was bitterly disappointed. Desperately wanting to ward off the bad luck of more daughters, he named Mother Kafia, which means 'enough' in Kurdish. But his name charm was futile. Three more daughters followed Mother before finally two sons were born, with Uncle Aziz being the youngest and last child of the union.

As the youngest son in a family with seven older sisters, it was no mystery that Uncle Aziz was greatly loved. But the daughters brought fame to the family because all seven blossomed into tall, slim beauties with exquisite faces and long black hair. Their celebrated good looks were a magnet for many suitors. It was said that many men dreamed of marrying one of the daughters of Officer Hassoon.

Mother was not only beautiful but studious as well, and she was allowed to attain the highest level of education for a Kurdish girl at that time, which meant six years of schooling. Her education left her with a love of learning and she was always an avid reader, entranced by the beauty of Kurdish poetry.

But Mother's happy childhood and promising future came to an abrupt end when her father's appendix burst, releasing poison into his body. No one could save him. And with his death, no one could save my mother from her fate.

At that time, my father's mother was searching the country for a suitable bride for her deaf-mute son. While the best families in Baghdad usually intermarried, few were tempted by a man considered handicapped, despite his wealthy family and his European education. Most people erroneously believed that my father's deafness could be passed through to any children he might father.

My father's mother sent a representative across the country to report on marriageable girls from good families, and the representative heard about the beautiful daughters of Hassoon Aziz. Mother was sixteen years old, which was considered the perfect age for marriage. After several meetings, my father's family proposed that the two families be joined by marriage.

Mother, who by this time had received many marriage requests, was secretly in love with a Kurdish boy who she hoped would one day be her husband. She baulked at the prospect. She did not wish to marry a man who was not only a stranger but an Arab stranger, as she was aware of the scorn Arabs expressed towards Kurdish people. She did not want to marry a man who was a deaf-mute. She did not want to marry into a family that lived so far away from her family. In those days people rarely made long trips across the country. Mother understood the reality of the situation: that once in Baghdad she would be marooned and lucky if she saw her family once a year. Unable to speak Arabic, Mother realized too that living among Arabs in Baghdad she would be socially handicapped and isolated.

But Grandmother Ameena was a widow in a precarious situation. She recognized the chance to forge a union between her family and one of Iraq's most prestigious families. Going against Mother's wishes, Grandmother Ameena accepted the proposal on Mother's behalf.

At only sixteen, my poor mother had no choice but to leave the paradise of Sulaimaniya to marry a man she did not know and live among strangers in the unappealing, hot Iraqi capital of Baghdad. She was devastated, but in those days girls had no option but to do as they were told.

And that is how I came to be born in Baghdad with an Arab Iraqi father and a Kurdish mother.

Later that day, I reclined in an easy chair at Grandmother Ameena's spacious home, with my arms crossed in front of me on my black doll. We had been there for only a few hours, but I was still fatigued by the stressful journey. Mother, Grandmother and three aunts were in conversation, believing me to be asleep, but I was merely resting, while secretly listening in.

Feeling a pang of hunger, I opened my eyes, thinking of persuading Mother to allow me a sweet. But just at that moment Auntie Aisha, my mother's sister, who was also visiting, began to speak, whispering, 'Kafia, Aziz? Tell us how he is faring.'

I hastily closed my eyes, feigning sleep once again, curious as to what might be said about my beloved uncle. The arrest and torture of Uncle Aziz was the one topic rarely discussed in our family. If I remained quiet, perhaps I would learn additional details of his arrest and subsequent troubles.

Mother sighed noisily and made a series of clicking noises with her tongue.

Grandmother Ameena urged her on. 'Kafia?'

'He is as he was before,' Mother finally admitted, with another sigh. 'He spends his days playing with Joanna, or, when he is in a melancholy mood, he seeks out his *nay*.'

Uncle Aziz was a talented musician and singer. He played the *nay*, a vertical flute made of a long piece of cane, with six fingerholes on the front and one on the back. Although most *nays* were simple, his was beautifully decorated with ancient patterns.

Grandmother Ameena made a low humming noise in her throat and then in a regretful tone said, 'If only I had not asked him to drive me on an errand that day.'

'Mother, how could you have known there was a roadblock at the market?' Auntie Fatima reminded her.

'Yes, that is true. I did not know about the roadblock. But I knew there was trouble on the streets. I should have kept Aziz safe.'

Auntie Aisha, who was known in the family for her passionate religious beliefs and even stronger personality, would not allow her mother to take the blame for that dark day. 'Everything happens only if Allah wills it, Mother. And Aziz was young. Young men feel invincible. If he had not been out with you, he would have been with someone else. The result of that day was Allah's will. Do not question Him.'

'All young men were at risk. I knew that,' Grandmother Ameena stubbornly remarked.

Auntie Muneera, who was left blind at the age of four when she contracted a mysterious disease that caused a sudden, horrifying deflating of her eyeballs, was busy knitting a sweater for one of her daughters, her steel needles clicking. She was a great beauty even without eyes, and after a lucky suitor won her hand in marriage she had given him a large family. She was so dextrous that she never allowed anyone to assist her in her home. She also always saw the positive in every situation. 'Be thankful, at least, that Aziz is still with us,' she reminded everyone. 'We could be visiting the Gerdai Shhedan, you know.'

I cracked open one eye. My mother, grandmother and three aunts were sitting as still as stones, their eyes locked on one another and their lips compressed tightly.

Like all Kurds, I had heard the story of the Gerdai Shhedan or Hill of Martyrs. It had become a shrine, a place many Kurds visited and where relatives of the dead went every Friday, the Muslim holy day, to weep and pray for the innocent souls who were murdered on that hill. Kurds had always been persecuted by those in power in Baghdad and there had been so many massacres of innocent people that it was virtually impossible to keep count. But the massacre on the Hill of Martyrs was the most haunting in modern memory.

Soon after I was born, there had been a lot of violent skirmishes between soldiers and Kurds. One day the Iraqi army occupying Sulaimaniya began to round up students and other young men between the ages of fourteen and twenty-five. The soldiers marched the young Kurdish men through the streets of the city to its highest point, a hill visible to many people in Sulaimaniya. There they gave the prisoners shovels and forced them to start digging.

A great dread came over the crowd of onlookers, as well as the young men digging, because they assumed the young men were about to be shot and were being forced to dig their own graves. After the holes were dug, most of the men were told to step into the holes. Then the soldiers ordered the remainder of the men to shovel earth over their friends and relatives, up to their chins. The Iraqi soldiers then shoved the remaining prisoners into the holes, where they, too, were buried in dirt up to their chins.

The resulting display was eerie. Nothing was visible above the ground other than rows and rows of squirming human heads.

It was said that the crowd was mystified but relieved. This was not the government's usual method of killing. Onlookers experienced a flicker of hope that the buried men would be left to bake in the sun for a time and then uncovered, released and allowed to go home, with only their pride wounded and the tops of their heads blistered.

But then a military tank was brought up the hill. To the horror of the crowd, the tank commander was ordered to drive his tank over the heads of the young men and pulverize them.

And that was what happened.

The scene was one of chaos and carnage. The soldiers held back the crowd by firing their weapons, as it took a long time for the tank driver to smash all the exposed heads.

The Iraqi authorities did not try to hide the atrocity. They were proud of the massacre and invited family members to see for themselves what happened to people who persisted in fighting the central government.

But the Kurds were not intimidated; in fact, the event had the opposite effect. News of the massacre spread like wildfire. That bitter sample of Iraqi injustice sent a shockwave across Kurdistan. After such a brutal massacre, there was no longer any possibility of signing a peace agreement. Incensed *peshmerga* sprang from their hiding places and made several daring but unsuccessful attempts to assassinate the man who had ordered the death of the young men: Abdul Salam Arif, the President of Iraq.

The fight escalated, and even more Iraqi soldiers poured into the north. The Kurds were victorious, for a time, and stubbornly refused to give in to the Iraqi President's demands. But as the fighting became more and more desperate, the full force of the Iraqi army arrived. Its numbers were overwhelming. The Kurdish *peshmerga* were finally defeated. With the fighters on the run, there was no one to protect Kurdish civilians and thousands of ordinary people were butchered. Livestock were shot. Wells were poisoned. Houses were torched. A conflagration of killing and destruction fanned out across the Kurdish countryside.

After shattering village life, the Iraqi army turned its attention to the cities. That's when they got their hands on Uncle Aziz.

His life was shattered because he was a dutiful son. When asked by his mother to drive her around in Sulaimaniya on some errands, he rushed to do her bidding. After the attempts on the Iraqi President's life, suspicion fell on every Kurdish man, even young students. Driving his mother, Uncle Aziz came across a newly erected roadblock. Although his papers were in order, and it was clear that he was a student and not a *peshmerga*, he was detained without explanation. Grandmother watched helplessly as her youngest child was roughed up, thrown into a military vehicle and driven away.

Frantic months passed before a relative managed to locate him. He was found in a prison notorious for macabre punishments and torture. While the family was greatly comforted to discover that he was still alive, they were dismayed to think of the condition in which they might find him. Frantic efforts were made to gain his freedom. Finally after bribes were paid he was liberated.

The gaunt silent man released to the family bore little resemblance to the handsome young man arrested months before. Although his body bore signs of torture such as burn marks and missing fingernails, the most crippling damage was invisible, at least in the beginning. For the first few days when he refused to speak or leave his bed the family believed that their beloved Aziz was suffering from the trauma of imprisonment and torture. But soon his catatonic behaviour revealed that Aziz's brilliant mind had vanished in prison. The young man they once knew was no more. He was no longer a gifted mathematician. He was no longer an ambitious student. He was no longer a sensitive son or supportive brother. He no longer spent hours playing board games with his friends. He no longer enjoyed sports. He was no longer interested in talk of marriage and children. Uncle Aziz was no longer connected to life itself.

No one in the family could uncover exactly what had occurred during Uncle Aziz's internment, but a student imprisoned in the same cell reported that every torture imaginable was applied to them. It was as though the torturers particularly hated students. That was no surprise. When it came to Kurds, the Iraqi Arab government policy had always been consistent: all Kurds are a danger, but a Kurd with a pen is even more dangerous. The cellmate was in awe of Uncle Aziz, claiming that he had been fearless during his torture sessions. But my uncle couldn't bear the suffering of others. He could not witness the torment of women and children, a favourite ploy of the torturers, without breaking down. According to his cellmate, my uncle's tough shell finally broke when they tied him to a chair and compelled him to watch the brutalization of a small boy.

From the day he was released from prison, Uncle Aziz had only been interested in entertaining the youngest children in the family, playing his musical instrument and singing. He had reverted to being a child himself, without working, without studying, without any discipline to his daily life.

His only crime had been to be a Kurd.

I drifted off to sleep while listening to the low buzz of the voices of the women in my family, as they spoke of the cruelties and perversions endured, seemingly forever, by Kurds.

3

Sprinkled by Stardust

Sulaimaniya
the following morning

When I woke up the following morning, it was sunny and fluffy white clouds were forming in the sapphire sky. Songbirds were singing. The house was filled with the sounds of children playing.

The carefree atmosphere in Sulaimaniya always made it feel like festival time. Grandmother's house overflowed with family. The adults would sleep on cotton mattresses laid out on the bedroom floors, while children slept on the flat roof. The women of the household would rise early to cook a feast. All our favourite Kurdish dishes were prepared, such as *kuftay Sulaimaniya*, ground rice pastry filled with mincemeat, *doulma*, vegetables stuffed with rice, and, my favourite, a special sweet called *bourma*, which was very thin puff pastry sprinkled with pecan nuts and drenched in honey or syrup. Tea was available at all times, kept hot in enormous *samawars*, special copper Turkish urns.

Children were allowed to play all day and into the late evening. Sometimes we went on a picnic. Our preferred place was Serchenar, a place of waterfalls. While the adults chatted, and the sweetest watermelons sat chilling in the cold spring water, the kids would play games. My favourite game was a test of endurance to see who could stay in the cold water the longest. To my disappointment, I never won.

On our first day of holiday, my sister and I received permission to accompany two of our female cousins to the central market.

Ra'ad was practically an adult, so he had better things to do than hang around with children. I overheard Mother say he was going to visit some Kurdish student activists who wrote and distributed pamphlets that pressed for Kurdistan to be free from Arab rule, for the Arabs forbade us from speaking our language, learning our history, singing our songs or quoting our poetry. Several years before, my brother had joined the Kurdish Democratic Party, and his hero was Mullah Mustafa Al-Barzani, the Kurdish hero and leader who fought the government in Baghdad at every opportunity. Mother seemed pleased with Ra'ad's political activities, so I didn't worry. I had no way of knowing that my brother had ventured into a risky arena that would very soon impact on all our lives.

As we were leaving the house Mother intercepted us at the front door to remind Muna to hold my hand, because five years earlier, when I was only five years old, my older sister, Alia, had returned home without me after taking me to the market. When questioned, Alia would say only, 'The gypsies got Joanna.'

Mother and Grandmother and Auntie Aisha launched a frantic search, but I was nowhere to be found. They feared that someone had indeed kidnapped their little Joanna and she might never be seen again. How happy they were when later in the day a friendly policeman brought me to Grandmother's door, explaining that I had been found wandering the main streets of Sulaimaniya, accosting grown-ups and asking them to buy me a lamb kebab and a cold soda.

So even though I was ten years old that summer, Mother demanded that I was carefully supervised any time I left her side.

Muna clung to me as though I was a treasure. Eventually I peeled her hand from mine, promising not to tell Mother we had disobeyed and pledging not to leave her sight.

Soon we came to the market place. To me, it was the most interesting place in the world. The combined scents of aromatic foods, exotic spices, sweet-smelling perfumes and freshly cut flowers were deliciously fragrant. Everything one could possibly need was on sale in the square. Fruits and vegetables were laid neatly on rickety tables or spread upon colourful fabric on the ground. Fresh yogurt was sold from huge bronze pots. To keep the yogurt from spoiling, each pot top was shielded by white meshed cotton fabric called *melmel*, and the fabric was covered with a wet loofah. After the yogurt was sold, the seller would sell these Kurdish loofahs, reportedly the finest loofahs in the world.

We browsed in a side section of the plaza devoted to beautiful jewellery, handcrafted by local artisans. At one stand I spotted three young women, who, judging by their striking physical similarities, were clearly sisters. All three smiled brightly as they hovered proudly over colourful stones set in necklaces, bracelets and earrings. They were so pretty that everyone walking past paused to stare openly at them. One had dark brown hair in thick plaits that fell to her waist, while the other two were sporting matching red scarves threaded with golden ropes, dangling with shiny coins.

As I gawked, one of our cousins pulled Muna and me to one side and whispered excitedly. 'I must tell you a saga about those sisters. Everyone in Kurdistan is whispering about them.'

'Go on,' I said eagerly.

'Well,' she said with a touch of importance, 'those three sisters are betrothed to three of Kurdistan's most revered *peshmerga*. Their parents and siblings were burned alive during the military assault of Qasim in 1961, when orders were given to wipe out Kurdish villages. When the village was torched, the *peshmerga* went there to avenge the deaths. They arrived too late to retaliate against the Arabs, but while there a handsome *peshmerga* caught sight of the eldest sister, who was only twelve years old at the time.' My cousin pointed her out. 'That one with the plaits. She was carrying water from a spring. He was instantly smitten, struck by a great longing. He asked around, and was told that this beautiful girl had two equally beautiful sisters. The area was in chaos and her parents were dead, and of course he couldn't approach such a young girl about romantic love, so, with some reluctance, he left. But he could not erase the image of her beautiful face from his mind. After many restless months of long nights he convinced two *peshmerga* friends to return to the area with him. But by this time the sisters had moved away to live with relatives.'

I involuntarily turned to glance at the woman. Her perfectly formed face was framed like a picture by those long plaits of shiny, chestnut-coloured hair.

My cousin pinched my arm. 'Listen, Joanna, there is more to the story. Do you want to hear it or not?'

I nodded. 'Yes! Yes! I am listening.'

'All right. The brave *peshmerga* was in love and he would not be discouraged. So he and his friends searched until they found the village where the sisters now lived. It didn't take much effort to locate the house because everyone in that village knew about the three beauties. This *peshmerga* was bolder than most, so he approached the eldest male in the family and asked outright for the eldest girl's hand in marriage, offering to wait a few years until she matured.

'The family called a conference. Although they respected these brave fighters, they did not want the girl to live the difficult life of a fighter's wife. She had suffered enough, they claimed. Also, with the girl being so beautiful and promising to grow more beautiful still, the family was counting on a substantial dowry. So they said no.'

'Did she run away?' I asked, thinking that that was what I would have done if a handsome *peshmerga* wanted me for his bride and my parents refused.

'No! The fighters are too honourable for that!' she snapped, irritated at my ignorance. 'But when the heartbroken *peshmerga* was leaving the house, the girl he loved was curious about this fighter who had followed her from one village to another, so she slipped out via the garden and walked past him as he was leaving, so as to have a look at him. He was too handsome to ignore and when their eyes met, she, too, was infatuated. The rest is history. In the face of young love, and the fair one saying she would jump into the well if she could not marry her brave hero, the family relented. The two have been betrothed since that day and the wedding is to be soon.'

I turned and gazed at the beautiful sisters once more. 'What about her sisters?'

'The fiancé's *peshmerga* friends accompanied him and when they met the two younger sisters, they, too, caught love fever. As time passed, the other two became engaged as well. They will all marry *peshmerga* fighters,' she said with such a satisfied air that one would think she had personally negotiated the marriage contracts.

'When are the weddings?' Muna asked in her girlish voice.

I looked at Muna with pride. Muna looked especially lovely that day with her luminous skin and big eyes, the colour of deep caramel.

In my eyes, she was as pretty as those three sisters. I was desperate to be as lovely as Muna.

My cousin replied, 'Soon, I have heard. And once they marry, they will live with their husbands in the mountains. They are heroines, too. For the rest of their lives they will live for Kurdish freedom.'

I stared at the young women. They were living my dream. Since I was very young, I had had a feeling that I would not live an ordinary life and that I would not be the usual bride, a girl who married the safe and respectful government clerk while draped in wedding white. My only wish at that moment was to be grown up, and to be so beautiful that I, too, would catch the eye of a brave *peshmerga* and go and live with him in the mountains, where I would fight by his side.

My legs trembled and I did not even follow my cousins and Muna, who had walked on until she noticed I was missing. Frightened, she retraced her steps, her white face turning red, and demanded, 'Joanna! You promised!'

But I could think of nothing but the three beautiful sisters, waiting to be married and join their romantic, courageous husbands in the Kurdish mountains, and I worried to myself that I was not considered beautiful. Although I had been told I was so pretty a baby that I had to be protected from the evil eye, that was no longer the case. In fact, lately I had been teased for being skinny and gangly. And it was true that I was a bony girl with legs too long for my body. For convenience, Mother kept my hair cut close to my head. I had rather large ears that stuck out on the sides of my head. I was also a dark-skinned person living in a country where lily-white skin was greatly prized. My skin turned darker with each passing summer. In contrast, my mother and sisters were extremely fair. Even Grandmother Ameena, an old woman, had very beautiful white skin. Other women were always complimenting them on their white complexions.

In that instant I resolved to grow out my short hair. I would also start protecting my skin from the darkening rays of the sun – I would carry an umbrella. Even so, I knew that it would be years before there would be the slightest chance that I would catch the eye of a brave *peshmerga*.

I leadenly followed my sister back to Grandmother's house.

★

That evening should have been fun for me, with women and girls wearing their most colourful dresses and the men and boys in wide pantaloons, called *sharwual*, with broad sashes wrapped around their waists.

As soon as the sunset dipped to the bottom of the sky with its display of reds and pinks, everyone gathered in the courtyard. The garden was as colourful as the sunset, with borders of red poppies and white narcissi. Our mothers had prepared a feast, and we began the meal nibbling at figs, apples, pears, almonds and walnuts. Steaming bowls of hot rice caught my eye and soon the family were being served several main courses, including *kubba* stuffed with meat and *dolma* or stuffed vine leaves, and barbecued chicken and kebabs.

Trying to fatten myself up, I ate more than I wanted. I was tired of being the skinny cousin. It did not improve my mood that my teenage female cousins appeared to have grown stunningly beautiful in one short year. For the first time I noticed that most of them had fair skin. With the wildest jealousy, I watched three of the prettiest girls swinging their heads as they spoke, purposefully showing off their shimmering black hair, which hung to their waists.

It didn't help my mood that no one seemed to notice or even care that I was not my usual self. The rejection stung. There was a nervous knot in my throat and my eyes began to water, but I refused to let anyone see me cry, so when I was eventually asked what my problem was, I pretended to have a foreign object in my eye.

After everyone had eaten, there was a call for music. Ra'ad found some tapes of Kurdish dancing music and soon the back garden came alive with the sound we all loved. Before long most of the teenagers and young adults were on their feet.

There is a saying: 'One who cannot dance is not a Kurd.' And that is so true.

Soon a circle was formed, with everyone holding hands, men and women together. Ra'ad was a leader because he was known for his talented dance moves. Despite encouragement from their cousins, Muna and Sa'ad refused to join in, for Muna was too shy and Sa'ad was too serious for such frivolity.

No one invited me to join the circle, but that was fine with me because I was newly ashamed of my short hair and long legs. I was content to sit next to Mother and merely observe.

The music grew loud and the dancers held hands, starting to sway, pull close together and press their shoulders against one another. The leading and trailing dancers began to wave colourful handkerchiefs in impressive intricate gestures. Changing direction, all the dancers managed to complete the complicated moves without breaking their original handhold.

When the dancers were exhausted, the evening finally broke up and I quietly followed my cousins to the flat roof where we were to sleep. Normally joining my cousins on the roof was my favourite treat, but that night I was too disheartened to take pleasure from anything.

The oldest boys and girls hauled up our bedding of lightweight cotton mattresses, pillows and thin blankets. After everyone had settled down, the older cousins talked quietly while we younger kids listened to the sounds of night, making a game of guessing whether it was frogs or crickets creating the interesting noises.

Slowly the night grew peaceful and the youngest children fell asleep. I bedded down without words, pulling the flimsy blanket up to my chin, and stared up to see a sliver of a moon in the star-scattered sky, casting a faint light. I felt even more depressed and insignificant under that infinite Kurdistan sky.

Just as I started hearing the heavy breathing sound of sleeping from some of the older cousins, there was a terrifying burst of noise. I knew from our experience with the bandits that I was hearing gunfire.

Before I could dash down the stairs to get off the roof, I was tackled and brought heavily to the floor. The breath was knocked out of me as I tumbled backwards. My brother Ra'ad was protecting my body with his own. He had me in such a tight grip that I could not wiggle.

He said loudly enough for everyone to hear, 'Stay down,' and then to me, 'Shush, Joanna. Don't move. Don't make a sound.'

Several of the younger cousins began to whimper and call for their mothers, but I heard an older cousin hiss a word of warning that it was too dangerous for anyone to stand upright.

Ra'ad instructed, 'He's right. Don't stand up. You are in no danger if you stay down. It is our fighters who are being attacked. No one knows that we are even here.'

I overheard a multitude of shouts coming from the thick of the treeline, as though orders were being given, but I could not clearly understand anything being said.

I stared into my brother's face as he whispered, 'Joanna, listen but don't be afraid. Something has happened. Some of our fighters have appeared in the city. Obviously their presence has been discovered by the army. But they will never find the *peshmerga*. No one who lives here will give them up. Besides, these streets are unfamiliar to the Arabs.'

Just then a lone bullet whizzed over our heads.

I quivered with suppressed excitement. This was war! Everyone hugged the floor with intense urgency.

There was further volleying of shots and shouts in the darkness, mixed together in what sounded like the wildest confusion.

We didn't move for a long time, until the sounds of gunfire grew faint as the soldiers moved away from our area. Then there was silence.

There were sighs of relief, and my younger cousins leapt to their feet and fled down the steps and into the house to be with their mothers. I remained on the roof, even though Ra'ad suggested that I should go down. I did not respond, wanting him to forget I was there.

The incident aroused the ire of older male cousins, several of whom claimed they were going to join the *peshmerga* as soon as they graduated. They believed they would be the generation to finally lead the Kurds to victory. 'By God we will soon be tapping on Baghdad's gate,' one of them boasted.

'Me too,' I whispered to myself, smiling faintly. 'Me too.'

That day was a turning point in my life. As surely as I recognized my own name, I knew that I, Joanna Al-Askari, would one day live the life of a *peshmerga*.

Being active in Kurdish causes, Ra'ad congratulated the *peshmerga*-to-be, and the talk veered to the injustices perpetrated against the Kurds. I listened carefully to all that was said. I wanted to know everything about my country and the Kurdish people I so loved.

The first significant Kurdish revolt occurred in 1806, when armies from the Ottoman Empire gained control of our land. It was followed by repeated waves of fighting against the Turks. Rebellions and wars were so frequent that they began to merge into one another.

In 1918, the British occupied our land. When we resisted, they attacked us with their modern weapons. On the order of Winston Churchill, who labelled the Kurds 'primitive tribes', the Royal Air Force dropped poisonous gas on the Kurds. That was the first time our people were massacred by chemical weapons.

In 1923, my Kurdish family supported Sheikh Mahmud Barzinji when he led a rebellion against both the British and the new Iraqi king, King Faisal. Barzinji defiantly declared himself King of Kurdistan, but in 1924 Sulaimaniya fell to the British soldiers. Kurdistan was occupied yet again.

Mother, born in 1928, once told me that she had no memory of a time when her world was not dominated by war. She had only the dimmest memory of the 1932 uprising, but well recalled the 1943 uprising against the central government, when Kurdish forces won control of large areas of land.

In 1946 there was a serious rebellion, after which the Kurdish leader Mullah Mustafa Barzani was forced by the Iraqi government to flee into exile in the Soviet Union. Kurdish calls for freedom grew weaker after his loss. But in 1951 a new generation of Kurdish nationalists revived the freedom movement, and Mullah Barzani was elected President, even though he was still in exile.

In 1958, after the overthrow of the Iraqi royal family, there was yet another revival of calls for Kurdish rights and our hero Barzani returned from exile, bringing renewed cries for freedom from government control in Baghdad. Kurdistan was attacked again, but the *peshmerga* were masters of guerrilla tactics and they won battle after battle, stunning the Iraqi government when they occupied and controlled the main road into Baghdad from Khanaqin, only 140 kilometres from Baghdad – something that had never before happened.

Within a few years of these victories, however, we had to endure yet more hated defeat.

And on that night in 1972 the tension was increasing once again.

I overheard a male cousin, who was near to Ra'ad's age, whispering, 'You know the truth, don't you? The crime is to be born a Kurd.'

Ra'ad made a small noise in his throat that seemed to signify agreement.

So I had committed a crime merely by being born.

I had no doubt that when I was finally old enough to hold a weapon there would be plenty of battles left for me to fight. Our battles were eternal, the only change being the face of our enemy.

Just then Ra'ad discovered that I was awake. He leaned in towards me, and as I admired his handsome face with its high, broad forehead and sensitive brown eyes, I was reminded that my older brother has always met the censure of being part-Kurd behind a mask of serenity. He is imbued with bravery unknown by most and, even then, was fighting the occupation in his own clever way.

Gently, Ra'ad reminded me, 'You must sleep, little Joanna. Tomorrow we are going to the mountains, to picnic and swim under the waterfalls.'

A happy image of plunging into the transparent waters of mountain waterfalls flashed through my mind.

He encouraged me again, 'Joanna, go to sleep.'

'I'm not sleepy,' I replied.

'Joanna,' he told me, 'look up at the sky.'

'I am.'

'Do you see the light of the stars?'

'I do.'

'Joanna, would you like to know a secret about the stars?'

I shivered in anticipation. I've always loved secrets. 'What?'

'I will tell you a scientific secret that few people know. Whenever the stars shine this bright, there is a reason. And the reason is: the brightest stars are showering stardust. As you sleep, you'll be sprinkled with stardust.' Smiling, he gently stroked my face. 'Stardust, Joanna. Just imagine it. Stardust all over your pretty little face.'

I was still young enough to believe him. Besides, for me, Kurdistan had always been a land of dreams. So I turned to my side, closed my eyes and slept peacefully through the night, my dreams shimmering with sprinkles of stardust.

The following day we were awakened to news about the previous night's attack. The battle we had heard between the Iraqi army and the *peshmerga* revolved around the three beautiful sisters we had seen selling jewellery at the market. A nest of Arab spies in the city had notified the Iraqi security of their romance with *peshmerga*. At the end of the day, as the three sisters were riding in a donkey cart back to their village, there was an ambush and they were arrested by Iraqi soldiers. The beautiful brides-to-be were used as bait to draw in their three handsome *peshmerga* fiancés. Falling into the trap, the moment the fighters heard that their betrothed had been detained, they slipped into the city to rescue the women they loved, but found that the three sisters had already been taken to a prison in Baghdad.

During the fighting that ensued two of the three warriors were killed but the third escaped. The fate of the sisters was predictable: they would be tortured, and then executed.

I grieved for the young lovers. As for so many Kurds murdered over the years, their dreams of love and marriage would never come true. I felt tremendous hate for the men who had destroyed their dreams. My anger hummed like slow, angry bees inside my head, driving me steadily onward towards my fate.

Perhaps a sprinkling of stardust would light my way.

4

Baathist Terror

Two years later in Baghdad
Thursday 4 July 1974

Time always passed slowly in dreary Baghdad. Nothing good ever happened there. Even my growth was stunted. I had hoped that by my twelfth birthday I would see a physical miracle and grow as beautiful as my Kurdish teenage cousins, but my body failed to blossom. I was still teased about my long legs, skinny body and flat chest, a cruel reminder that I still looked like a child.

Against Mother's wishes I grew my hair long. At least no one could deny its beauty. It was thick and shiny black, hanging to my waist, although I often wore it plaited in two thick ropes, just like the braids I had seen worn by the tragic Kurdish fiancée I had so admired in Sulaimaniya.

An image of those sisters often flashed before my eyes. My full heart was in the Kurdish cause, as theirs had been. While my family still considered me a child, I no longer thought or acted as a child. My awareness of Kurdish troubles made me older than my years. I was more knowledgeable about the politics and geography of Kurdistan than many adults I knew.

That summer when I was twelve years old, our trip to Sulaimaniya was delayed because Father was bedridden with a mysterious illness. He was suffering weakness and a loss of appetite. His illness disturbed and confused us all, because apart from his inability to hear and speak, Father had always enjoyed exceptional health. But he was now improving, and Mother assured us that if he continued to improve we would leave for Sulaimaniya only one week late.

I was desperate to return there, to Kurdistan, to paradise. But we never made it to paradise that summer. The trip was cancelled by a shattering event.

The tragedy erupted on a day in hot July, when Baghdad was strained for more reasons than the heat. The Baathist government was becoming more repressive. People no longer felt free to speak carelessly. There was hushed talk over unprovoked arrests, with rumours of many innocent people disappearing.

Tempers were not improved by the heat. Although we lived under the shade of large palms, the swelling heat of the day crept like a haze silently and insistently through the rooms of our little home, infiltrating every corner until it became unbearable. I could not stay inside for very long before the sweat ran down my body and darkened my clothes.

Only my father's shaded bedroom had the benefit of cool air, and none of us begrudged him. For longer than most Iraqis could remember, dwellers of the hot Mesopotamia region had utilized an ingenious method of air-conditioning, which consisted of twisting palm tree reeds into frames. These frames were criss-crossed with additional reeds, and then a layer of desert thorns called *agool* was sandwiched between them. The palm tree frame was securely affixed over windows. Every six hours we children would pour water over the branches and reeds. With each passing breeze, the ancient apparatus cooled the interior room. Although few Iraqis still used the antiquated method, Father clung to the old ways in this instance, enjoying the chilled air.

Everyone else sought the cool of the night on the roof, in the back garden or on the covered porch. Sunset found Mother, Muna, Sa'ad and me gathering on the covered porch, sorting our bedding and preparing for sleep.

Recently the number of people living in our little home had diminished. Uncle Aziz was away visiting another sister. Ra'ad no longer lived at home, since he had started his first year at university. He now resided with our older sister, Alia, and her husband, Hady, on the opposite side of the city, in the posh Mansour district. Alia's home offered Ra'ad two advantages: he was slightly closer to the Baghdad University of Technology and he had more privacy. Alia had given him his own room, saying that he needed a quiet area to study. Ra'ad was studying to be an engineer, like his father. Nothing was more important in the Arab and Kurdish world than for the eldest son to be educated, for one day he would be responsible for the well-being of our entire family.

Once our bedding was arranged we slowly settled down for the night, although we did not immediately fall asleep. Despite the severity of summer days in Baghdad, nights held a certain thrill and charm. That night was no exception. After the reddish-pink horizon of the setting sun dropped from sight, the night-time slowly broadened with a full moon shining through the grove of palm trees. Their branches waved like long arms from the gentle breeze. The gleaming, golden eyes of a large owl who had made his home in one of the palms seemed to be watching us. Seeing that owl, I suddenly ached for the companionship of Ra'ad, for many times he had pointed it out, talking me out of my old-fashioned fear that owls bring bad luck.

The sounds of voices wafted through the silence of the trees. I recognized the voices of our neighbourhood's night guards, called *charkhachi* from times long past. The guards dressed distinctively in ankle-length army coats with brass buttons. They wore colourful turbans on their heads and they were armed with obsolete rifles, courtesy of the British. Although the ancient rifles had ceased functioning, these men provided a sense of safety from thieves.

The sights and sounds of the Baghdad night slowly disappeared into nothingness as my thoughts floated to Sulaimaniya. My cousins were probably on the roof of Grandmother Ameena's house, their eyes drawn to the same magnificent moon. I would soon be there with them. Basking in that pleasant thought, I curled up in my bedding and soon was soundly sleeping.

A few hours later, my lovely dreams of Sulaimaniya were breached by an alarming noise. Someone was attempting to break down our front door.

Sa'ad jumped to his feet. Though only fifteen years old, he was larger and stronger than his age suggested. In the face of possible danger, he ordered, 'Stay!' Since Ra'ad had moved away, Sa'ad considered himself the protector of the women of the household – to my dismay, for I was a rebel child and didn't like taking orders.

Muna meekly obeyed and remained where she was, covering her face and head with the bedclothes. But Mother, like me, was a bit wilful, so as Sa'ad rushed from the porch we both jumped up and followed him through the kitchen and hallway, which opened into the large living room.

There we paused, standing shoulder to shoulder, listening. Was a thief loose in the neighbourhood? Had the guards come to warn us? My father had not made an appearance, but that was not a surprise: even if he hadn't been weakened by illness, his deafness would have made him oblivious to the commotion.

Sa'ad yelled, 'Who is there?'

The response was shocking and unexpected. There was a series of strong kicks at the door. I gasped in bewilderment as the heavy wooden door began to crack in various places, before bulging out in the centre and then splitting. A powerful force was coming for us from the outside.

Two large pieces of the door fell haphazardly on to the living-room floor, leaving jagged edges hanging on the frame. Whoever was kicking created an opening sizeable enough for a large adult to enter. Three men dressed in Iraqi security uniforms jostled each other as they pushed through the jagged gap, trampling over the splintered sections of what remained of our front door.

They were in such a rush to get to us that one man lost his footing, tumbling to the floor. In their haste, the other two men stepped on him.

The largest of the three had a red face cratered with pockmarks. He confronted Sa'ad, screeching, 'You! Spy! Where is your radio?'

Sa'ad was never afraid of anyone, not even that monster. With a sarcastic expression, he retorted, 'Spies? There are no spies here!'

'We have proof that this is a house of spies.' The man's tongue darted out between his lips two or three times like a serpent's.

I shivered with repulsion.

He shrieked, 'For the Israelis!'

The Israelis? I could not believe what I was hearing. If I had not been so panicked, I would have laughed at the man's preposterous claim. No one in our family had ever even seen an Israeli, as far as we knew. In fact, few Arabs or Kurds in Iraq during those days gave much thought to the Israelis. We struggled with too many uncertainties with our own government to be interested in the far-away conflict between the Palestinians and the Israelis.

The man continued with his mad rant, spitting, 'This is a home that supports Mullah Mustafa Barzani!'

While his Israeli allegation was blatantly ridiculous, this charge caused me a nudge of anxiety. Undeniably, Mullah Mustafa Barzani, the famous Kurdish leader and fighter, was considered a hero in our Kurdish home. I suddenly remembered a poster hanging in Ra'ad's room. The hero's image was hanging there for these men to find. Although since 1970 we had been given the legal right to support our Kurdish heroes, such as Mullah Barzani, I had lived long enough to understand that mere laws were no protection for Kurds.

Something told me that that poster would doom us all.

The men were preoccupied with Sa'ad, so I slipped away and walked rapidly to Ra'ad's old bedroom.

The poster of Barzani covered the wall over Ra'ad's bed. That poster had been a part of Ra'ad's life since March 1970, when the Iraqi government finally concluded that it must negotiate with the Kurds, who were defeating the Iraqi army on the northern front. An agreement was reached that granted Kurdish autonomy. The accord promised to recognize Kurdish as an official language. An amendment to the constitution stated, 'The Iraqi people are made up of two nationalities, the Arab and the Kurd.' From that time, we were given the right to support Kurdish parties. But in reality, the Iraqi government broke the agreement from the moment it was signed. Kurds who took their newly granted civil liberties seriously were targeted for imprisonment and worse. In their naivety, many Kurds had been murdered for showing support for Kurdish leaders.

Perhaps they would murder Ra'ad.

I well remembered the day Ra'ad brought home the poster and hung it. He was the proudest boy in Baghdad as he measured the perfect spot for his hero. On the bottom of the poster he had joyfully inscribed: 'The Lion of the Mountains and the Father of the Kurds.'

Regretfully, I climbed on the bed and began pulling at the edges.

Breathless with nerves, I ripped Mullah Barzani's likeness into small pieces. Pulling up my nightgown, I poked the fragments into the waist of my pants – not a minute too soon, because I next heard the men stomping through our house. I overheard the leader order one of his men to guard the front door and the stairway to the roof so that anyone trying to flee from the house would be apprehended.

I froze in place when a gravelly voice loudly announced, 'We are looking for the spy Ra'ad Al-Askari. Where is he?'

I anxiously looked around the room for any other incriminating materials but could see nothing. I glanced over at Ra'ad's desk, worrying that flyers or brochures promoting the Kurdish cause might be in the drawers, but there was no time to investigate. The men were coming down the hallway in my direction.

I was horrified to feel tiny pieces of the poster sliding down my legs. Gravity was doing its work. If I could not find a solution, my deed was bound to be discovered. My young age would not save me. I was struck by a dreadful thought: perhaps I would end up like Uncle Aziz, imprisoned and tortured until I lost my mind.

With no time remaining, I snatched up the poster pieces on the floor and then jumped on to the bed. I wiggled under the sheets, pulling the bedcover up to my chin, and simulated sleep.

Two of the men were upon me before I could inhale, and I opened my eyes, affecting surprise at their presence.

I caught a brief glimpse of Mother and Sa'ad on the heels of the security men. No one was more astonished than they were to discover me in Ra'ad's bed. I watched their faces as they glanced up at the wall over my head. I was rewarded by their reactions. A triumphant gleam flashed in Sa'ad's eyes and visible relief washed over Mother's face.

As the men tore apart the room, Mother lightly slapped her face, something Kurdish women of her age do when they are distressed. But she did not shriek or cry. Mother did not understand Arabic very well, yet she knew enough to realize what those men were after. Their only goal was to collect evidence to indict her oldest son. If they found anything incriminating, all would be lost.

To give myself courage, I silently recited a few of my favourite verses of the Kurdish anthem:

> *The Kurdish youth have risen like lions,*
> *To adorn the crown of life with blood,*
> *Let no one say Kurds are dead.*
> *Kurds are living,*
> *Kurds are living; their flag will never fall.*

Perhaps because I was small for my age and childlike in appearance, the men ignored me. Whatever the reason, the men did not heed me as they stomped around the room, holding books dramatically up in the air and thumbing the pages before tossing them to the floor. They crouched on their knees to peer under the bed and pounded the curtains with their hands, as though they believed a grown man might be hidden behind the nearly transparent fabric. One man tapped on the walls. Not to be outdone by his partner, another man climbed on the desk chair and began to knock on the ceiling. It was unsettling, even at my young age, to know that such dim-witted men held our fate in their hands. Their tactics would have been comical if not for that daunting fact.

I watched Sa'ad carefully. His dark eyes flickered between anger and despair. His lips were puckered with the effort of keeping quiet. How I hoped he could suppress his famous temper; otherwise he would use his fists to stop these men. If that happened, everyone in our family would be arrested. Mercifully, Sa'ad maintained perfect control. The traumatic day revealed a new quality in my brother's temperament: restraint.

Soon, I hoped, they would leave. Then we could warn Ra'ad.

After searching every inch of Ra'ad's bedroom, the men moved on to the rest of the house. When I heard them in the kitchen throwing heavy pots and pans, I took a moment to gather all the pieces of the poster from under my clothes and from the bed and placed them under some papers the men had examined and thrown to the floor. Satisfied that my secret was safe, I scampered from the room to join Mother and Muna, who had finally come in from the porch.

With Sa'ad looking on, we women formed a semicircle at the door, watching as they wrecked Mother's orderly kitchen. Mother kept slapping her face while Muna took sharp gasps with every dish that was hurled and every glass that was broken.

The men theatrically emptied bags of salt, flour and sugar across the table, cabinets and floor. They even broke the four eggs sitting on the cabinet top. Such actions puzzled me. Would any spy hide evidence inside unbroken eggshells? And, if so, how?

There was wild confusion. As they worked they cursed and made threats about what they were going to do to the Israeli spy Ra'ad Al-Askari.

There was a dreadful moment when Mother's treasured tray of tea glasses was dashed against the wall, the thin shower of broken glass dropping to the floor and tinkling like delicate bells.

Muna's face paled. She swayed, about to faint. She couldn't take the drama. I was afraid she was losing her mind.

The leader of the gang brusquely ordered us to sit in a corner of the room. We did as we were told, clinging to one another as the men worked their way through the house, up the stairs to the roof and back down to the back porch and into the garden. Mother and Sa'ad trailed them, Mother sad and Sa'ad sullen, watching the destruction of our home.

It seemed strange to me that the men did not challenge my father. I supposed their offices had a full security file on our family, and that they knew that there were two reasons my father could not be a danger to the regime: he was not a Kurd and had never participated in any Kurdish political activities, and his deafness further ensured that he could not be a threat to the government. Or perhaps it was the simple matter of the sleeping pills Mother gave him at bedtime: he was probably in such a deep slumber that they couldn't easily rouse him. Whatever the reason, I concluded that being deaf had its advantages that night. While we were all frightened out of our wits, my father was enjoying a splendid sleep, unaffected by the most traumatic event of our lives.

A few hours later the men finally departed. As they made their way back across the broken door, they hurled curses and threats at us, but their hands were empty. They had found nothing in our home on which to hang their ridiculous accusations.

I joined Mother and Sa'ad to watch from the front porch as the three thugs stomped down the pathway, jumped into their car and drove away, their tyres spinning as if they had been called to a fire at the President's palace.

For me, that night was the first time terror had a face.

I listened quietly as Mother and Sa'ad discussed the best action to take.

Sa'ad told Mother, 'I'll go to Alia's. Ra'ad must leave Baghdad. Go to the north. He can wait there while we find out the source of this trouble.'

Sa'ad's words excited me. Perhaps Ra'ad would become a real *peshmerga*. Rather than distributing flyers and putting a gentle face on our struggle, he would become a warrior. I made up my mind in an instant: if so, I would join him in the mountains. I would be the youngest *peshmerga* in Kurdistan.

I squirmed with pleasure when Sa'ad turned to me and said, 'You were very crafty, Joanna. That Barzani poster would have fed their anger and given them evidence against Ra'ad.'

Sa'ad then hurried to change into street clothes. When he rushed back past us to leave the house, he took a few dinars for the taxi fare from Mother's open hand.

My entire body trembled with anticipation as I contemplated the new danger stalking my family. The night's event had been a personal test for me. If I was going to be a fighter, I must be cool and calm in times of crisis.

Mother drew me into her arms, tucking her fingers under my chin, pulling my face up to face hers and praising me. 'Joanna, you were a very clever girl.'

Yes, I had passed my first test. *Peshmerga* must react quickly even when under pressure of investigation.

My mother and sister sat quietly while I fidgeted, looking around our destroyed home.

Mother grimaced. 'We must clean this up. Your father must not know about this night. There will be big problems if he discovers Ra'ad is in danger. We must keep this night a secret from him. And Aziz.'

Mother was right. If told of the night's threats, my father would rush to the local Iraqi internal security office to settle the score. He had never been afraid. A physical fight would ensue, and he would end up in prison. And, even though I was young, I knew that times in Iraq were more dangerous than ever. My father might not survive prison if the Baathists got him. And Uncle Aziz had to be shielded as well. Otherwise he could easily relapse to a dark and unreachable place.

'Joanna, your father is feeling stronger. He might make the morning tea tomorrow.'

Ever since I could remember, until his recent illness my father had always risen with the sun to make a pot of morning tea. He had to have tea with his bread and jam in the mornings.

Mother's voice trailed off to a weak sigh. 'We must straighten up this mess.'

I jumped to the task, while Mother took Muna with her to the kitchen.

As I was placing items back in their rightful position in the sitting room, I heard thundering feet racing up the path and on to the porch.

I turned to flee, believing that the men had returned. To my relief, it was only Sa'ad, but his face was puffy and his eyes dark with fury. He pushed past me, looking for Mother.

I followed him into the kitchen, where Mother was scooping sugar off the floor.

'We were too late.'

'Too late?'

'They have taken Ra'ad. And Hady.'

'Taken?'

'Yes. We should have known. The searches were coordinated. While those security officials were here, five men from the same unit appeared at Alia's house at the same time. They wrecked her home, searching for evidence to use against Ra'ad. They claimed to have found incriminating documents, and when they left they forced Ra'ad and Hady to go with them.'

Muna cried out.

Mother faltered for the first time. She sagged, her knees buckling, but she broke her collapse to the floor by gripping the back of a chair. 'They have my son?'

I was frozen to the spot. Ra'ad? In prison? Uncle Aziz had been in prison. Unpleasant thoughts flickered in my mind. Would Ra'ad return to us mentally impaired too?

And Hady – what would happen to him? A relative even before he married Alia, my brother-in-law was a gentle man. He was so in love with Alia that he was teased by other men for pampering his wife – uncommon behaviour in our culture. He and Alia were the parents of two small boys, four-year-old Shaswar and two-year-old Shwan. They would be miserable without their father.

Mother quickly regained her composure. 'Go, Sa'ad. Go to Fatima. Tell her what has happened. Then go to Othman. He can help us.'

Daddy's sister, Fatima, the woman who had given me my black doll, was an influential woman in Iraq, married to a prominent man. Uncle Othman was Daddy's younger brother. He had important connections too.

Mother lightly tapped Sa'ad on his arm. 'Before he went to sleep, your father said he was going back to work tomorrow. While he is there, we will visit the security officers for this area.' Her voice was fiercely protective. 'We must keep this secret from your father.'

Sa'ad understood without further explanation.

After Sa'ad had left for a second time, Mother and I cleaned the house more rapidly than I would have believed possible. Muna followed us, wanting to help, but she was too upset to be of much use.

The sun was rising when Muna and I returned to bed. It seemed as if a lifetime had passed in only a few hours. We had been frightened out of our wits. Our home had been wrecked. Ra'ad and Hady had been arrested. Yet Sa'ad was already working to get them freed. Mother and I had restored our home to its normal impeccable condition; no evidence remained of our terrifying evening, other than our smashed front door. I had no idea what Mother would tell Father about that door.

Not surprisingly, Mother could not sleep. When I closed my eyes, she was spreading her prayer rug, facing Mecca, lowering herself to her hands and knees, and praying.

When I awoke a few hours later, Muna was still sleeping beside me. Our home was gloomy and quiet. I was thankful to discover that Daddy had returned to work for the first time in ten days.

I found a scribbled note from Sa'ad under a heavy pot on the kitchen table, instructing us to take care of ourselves for the day. He had also cautioned that we were not to leave the house.

Muna and I barely exchanged a word. I searched for food. I nibbled a piece of dry bread and a small chunk of cheese, but it was difficult to swallow. Unaccustomed to being alone in the house, we wandered aimlessly. We saw that the destroyed sections of the front door had been removed, but the splintered gap remained. I was glad that I had slept through my father's reaction when he had seen the condition of that door.

I paced, trying to escape our troubles, but the image of Ra'ad's face followed me. I felt hollow and frightened inside. Ever since I was born, my older siblings had pampered and protected me, and none more than Ra'ad. There were good reasons for this.

It's difficult to believe, but Mother tried to kill me when she discovered she was pregnant with her fifth child. She had been overwhelmed with troubles and felt incapable of enduring another pregnancy. After the 1958 revolution, when my father's furniture factory had been destroyed, my parents became suddenly very poor. The twins had recently been born. She did not know how they could afford yet another child. She was so distraught at my coming that she embarked on desperate measures to stop me. She threw herself down stairs and jumped off the dining-room table. When she failed to accomplish her goal, she even swallowed pills – poison pills that the doctor claimed came within a few heartbeats of killing us both. Mother gamely admitted these acts.

When the doctor informed my father and older siblings about what my mother had tried to do, they were horrified and shocked, and assumed guard over her in order to ensure my safe arrival. When I was born healthy, everyone was so relieved that they spoiled me.

Ra'ad had been the most commanding presence in my life. Ever since I was a toddler, I had been a small shadow to him, even following him out of the house and over to the River Tigris. I would often sit on the sloping banks and admire his swimming. He was so sleek in the water that onlookers affectionately called him the Crocodile of the Tigris.

Now Ra'ad, the brother I so loved and admired, had been taken from me.

Images of the torture my brother might be enduring pursued me miserably. Tears began to edge around my eyelids, making crooked tracks down my face, which was dirty from the previous night's house cleaning.

We knew nothing. We had only our imaginations.

★

Slowly a month passed, and then another. Still their fates remained unknown to us.

Summer faded. The heat lifted.

Mother's prayers filled the cooling air.

And more agonized waiting filled our home.

5

Ra'ad and Hady Return

Baghdad
October 1974

Mother always said that true joy is an answered prayer. She had been praying continually since Ra'ad and Hady had been taken, so her shrill, piercing cries of joy could mean only one thing. She was the first to see them stumble out of a taxi parked a short distance from Alia's house. At the sound of her cries, Alia, her two boys, Sa'ad and Muna came running from inside the house.

Then Mother's joyful cries paused and ceased altogether.

My brother didn't bear the slightest resemblance to his former self. He was so white that he looked like a ghost. He was so bent over that he appeared to be crawling. The last time I had seen Ra'ad he had borne himself tall and strong, but now his lean, muscular body had greatly diminished, and his clothes were so tattered that I could not identify what he was wearing. Was he swathed in a ragged sheet? Or were those shredded rags the last of the pyjamas he had been wearing when he was arrested? It was impossible to tell.

Sa'ad ran over to him, and Ra'ad clung to his younger brother's arm, moving tentatively like one of the cripples or old men I had seen shuffling through the streets of Baghdad. But those pitiful men would have appeared healthy and prosperous next to my brother.

My eyes followed a slow movement behind him and there was Hady, who looked much the same as Ra'ad. His face was ashen and listless, his usual broad smile absent.

Despite their pitiful condition, my sister Alia was overcome with happiness. She broke loose from Mother's arms and rushed to her husband.

I wanted to warn her that Hady was too frail to touch, but I could only choke out a croaking sound.

Tears formed in my eyes when Mother ran to her eldest son and reached out to hold his face between her hands. She pulled him close. She had not seen him for nearly three months, and during much of that time she had feared that he was dead.

Those long months had been an excruciating wait as Mother, Alia, Sa'ad and other relatives struggled to discover Ra'ad and Hady's whereabouts. They were finally found in the prison system. Negotiations had commenced, and earlier that day many thousands of Iraqi dinars that our relatives had pooled had been paid to gain their freedom. Although there was no guarantee that they would be released immediately, we had felt compelled to wait with Alia at her house, just in case.

And that is where they returned, finally. Alive, but barely.

When Ra'ad finally stepped on the porch, he was panting like a man who had competed in a long race. Everything about my once impeccable brother was a mess. His hair was long and dishevelled and his beard sprouted shabbily. His lower lip was so cracked that it was bleeding, and it was hanging open, exposing his teeth, once sparkling white but now coated with the filth of months of imprisonment.

I could not bear to look at him, but I glanced at Hady, whose bloodshot eyes were focused on Alia. His once slim face was now hollow and gaunt.

Both men drank a small glass of water offered to them by Muna, who was so shaken by their condition that her hands visibly trembled.

Mother and Alia led them into the house, where they could have some privacy to eat, have a bath and take a short rest.

Muna and I stared at each other, unable to speak. Muna finally went inside, but I sat alone on the porch for nearly an hour, nursing my grief and anger.

Later in the afternoon our moods lifted slightly and everyone gathered in Alia's living room. A celebratory atmosphere was overtaking the house, as a number of relatives had been told the good news that Ra'ad and Hady were back and had popped in to see the freed prisoners for themselves. Most importantly for me, Auntie Aisha had arrived. When Ra'ad was first taken, she had travelled from Sulaimaniya to support Mother, and had endured every waiting moment with us. I loved that aunt more than any other aunt and cuddled contentedly next to her.

Mother sent a cousin to our home to tell Father that Alia was not feeling well and that we could not return until later in the evening.

Amazingly, and despite all the activity involved in finding Ra'ad and Hady, Mother had succeeded in keeping news of their arrest and imprisonment from Father. Our daily life had been a confusing trail of lies, with Father believing that poor Alia was often ill, hence our frequent visits to her home, and that Ra'ad had been lucky enough to gain permission to travel to Europe – hence his long absence. But living such a lie had been stressful, with the constant worry that someone would accidentally slip. I was looking forward to the day when Ra'ad regained his health and we could behave normally with Father once more.

Once everyone had settled in and around on the sofas, the once humorous Hady was strangely silent while Ra'ad began to speak.

'I will share the details,' he began.

I squeezed Auntie Aisha's hand. She lightly patted my head.

It was distressing to hear Ra'ad communicate in that strained, rustling voice, no longer rising and dropping as I remembered.

'The night we were arrested, everyone had gone to bed. Alia, Hady and the boys were sleeping outside in the garden, but I was on the roof, not yet asleep. I was listening to Monte Carlo radio while watching the full moon through the swaying palm trees. Suddenly I felt there was someone with me. I thought perhaps Hady had remembered something he must tell me, but to my shock, when I looked up, I saw five men I didn't know, all wearing civilian clothes and holding assault rifles. I had no idea how or when they had entered the house, because I had not heard any unusual noise.

'There was no time to speak. Three of the five men jumped on me and started hitting me while pulling me to my feet. One man grabbed my radio and smashed it. They were screaming curses and ordering me to go down and point out my bedroom.

'They practically threw me down the stairs. They already had Hady. Poor Alia and her two babies were terrified witnesses.

'As I was being hustled into my bedroom I overheard Hady asking them who had done anything wrong in this house. That's when I heard the first of many baseless charges: one of the men said that I had been seen spying for the Israelis. And for the Kurds.

'I told them that if they were talking about my membership of the Kurdish Students Union, it was legalized by the March 1970 agreement. But nothing I said registered with those crazed men. I had recently heard that other students had been targeted for being Kurdish, so I assumed they were rounding up all the members of the Kurdish Students Union. Then I remembered that a few days before I had been approached for membership by the Baathist Student Organization. Of course I had refused to join. Perhaps my refusal had triggered the investigation.

'The men started trashing my bedroom while I stood helplessly watching, still in my pyjamas. They refused to give me permission to change my clothes or put on my dressing gown, although I managed to slip my feet into my slippers.'

I nodded along with Ra'ad's telling, remembering how crude and brutal those men were who broke into our house.

While Ra'ad drank a cup of tea, Hady spoke tentatively. 'There was nothing illegal in the house. They found a pamphlet Ra'ad had been writing, telling the history of the Kurds and praising the government for allowing Kurds to speak the Kurdish language and study Kurdish history. Yet when they began to wave it around I knew we were finished. Out came the blindfolds. First Ra'ad. Then me. Alia cried, pleading with them not to take us.' Hady shook his head. 'Those men appeared as deaf as her father Muhammad. We ended up at the security intelligence headquarters in the Mansour area. I've seen that place many times. It's in a huge old house there.'

Hady was struck by a coughing fit so severe that he had to leave the room, so Ra'ad resumed the story.

'I was pushed into a chair and the blindfold removed. I was facing an aggressive interrogator. He was cruel. And stupid. He claimed I had been reported transmitting from a wireless radio. I was racking my brain, trying to think where they could have got such a false impression. Then I remembered that one day Hady had loaned me his car so that I could visit Auntie Fatima. When I came out, I noticed that his car aerial was loose and I removed it so that I could repair it. While I was standing there with the aerial in my hands, a neighbour kept walking past, staring first at the aerial and then at me. Looking back, I know now that he must have been a Baathist who drew false conclusions.

'The interrogator said that while I was holding the aerial I was overheard speaking Hebrew to the Israelis. He claimed I then moved the aerial to a different spot in the yard and spoke Kurdish to the Barzani party headquarters up north.'

Several family members laughed loudly at the idea of a spy so clever that he spied for two such dissimilar groups, yet so stupid that he boldly spoke in a foreign language in plain view of witnesses.

Ra'ad smiled thinly. 'The accusations were so absurd that I asked the man why didn't they arrest me on the spot, which is what I would have done if I were a security official and witnessed such a busy spy. Indeed, I told him that if I was a spy, that I was a most in-efficient one! I asked him to tell me the exact day and the time all this occurred. The man named a certain date. It was not even the same day I had visited Auntie Fatima. Then I remembered where I was on the day he was claiming I had been spying. I had been swimming in the river, and afterwards had played a game of football with a group of friends. There were twenty-two swimmers and foot-ball players who could attest to what I was saying. I insisted that he check out his facts.

'When he called out for an assistant to take down the names, I instantly regretted my words. When I was recruited to join the Kurdish Students Union I was told that should I ever be detained, I should never reveal names of anyone I knew. One of the more experienced student members gave wise advice: part with your head but not your secret. I decided it was best for me to shut up.

'When I grew silent, the interrogator furiously rang a bell. Two strange men entered the room and clumsily testified that they had seen me on the very day I was claiming to have been swimming and in a football game. They claimed I was lying, and that I had been seen transmitting with an aerial and speaking first in Hebrew and then in Kurdish. I said I had never even heard Hebrew being spoken and would not recognize it if someone started speaking it at that very moment.

'Just then they pulled poor Hady into the room and questioned him about his relationship with me. He confirmed that he was my brother-in-law. They accused him of being a Kurdish sympathizer. Hady admitted he was a Kurd, but said that he was a peace-loving husband and father, working as an engineer. The men knew that Hady's brother was a *peshmerga*, though, and that Hady had recently gone up north to drive his brother's car back to Baghdad for safekeeping.

'Then we were blindfolded again, and taken out of that building and put into another car. I could think of little besides Uncle Aziz and how he had been tortured, and in particular how he had been hung upside down from the ceiling and beaten for a week. I expected something similar and I was dreading it.

'Soon the car stopped and our blindfolds were removed. We were pushed into a dark area surrounded by a high wall. I presumed we were in a prison yard. Hady and I were ordered to stand side by side, so I assumed they were preparing to shoot us and bury us.

'The full moon cast light on the scene. By the dim light I could see that we were standing next to a large metal cover. Then one of the guards walked our way, struggling with a ladder. The metal cover was lifted off the ground and I looked down into a deep, dark pit. One of the guards lowered the ladder into the pit. Hady and I were ordered to go down. I thought we were going into a pit of snakes.'

Hady had returned to the room by this time, and he spoke in a weary voice. 'Snakes I would have preferred. It was like going into the grave.'

'Exactly.'

Mother looked shattered. She walked over to Ra'ad and rubbed his neck and shoulders. 'Perhaps you can tell us the rest later, son.'

Ra'ad looked up. 'I must tell this while my memory is fresh. Perhaps one day the world will be interested in knowing what innocent Iraqis and Kurds have endured under this insane government. There we were in the grave, standing in a dark pit. Then true terror: the metal lid was closed on us. That was the blackest black you can imagine.'

Hady interjected, 'But that was not the worst of it. I was already terrified and what did I hear? Ragged breathing. I shouted "Who is there?" It was so black that I could see nothing. But I could hear. And I could smell. What a stench! Something or someone was coming at us. I believed that we had been put in a pit with wild animals. I put up my fists, ready to fight man or beasts. Then some poor man spoke, saying, "Do not be afraid. I am a prisoner too. I have been alone in this hole for many weeks. I'm from Najaf."'

We knew about Najaf, a large city south of Baghdad. It was the seat of Shiite political power, and considered a holy city by the Shiite Muslims. It was where the tomb of Imam Ali was located, Prophet Muhammad's son-in-law. The Shiites had bravely struggled in vain against the Sunni powers in Baghdad, and Saddam was the most repressive Sunni ruler of all. Obviously, my brother's pit companion was of the Shiite sect.

Hady continued, 'I was so relieved that the stench was apparently human that the smell no longer bothered me. In fact, I felt like embracing the man.'

Ra'ad laughed hollowly. 'He quickly related his story. His brother was a politically active Shiite, belonging to the Al-Dawa Islamic party, which as we all know has recently become even more active against Saddam. When the brother heard he was going to be arrested, he fled to France. Our poor companion in the pit, who had never been political in his life, was arrested and held hostage in his brother's place. He had been told that if his brother didn't return to accept his death sentence, he would die in prison in his stead.

'We talked all night, partly to take our minds off the misery of being in that hole, but the man's spirits were so low that he didn't make us feel any better. He kept repeating that it was written that the three of us would die in that pit.

'He predicted that I would be the first to die. He said that students were not accustomed to hardship and always perished quickly. He reasoned that he would be the second to die, because he had become so weakened by his ordeal. Hady, he decided, would survive for several weeks before he died.

'We thought then that we knew true torment, but that came with the morning sun. We were fried under that metal top. The heat intensified the toilet stench. Our pit was a toilet which had never been cleaned out. The smell was indescribable. I realized then that the prisoner from Najaf was correct. We were going to perish. I didn't think I could last a day.

'I was the lowest on that first day, because I still had enough intellect to think. I believed that my life was basically over, one way or another. I knew that once I had been arrested in Iraq, my future was doomed. I would forever be in the shadow of the internal intelligence officials, never again allowed to move freely.

'Later in the morning they opened the metal lid to lower a plastic pitcher of warm water. The pitcher was tied by a rope. Most of the water spilled out on the way down. We were given a single loaf of bread to share, but I couldn't eat anything on that first day. Hady tried to eat, but couldn't, so our fellow prisoner happily ate our share and his.'

Hady interrupted. 'He no longer had any teeth. His interrogators had pulled out his teeth as a part of his torture.'

Ra'ad added, 'They had extracted his fingernails and toenails as well. I expected the same to happen to me.' He scratched his head. 'Lice,' he confirmed in an apologetic tone.

I gasped and looked at Auntie Aisha. Lice! On Ra'ad!

'One day turned into the next and we lost track of time. The heat and the stench never ended. And the waiting – nothing was more upsetting than the waiting.' Ra'ad glanced affectionately at Hady. 'I was most concerned for Hady. Every day I thought, This will be his last day.'

Hady laughed sadly. 'And I thought the same of you.'

Ra'ad grimaced and said, 'But I was the first to collapse. One day I just lost it. We faced constant hunger and I grew weaker by the day. One minute I was sitting there plotting how we might get word to everyone where we were being held and the next minute I passed out.'

Hady told us, 'Ra'ad looked dead. While I shouted for the guards, our pit mate took one look at him, felt his neck, and pronounced him dead. That was the worst moment. I couldn't get the attention of the guards, so I took out of my pocket a few pebbles I had gathered from the ground and started flinging them against the metal lid. The guards soon appeared and I yelled at them that Ra'ad Al-Askari had died. They pulled him up and out. They threw water on him. Soon I heard them exclaim that he was alive. With that, they put the lid on us again. I don't know what happened to you after that. Ra'ad?'

'As it happened, it was the fourteenth of July celebrations, commemorating the revolution that had brought the Baathists to power. The guards were drinking beer and *arak* and dancing together. They dragged me into the middle of the festivities and chained me to a palm tree. I sat watching a bunch of fools drinking alcohol and dancing.'

Sa'ad grunted in disgust. Sa'ad was the most religious of my siblings, never missing a prayer and guarding his sisters' morals. The idea of government officials drinking alcohol and dancing while keeping innocent men in holes in the ground rankled mightily.

'My head was hanging to my chest, but I saw feet walking in my direction. It was a drunken officer undoing his trousers. He was going to pee on me. I found the strength to shout, startling him. He saw me, and said, "By God! I know you. You are Ra'ad Al-Askari."

'He had seen me at the Al-Aadamiya sports club, where I played basketball. I told him that I needed help and that I had been wrongly accused. He replied that his rank was low and he couldn't even help his own relatives, some of whom were in prison. I made a request that he call my family at least. He tapped his head, asking, "Do I look insane to you? If I call your relatives, I'll end up chained beside you."

'He disappeared, leaving me chained to the tree. When the sun came up, it was the first time I had seen that grove during the daytime. And what did I see? Hundreds of metal covers plastered the ground. Each represented the most acute human misery. Moans of anguish hummed from the covers, sounding like one long groan. The agonized cries corroded any confidence I might have had that a single prisoner would get out of that hell alive.

'I remained chained for up to two days, tortured by those pleas for help. Finally I was released from bondage and taken inside the building for further questioning.

'I was faced with a different interrogator. He was a tall, dark man, much more dangerous-looking than the first one. He was armed and

waved his pistol around in a very unprofessional manner. Then he
held it to my head, accusing and threatening, telling me, "You are a
low-down dog. You are a Barzani follower. You are a mutant. Why
don't you confess and save me the trouble of making you?" He was a
madman. He was interrupted when another prisoner was thrown
through the door. He was crying out in Kurdish for help. My
interrogator left. I was cautious, since I had been warned that a
favourite tactic was to bring together prisoners with the same
loyalties. I assumed they wanted me to confide in this man and
confess that I was working for the Israelis, or some such nonsense.
Nevertheless, I asked the man why he had been arrested. He said he
had been caught listening to Kurdish radio broadcasts. As far as I
knew, listening to Kurdish broadcasts was no longer a crime after
1970, but I said nothing.

  'I was not prepared for what came next. Suddenly the door flew
open and three muscular men rushed into the room. Without a word
of warning, they attacked that poor man, beating him viciously. I
heard harsh breathing sounds and then nothing. I think he died. They
pulled his limp body out of the room.

  'Yet another officer came in. He spoke so softly that I could barely
hear him. There was a window covered by curtains. He opened the
curtains and the palm grove became visible. I stared at the trees,
thinking about all the men buried alive in that grove, and how no
one in the world knew about, or cared about, that dreadful place.
Billions of people throughout the world were carrying on with their
lives, numerous foreign governments were friendly with Saddam
Hussein, and all the while innocent Iraqis had been thrown into holes
in the ground and were being tortured and killed for no reason.
Where was everybody? Why didn't anyone care?

  'The officer gazed at me with strange sad eyes. He asked me, "Why
did you commit this corrupt deed against your own country? Don't
deny it. We have witnesses that you had a wireless device, and
that you were contacting the Israelis and spying for them. Then you
contacted the Kurdish rebel forces in the north. All this was so as to
harm your own government."

  'I don't know why, but I decided to appeal to this officer. I told
him that I speak Kurdish only because my mother is Kurdish. I
admitted that I was active in the Kurdish Students Union, but only

because I was allowed the right under the treaty of 11 March 1970 between the Iraqi government and the Kurds. I told him that I had never travelled out of Iraq in my entire life. I told him that I had never met an Israeli. I told him that everything he had read about me in the report was simply not true.

'I felt I was getting somewhere with him, so I said that when I told the truth, everyone got angry with me, but if I lied and confessed to the things they were accusing me of, it was only to humour them. I told him that he seemed an intelligent man and I doubted that he wanted to hear lies. I repeated what I had said before: that I had been swimming and playing football on the day in question, and that it was physically impossible for me to have been in two places at the same time.

'He didn't acknowledge a word I said. He raised the subject of Great-uncle Jafar, saying that I should honour the memory of the man who had been the first Defence Minister of Iraq, the man who had helped to form modern Iraq. He claimed that Uncle Jafar would be ashamed of his nephew for engaging in such traitorous activities. Without waiting for an answer, he then said that the Kurdish movement consisted of criminals and Israeli spies.

'To my despair, I was sent back to the pit. Hady had been told I was dead, so he was amazed to see me. I was pleased, of course, to see that Hady was still alive, but terribly sorry to be back in that hole. While I was away, Hady had been interrogated too, and knocked about. After what I had witnessed, I was grateful that we were both alive.'

'Ah, praise God for that,' Hady mumbled.

'For five more days we stayed in that hole. Our pit mate was near death. Then on the sixth day, they came to take us away. Although terrible days were still ahead of us, that was the last we saw of that pit, thank God.'

Auntie Aisha asked, 'What about that poor soul from Najaf?'

Hady said, 'As they were taking us out of the pit, they replaced us with three other prisoners. But the poor man had been there for four or five months already. He was no longer talking. He would just rouse himself slightly when the bread and water was delivered and then fall to the ground and hold on to his bread. He had lost control of his bowels. He is dead by now, for sure.'

Mother was visibly shaken. 'What happened then, son?'

'For that move, we were each forced to wear glasses with blacked-out lenses. But I discovered that if I held my head in a certain position, I could see a little from the sides. We left the pit prison and were driven west, out of Baghdad. The trip took only about an hour. I knew the direction we were going. I hoped I was wrong, but I soon realized that our destination was the Abu Ghraib prison. I lost all hope at that point.'

Although safe in Auntie Aisha's arms, I shivered in fear. All Iraqis knew the history of the notorious Abu Ghraib. The British had built the prison at about the time I was born, in the early 1960s. It was a huge prison complex, an independent city, with five large compounds. It was now a prison mainly designated for political prisoners, such as Kurds calling for Kurdish rights or Shiites demanding religious freedom, or even Sunnis who were against the Baathists. From the day it had been built, the name Abu Ghraib had been linked with torture and death.

Ra'ad described the place for us. 'They registered us and put us in a crowded cell block. There were Kurds, Shiites and even non-Iraqis such as Lebanese and Palestinians in our block. We met a Spanish journalist who had been there for over a year. The cells had bars, so we could see prisoners in other cells and even talk to them when the guards were out of hearing range. There was no privacy. A single small bowl served as a urinal.'

Hady tittered, 'It was heaven.'

'Yes. You are right. Terrible as it was to be in Abu Ghraib, compared to the hole in the ground it was heaven, at least at first. We heard there was even a dining hall, an exercise room and a prayer room, but that was a joke. It was not a social club. No prisoners were ever allowed in those areas, as far as we knew.

'Soon after our arrival we were told that one of three things would happen: we would be set free, we would be sentenced to life imprisonment or we would be executed. The decision was to be made within a few days. For me, those were the most torturous days of all, when we didn't know if we would live or die. Or ever see any of you again.'

I glanced at Hady. Alia was sitting close by his side. She was holding her youngest son, Shwan, in her lap, while her oldest, Shaswar, was sitting beside his father. They were a perfect little family. I had to fight back my tears.

'After more than seven weeks in that place, we had heard nothing of our fate, while prisoners all around us were regularly being taken out to be executed. Then one day I was taken to see a doctor. The doctor gave me a courteous examination, asking me if I needed any-thing. I had been warned by other prisoners that the doctors often prescribed poisonous pills or gave deadly injections. So I told him that I was just fine and I only needed my freedom.

'I think he was sincere. He told me, "Son, when people are brought to me, it is usually before their release. But there is one thing you should remember: never tell anyone about what you have been subjected to or what you have seen in this place. If you talk, you'll be back."

'Then I was escorted back to the cell. I was upset to find that Hady had been moved while I was away. Where had they taken him?

'I didn't have time to worry about Hady for very long. The moment the cell door closed behind me, my cell mates began to claw at me. Everyone appeared to have gone mad. Perhaps they had received orders from the prison authority to murder me. I fought, to no avail. They pushed me to the floor, on my stomach. They started pulling at my pyjama top, or at least what was left of it, as I had been wearing it for over two months. I pleaded for mercy.

'One of the men clawing at me said, "Relax, relax. When a prisoner is taken to the doctor, often the next step is release. We are going to write our home telephone numbers on your back. When you get out, have a family member copy the numbers down. Take this list and go to a public phone. Call all the numbers and tell whoever answers that you have been at Abu Ghraib, in the political section. They will know who the message is really from. Say nothing more."'

Curious, I slipped from Auntie Aisha's arms and went to stand behind my brother's chair. When I looked down the neck of his shirt, I could see evidence of numbers scrawled on his back.

'Sa'ad will write down those numbers later,' Ra'ad promised. 'Then we'll call these people. It's the least I can do.'

I stared at my big brother in awe. I loved him.

Ra'ad smiled weakly. 'Little Joanna,' he said, 'I am very happy to see you.'

My face flushed red. I longed to tell my brother so many things. I wanted to tell him about the owl with the golden eyes, and I wanted to tell him that at the very moment when he had been staring at the full moon and the star-cloaked sky, I had been doing the same. Despite the lice in his hair, I reached over and kissed him on the cheek, before sitting down to hear the end of his tragic tale.

'This happened this morning. Hady was never returned to our cell, so that is why his back was not used as a message board.'

I was glad to hear Hady chuckle, coming back to life.

He reported, 'That's because I had been taken to my place of employment. The guards said they must have a guarantee from an Iraqi company that I would be employed if released.' Hady swung his head back and forth. 'You should have seen the faces of my employers when I appeared in the office after an unexplained absence, surrounded by prison guards, in torn pyjamas and bringing a stench of unwashed bodies. But they signed the guarantee and told me to come back to work as soon as possible.'

'Praise Allah,' Mother murmured automatically, for many companies would have refused to keep on a former prisoner.

Ra'ad suddenly seemed in a hurry to finish the story. 'A few hours ago, Hady and I were thrown out of the front gate of the prison. Our dream of freedom had come true. We were released.' He snapped his fingers. 'Just like that!' He cleared his rasping throat. 'There we were, looking like two lunatics with long beards and hair, stumbling in the streets, weak, hungry and cringing from the blinding sunlight. No taxi would stop for us. Cars actually veered away when they saw us. Finally an elderly taxi driver stopped. We told him that we had been wrongly arrested. He believed us because, he said, his own son had been falsely arrested the year before. His kind heart wouldn't let him refuse us.' Ra'ad clapped his hands together. 'And that's it. We survived.'

Mother, Alia, Auntie Aisha and several other aunts jumped up to push tea and juice into Ra'ad's and Hady's hands. Our two men were home, safe, back where they belonged. Nothing else really mattered to any of us. The celebration began.

For that moment, my heart was throbbing with energy and hope that our troubles were over. But both Ra'ad and Hady sat quietly, their eyes leaden, unable to take pleasure from the festivities.

Thinking back, I believed that they had looked into the abyss, and there they had seen Iraq's future and our own.

In fact that terrifying episode was not an end but a beginning.

Tragically, our troubles had only just begun.

II Joanna Grows Up

6

Death

Baghdad
October 1976

Should I live a hundred years, memories of Ra'ad and Hady's narrow escape from those Baathist thugs will never leave me.

After regaining his health, Ra'ad resumed his university studies, but he was required to submit to a humiliating security procedure every six weeks. He appeared at the local internal security offices to answer questions and file reports, documenting that he no longer 'committed criminal acts against the state'. My law-abiding brother was mortified to be treated as a criminal. If he still participated in the Kurdish Students Union, he did not tell us.

Alia's anxiety over Hady's safety settled over her household like a fog. Hady returned to work, but looked shrivelled and wan, his features sharp. Alia tearfully confided in Mother that her husband's vivid nightmares about the pit prison provoked nightly mayhem. There were constant alarms with Shaswar and Shwan as well, two little boys who had once led carefree lives and now wept more than they laughed. The one joy was that Alia was pregnant with her third child and due to deliver.

Muna's torment was painful to witness. My timid sister was traumatized by her brother's ordeal. She would sit in a huddle and draw her small body into a tense ball.

Sa'ad was born with religion in his veins, but since Ra'ad's arrest he had become even more dutiful and dedicated, never missing a prayer. He insisted that Alia's two boys sometimes accompany him to the mosque, despite the fact that at six and four they were quite restless during prayers.

I believed that Sa'ad was on the path to becoming a cleric. Such a decision would have brought joy to my devout mother, although I would have greeted the news less enthusiastically, for Sa'ad's religious fervour promoted authoritarian conduct. I did not want nor need a guardian of my morals.

Although Mother strived to maintain a calm demeanour, I knew that her heart was bruised. I noticed a new fresh web of worry lines bordering her eyes and mouth. Living in Baathist Baghdad was ageing my beautiful mother. Despite Ra'ad's close call, however, Mother did not falter in her support of the Kurdish cause.

I was relieved, for I now had plans for my future. I was determined to join the Kurdish cause when I was old enough. No one could stop me. Yet Mother cautioned that we had entered a new and even more dangerous period in our Kurdish history with those brutal Baathists at the helm. She said that each of her children must become his or her own policeman, watching everything said, cautious of every action taken. I promised Mother that when the day came when I was old enough to join a Kurdish political party, I would be careful.

Only Father was oblivious to our worries. With sign language perfected after years of marriage, Mother had convinced him that thieves had kicked down our door, but had fled at the sight of Sa'ad armed with a carving knife. My father, who was a master builder and craftsman, soon fitted our home with a sturdy wooden door equipped with unique locks. I had never before seen such a door. A military tank could have broken it, perhaps, but human feet, never.

Certainly, life would never be the same for me. When an unfamiliar car turned up outside our home, I breathlessly rushed to peer from behind the curtains, poised to shout a warning for all to flee into the back garden and over the fence to safety. I even practised for speed. I was proud that it took me only one minute to shout a warning, seize my emergency bag, packed and hidden under a covered table in Ra'ad's bedroom, and make it to the garden wall.

I made these practice runs daily. My mother and siblings would exchange patronizing smiles, as though I was playing a childish game, but I believed that such preparation might, one day, save all our lives.

I was surprised to hear Mother claim that many citizens of our country supported our Baathist President, Ahmed Hassan Al-Bakir, and his second-in-command, Saddam Hussein, known as Mr Deputy to Iraqis. Supposedly, Mr Deputy was the true power in Iraq these days, but Mother scoffed at the idea there was any difference between the two men, saying that when one laid the eggs and the other one hatched them, it was all one and the same.

Some people claimed that Iraqis had never had it so good, with new government laws guaranteeing rights for women. A new law, called the National Campaign to Eradicate Illiteracy, had been passed, requiring that all Iraqis be educated. Even elderly villagers who had never stepped inside a school room were suddenly obligated to attend reading classes. Undoubtedly, such social reforms were beneficial, yet the repressive atmosphere and fear of arrest and torture tilted the balance against the Baathists for most Iraqi citizens.

During that year of 1976 I celebrated my fourteenth birthday, feeling a big girl. I sailed along during the summer but was pleased to return to school in September. The following month, October, just when I felt the family at last might be getting over the terror of Ra'ad's imprisonment, death paid us a visit.

The moment I heard, I was struck by the most unbearable agony. For some inexplicable reason my first reaction was to take off my shoes and fling them in the air. Shocked faces greeted my action but I didn't care. Next I ripped up school papers and threw them to the wind.

Then I heard excruciating screams. I wondered where they came from, not realizing that the screams were my own. I ran into the house and raced through one room after the other, overturning chairs and small tables. I sprinted through the kitchen and the back door and dashed into the garden. I shrieked so loudly that the neighbours called out over our garden wall in alarm, asking what the trouble was and shouting for someone to alert the police that a massacre was occurring at the Al-Askari home.

I didn't care.

I concealed myself behind one of the largest date palm trees in the garden. With open palms I struck my forehead as I leaned against the prickly bark of the old tree. When I stared upwards through the branches at the blue Baghdad sky I could not believe that everything still looked as it did yesterday, that the earth was still revolving around the sun, which was still shining brightly while white clouds floated past.

The sky and the sun and the clouds should all be draped in black, in mourning.

My backside slithered against the trunk of the tree as I slowly collapsed on to the earth. In my anguish, I rolled around on the ground, feeling sand grind into the pores on my face.

But I didn't care.

The loose sand edged my lips as I choked out the words, 'Daddy! Daddy! Daddy!'

Ten days before, he had collapsed at the railway offices and been rushed to the hospital. When word came, Mother, Sa'ad, Muna and I sped across the city in a taxi to the Al-Numan Hospital located in the Adhamiya neighbourhood, Mother staring straight ahead, praying, Sa'ad dark and still, and Muna pale and trembling. I was in an unmoving stupor, yearning to cry but unable to shed a single tear.

Alia was there to meet us, despite the fact she had given birth to her third son only a few weeks before, a precious little boy named Shazad. I had never seen my sister so distraught, not even after Hady was arrested.

When we were led to Daddy's bed, his features were drawn taut with pain, and one side of his mouth drooping and sad. He was restless, trying in vain to shift his partially paralysed body.

A new and horrible side of life was suddenly revealed to me. My parents could sicken and die and leave me. I reached to grasp Daddy's hand but Mother pulled me away, saying, 'Later, Joanna. Later.'

I then tried to catch my father's eye, but he was in too much pain to even notice me.

Shattered, I huddled behind Mother, waiting impatiently for a doctor while listening to the sounds of tired toddlers crying from the nearby hospital corridor. Finally, a short, stout doctor with heavy jowls appeared.

Father would live, we were assured. But in the next moment we also learned the frightening news that he had suffered a serious stroke, and that he was disorientated and possibly in severe pain.

I told myself that if he could only live, I would spend every spare moment by his side, doing whatever he needed. No task would be too difficult, no burden too heavy.

I longed to stay at the hospital, but the decision was not mine to make. Mother remained there at Father's side while Sa'ad, Muna and I were sent home. Auntie Aisha would soon make the trip from Sulaimaniya to stay with us.

Although I never had the comfort of making contact with my father before leaving him, to pass a secret message of my love, I did kiss his hands and face and squeeze his shoulder. I left the hospital in the naive belief that soon all would return to normal.

But the doctor had lied to us. He knew that my father was not going to recover. In those days, at least in Iraq, doctors thought it best not to reveal the saddest truths. That night at the hospital was the last time I saw my father.

Ten days later as I hurriedly walked from school, my steps slowed when I saw large numbers of sad-faced relatives congregating at our home. My heart told me that the gathering crowd was connected to my father's illness. I knew then that nothing would ever again be the same.

Wanting to avoid the news obviously awaiting me, I considered hiding in a friend's house, but a relative saw me and came running, pulling me aside to tell me that my father was dead.

Dead!

No one could make me stop screaming, not even my dear Uncle Aziz, his worried face looming over my own, calling my name repeatedly, 'Joanna! Joanna! Joanna!' With tears rolling down his face, he lifted me from the ground, carried me to my room and gently put me down on a bed and covered me with a blanket.

There was a deafening commotion, with everyone speaking at once, all offering advice as to what should be done with me, a brokenhearted girl who was screeching to see her father one more time. I called out for my mother but she was still at the hospital where Daddy had died. She would go straight from there with my brothers to the grave to make plans for the funeral tomorrow because Muslims must be buried within twenty-four hours. So it was uncertain when Mother would be home.

Auntie Aisha had arrived from Sulaimaniya. She rushed to sit by my side. She was the only one who could comfort me. She ordered everyone to leave my room.

Yes, I wanted to be alone with my memories of my father.

Although because of my father's inability to speak he could never tell me anything of his life, I had learned much about him from Mother, Ra'ad and Alia, as well as from older relatives who had known him from the time he was born. My thoughts brought him back to a sort of life, if only in my own mind.

Unlike ours, my father's childhood was privileged. The Al–Askari family were very powerful in 1914, the year my father was born. Later, the family became personally and politically aligned to Iraq's royal family, which ruled the country from the end of the First World War until the revolution of 1958.

My father grew up in a large home in the Aiwadiya area in Baghdad, a gracious villa shaded by swaying Iraqi palm trees. He and his younger brother Othman spent many hours lazing on the banks of the ancient Tigris, a place of dreams for men since the beginning of civilization. There they would watch the river craft drifting by, two young men dreaming of the days when they would take their rightful place in Baghdad society.

But my father's dreams ended when he was only seven years old. The first sign of trouble came quickly. One morning his throat was so painfully sore that he could barely swallow. A high temperature followed. His parents worriedly discussed a red rash that developed on his neck and chest. It was said that his rippled red skin had the rough texture of sandpaper. His tongue became swollen and red. Soon he was slipping in and out of consciousness.

He recovered, but when his parents came to assess his condition, he cried out, 'I cannot hear you!' He had not yet lost his ability to speak, and he began to sob softly, his panicked cries gaining momentum until harsh sounds of despair exploded throughout the house. His gentle father, a physical giant of a man, clasped his son's small hands in his own and wept with him, while his mother stood still and silent, a wooden figure, her brown eyes glowing dark while her very white skin faded whiter still.

Father's parents were wealthy, and every medical specialist in Baghdad was consulted. None offered hope.

Father's anguish increased when he began to lose his ability to articulate properly, for when children go deaf they generally lose their ability to speak as well. He was so ashamed of his infirmity that he withdrew into himself and became isolated.

In 1921, the year Father was stricken, Iraq was not equipped to deal with such medical problems. Most children struck by similar calamities were banished to a hidden area in the home, ignored by their families, who felt a handicapped child was a shame and a burden. But Father was more fortunate than most. His family were highly educated. There was money. Most importantly, he was the nephew of the renowned Jafar Pasha Al-Askari, an admired military genius of the First World War, a budding diplomat, and a treasured friend of many leading Europeans and Iraqis. I never knew that uncle, as he died twenty-six years before I was born, but it was an accepted fact that he was exceptional.

Jafar Pasha announced that his handicapped nephew must be educated and trained in a productive career. And so my father's future was arranged. When he was eleven years old, he was sent to a special school in France for the deaf-mute. He prospered there, becoming a master wood-carver and earning a university degree in engineering. He was so contented in France that he remained there for twelve years, only reluctantly returning at the request of his family when his beloved uncle, Jafar Pasha, was assassinated in 1936.

His uncle's assassination was only the first in a long line of family sorrows. On 22 March 1937, approximately five months after the death of Jafar Pasha, Father's own father, my grandfather Ali Ridha, killed himself. In a spiralling bout of depression caused by his brother's assassination, he shot himself in the head. His death was a terrible blow to everyone in the family, and especially to my father.

The next big setback to my father's happiness happened on 14 July 1958, when the royal family was massacred. During that upheaval, his booming furniture factory business was destroyed. My father was doomed to be forever poor.

The following morning my father came home from the hospital, but not in the manner I had hoped or imagined. He came to us in a wooden coffin that was placed in the middle of the living room. Our home was overflowing with many grieving relatives, friends and acquaintances, as my father was a well-respected gentleman. But the only thing I could see was that coffin. Father's face was not visible, since the coffin was kept closed, but my imagination took me in there with him.

I could not bear the idea that my athletic father was so tightly encased in that small box. I refused to leave him and I lingered around the periphery, watching everything through a haze, seeing the faces of well-wishers, distinguishing the movement of lips as mourners spoke of their sorrow but not hearing exactly what they said.

Alia was inconsolable. When she saw the wooden box she broke down completely, throwing herself on the coffin, crying and pleading for Father to come back to her. It took both Hady and Sa'ad to pull her off the coffin. Mother and several aunts followed and tried to comfort her.

I stayed with my father. I moved closer, staring at the small box and whispering 'Daddy' under my breath, willing him to reclaim life and open his eyes and use his strong arms to push the coffin cover away, look at me, smile at me, open his arms and pull me to him.

But he did not. He stayed in that little box.

I remained in the living room until the men designated to carry the coffin came in to take my father to the Sheikh Maroof Al-Karkhi cemetery.

Women in my country did not attend burials, although we could visit the grave later. Yet I knew exactly what would happen. At the cemetery they would lower my father into a hole in the ground and then cover him with earth.

Although discouraged by my aunts, I followed the procession down the street, watching the coffin until my father was out of sight. And my darling father was gone, just like that, never to return.

7
My Mother, My Father

Baghdad
October to November 1976

My father's kindly heart was filled with riches, yet he died a pauper.

After his death, apprehension about the future kept our home in turmoil. The need for money was so urgent that soon after the funeral Mother, Alia and Auntie Aisha searched through Father's possessions. They found a mere sixty dinars. For me, they found other, more important items that revealed what my father truly treasured. There was a stack of grainy photographs of his children, his parents and other dead relatives, all delicately wrapped in wrinkled tissue paper. Under the photographs he had amassed cherished notes that his children had written him over the years. Since he could not hear or speak, our main method of interaction with him was through the written word.

Sixty dinars would last us but a few weeks. Mother had four children still in school. Only Alia was married and no longer looking to Mother for her well-being. With money problems looming, our Kurdish relatives urged Mother to return to her childhood home in Kurdistan, so that we might benefit from our large and loving family there.

Of course, I wanted to go to Kurdistan. But because of my young age, no one cared about my opinion.

Alia heard me pleading, but cautioned me not to wish for such a move, saying that our lives would be very different in the north. The Baathists were becoming even more brutal with the Kurds in Kurdistan. Violence was escalating in our torn land, with government raids, sieges and murders of innocent Kurds.

I had a lot to think about. Suddenly I was discovering that nothing about adult life was easy.

Mother was anxious that the government would order us to vacate our home, as we were living in a house that belonged to the railway. Before the revolution in 1958 my family had enjoyed living in a lovely large house in the Salyiya district, but after the revolution, when my parents had lost everything, including their home and my father's modern furniture factory, they were fortunate that Father was quickly appointed as a mechanical engineer for the Iraqi railway. A benefit of his job had been assigned housing in the unpretentious district where I grew up.

Although in our teeming family life there had never been any privacy, I enjoyed living in our crowded modest yellow-brown brick bungalow. It had been built during the 1940s by British officials. Many British had lived in Iraq during the years when they ruled the country through their puppet king, King Faisal. When the British finally quit the country they were thoughtful enough to leave behind our cosy bungalow with its front garden hedged in by *yass* bushes, which had a citrus fragrance that, when in bloom, perfumed the entire area. It had a small front porch that opened into a sitting room, where sofas were arrayed around the walls, three bedrooms and a bathroom. A tapered, tight stairwell gave us access to the roof, which was handy because during the hot summer months most people generally sleep outside on the roof. Mother did most of her cooking in the small kitchen which adjoined the most popular room in the house, a sizeable veranda furnished with large tables and plenty of chairs. Best of all, the house was situated in the heart of a vast palm garden with trees so tall that they blocked out the hot rays of the Baghdad sun.

As we were worried about being evicted, it was a pleasant surprise when government officials told us that we could continue to live there during Mother's lifetime, and that Mother was entitled to a small pension from the railway company. We would have just enough money for food and clothes. In a few years Ra'ad would graduate from college and, as the eldest son, he would automatically assume responsibility for our well-being. Suddenly, our future seemed less bleak. With this good news, Mother decided we would remain in Baghdad.

After the funeral, our closest Kurdish relatives remained with us for many days. One night after dinner, when the women of the household were gathered in a morose group on the back porch, Mother's sister Fatima became unusually animated, and said to Mother, 'Kafia, it is time for the weeping to stop and the living to begin.'

I was a bit dazed by this kind of talk, as I could not envisage finding joy in life then, or ever. My fatherless heart was raw.

Auntie Fatima had an impish smile on her round face and her brown eyes were sparkling as she peered at Mother and asked, 'Kafia, have you ever told your girls how much your husband loved you?'

Mother shifted uncomfortably in her chair, frowning at her sister and refusing to acknowledge her improper question.

Mother possessed many exceptional qualities. She was a selfless mother, a devoted wife, a devout Muslim and an accomplished cook. She was so welcoming to visitors that our home was always filled with visiting relatives and people who would rather be at our home than at their own. Her children had always been proud of her in other ways, too. She was a regal beauty. Her skin was fair, her eyes dark and lively. She was tall, and had a mane of shimmering black hair that was the envy of her sisters and daughters. Even her hands were exquisite, with slender fingers and perfectly formed nails. It was no surprise to me that she had won her husband's affection, despite the fact their marriage was arranged.

Auntie Fatima looked around at the large circle of women and said, 'Why, Muhammad was so captivated by Kafia that once he even threw himself under the wheels of a bus.'

I perked up. I had not heard this story.

Mother glanced at Alia, Muna and me, cupping her hands over her mouth, embarrassed, I supposed, for her daughters to think of her as a desirable woman.

Auntie Fatima slapped her hands together. 'If Kafia won't tell this story, I will. Girls, I'm sure you have heard about Muhammad's mother, Mirriam. Everyone in Baghdad knew that she was malicious to all her daughters-in-law, and that she hated Kafia most of all, making her life miserable. When Kafia became pregnant, what did Mirriam do? She threatened Kafia that she was going to forbid a doctor to assist her in her first labour!' Auntie Fatima looked round the circle. 'Tell me now, what kind of woman wishes another woman to suffer needlessly during childbirth?'

A murmur of horrified disbelief went round the room.

'Sixteen-year-old Kafia was terrified of having her first child attended by her cruel mother-in-law, a woman capable of almost anything. Mirriam often expressed her hatred of baby girls, so Kafia had good reason for concern, thinking that Mirriam might go so far as to harm her child, if it happened to be a girl.

'So one day, while Mirriam was napping, Kafia slipped from the house and posted a letter to Mother in Sulaimaniya, saying that if Mother didn't send someone to rescue her from her mother-in-law she would throw herself into the Tigris.'

I glanced at my sister Alia, thinking that she, as I, had been in great peril while in our mother's womb. Alia had been threatened by drowning and I had been poisoned. It was a miracle that we both existed.

'As you can imagine, Kafia's letter created the greatest uproar in Sulaimaniya. The postal date on the envelope was illegible. Mother became frantic, worrying that it was already too late. Without stopping to pack, Mehdi – our wise brother – and I boarded the first bus to Baghdad. We arrived while Muhammad was at work. You should have seen Mirriam's face when we told her that we had come for Kafia. She vehemently protested, determined to keep her hated daughter-in-law within her sphere of influence. But Mehdi was diplomatic. He didn't accuse Mirriam of cruelty, which is what I wanted to do, but stressed Kafia's youth and inexperience, saying that it was only right for such a young bride to be with her mother when she delivered her first child. Mirriam reluctantly relented.

'Certain that Mirriam would change her mind and prevent her from leaving, Kafia was in such a rush to leave that she forgot about Muhammad.' Auntie Fatima burst into laughter. 'When we left the house, we saw one of the city buses conveniently passing by Mirriam's house. I took it as a sign and said, "Run!" The three of us ran as fast as possible with the very pregnant Kafia hiking up her dress and scurrying like a duck.

'As fate would have it, just as we were boarding the bus, Muhammad turned the corner and saw us. I suppose he believed that Kafia was leaving him, never to return. Now, don't forget, this was a man who couldn't shout "Stop" or "Wait". Instead, he did the only thing he could to make his point: he dropped his parcels and ran to the front of the stationary bus. He threw himself under one of the front wheels.' Auntie Fatima laughed lowly, shaking her head. 'That poor man went so far as to position his head under one of the bus tyres.

'There was instant bedlam. The angry bus driver was blowing the horn. We were pushing to get off the bus. A crowd gathered. Everyone was shouting. No one knew that the would-be suicide was deaf and couldn't hear a word they were shouting.

'It took us a few minutes to push through the crowd, but finally we saw Muhammad. Girls, it was the strangest sight! Your father was flat on his back. His arms were crossed over his chest. His eyes were closed, like this.' Auntie Fatima demonstrated for us.

Everyone laughed. Mother did not look displeased. She had a dreamy, faraway look in her eyes.

'By now Mirriam had heard about the excitement. Someone must have recognized Muhammad and run to tell her. She forced her way through the crowd like a tank or a strongman from the circus, lifting and throwing people aside.' Auntie Fatima jumped up from her chair. 'Like this.' My breath shot out of my body as she pulled me from my chair and tossed me across the room.

Everyone but me thought that was funny.

'When Mirriam realized that the potential suicide was indeed her son, what did she do? That crazy woman began yanking on his arms.'

I hurriedly moved a safe distance from Auntie Fatima, not wishing to be the victim of yet another demonstration.

Auntie Fatima carried on. 'Kafia squatted as best she could, considering her big belly. There they were, the wife and the mother, both pulling on Muhammad. Oddly, he refused to open his eyes. His lips were moving slightly. I suppose the poor man was saying his final prayers, preparing to meet his God. Mirriam didn't hesitate for a second. She reached with those strong fingers of hers and forced open Muhammad's eyelids.

'When Muhammad saw that his wife was there, too, he gave her

an accusatory stare, thinking she was leaving him. Kafia knew enough
sign language by then to explain what was happening: that she was
just going to her mother for help in delivering her first child and that
she would return. A suddenly hopeful Muhammad pushed himself up
on his elbows and leapt up. Of course, that incident made Mirriam
even more bitter and jealous. It was obvious that Muhammad was
very much in love with his wife if he would rather die than face living without her.'

Auntie Fatima's story had fulfilled her purpose. I forgot, if only for
a brief time, that my father was gone from me for ever. I felt cheered
by reflecting on the happiness my father and mother had derived
from their marriage. When I retired later in the evening, for the first
time since my father's death I did not cry myself to sleep.

I was not yet mature enough to understand that the winds of
fortune veer continually and that soon I would have a meeting that
would be the most pivotal event of my life.

8

Love in a Torn Land

Baghdad
1977

It was a Thursday evening when Alia telephoned Mother to complain about her life. Mainly my sister was exhausted. With two rambunctious sons close in age and a toddler, Alia was becoming haggard at a young age. Of her three daughters, Mother loved Alia most of all, so she quickly promised Alia that she could 'have' Muna and me: she said we must go and babysit for Alia for the next few days, even though that meant we would miss two days of school.

The following afternoon while my three nephews were taking a nap I heard loud voices. I was frightened. My first thought was that men from the internal security office had reappeared to apprehend Hady and Ra'ad. My heart thumped loudly as I leaned against the wall to listen. One of the voices was Hady's. My brother-in-law was arguing about the increasing tensions facing Kurds under the Baathist regime. Then I heard Alia's cheerful voice break through what seemed to be an affable dispute. The two men and Alia were in Alia's kitchen.

With a rush of relief and a spark of curiosity, I walked down the short hallway to see for myself the owner of the other loud, almost strident voice.

I stopped a few steps short of the doorway. I knew the visitor. It was Hady's nephew, Sarbast. He had been on the perimeter of our family life in Kurdistan since I was a little girl, yet I had never really noticed him until that moment. Suddenly I was struck by his good looks.

As I stared, I became captivated. My face felt flushed. My stomach took a dive. My heart was beating faster than normal. What was happening?

I had a sudden memory of the handsome *peshmerga* in love with the beautiful Kurdish girl. I felt a weird but wonderful kind of foreboding.

I tried to remember everything I knew about Sarbast, which was not much. I had seen him infrequently during our summer holidays in Sulaimaniya. He was older than me by three or four years. He lived in Kurdistan.

He was so very handsome. He was not very tall, but tall enough. His body was compact but well built, with a large chest and muscular arms. His face was handsome, his skin olive and his moustache full for a young man, masking his upper lip. Most strikingly, his chiselled face was framed by abundant curly dark locks. His hazel eyes were animated but earnest under a furrowed brow.

Sarbast was expressing his ideas loudly and emphatically. Hady, on the other hand, was responding calmly. Sarbast seemed to be being unreasonably obstinate with his uncle, but I found his passion strangely charming.

He waved his hands for emphasis and said, 'I am not afraid of the Iraqi government. Listen, Hady, the trick is to expect to die. Then if you live, your life is a bonus. I will fight them to the death!'

My entire life transformed in that instant. Yes! Here was a true *peshmerga*! Suddenly my happiness depended upon a man I barely knew.

It was then that I saw my sister smiling at me with a perceptive expression. I decided to beat a hasty retreat to my bedroom but before I could turn, Alia held out a hand. 'Joanna, come. You have not said hello to Sarbast.'

The men ceased talking. I sensed Sarbast turning to glance at me.

I patted my hair with my hands. It was hanging long and straight without any style to it. My fingers tugged on my skirt. It was not one of my favourites. I had no desire to talk to Sarbast in such a dishevelled condition.

Alia was persistent. 'Joanna?'

Sarbast broke in, his unthinking words plunging into my heart like a dagger. 'Alia, your little sister?' He looked at me and smiled. 'Oh? Yes! Joanna! Is this the same Joanna who was always so naughty?' He studied me more closely, and laughed. 'Little Joanna is still skinny!' Amused, he glanced at Alia. 'Don't you feed this child?'

Tears started to form. Although I was fifteen years old, and felt quite the adult, I was often teased by relatives who told me that I looked no more than twelve or thirteen, even though I was very tall and slim. Sarbast thought of me not only as a child but as a skinny child.

Alia laughed with him, saying, 'Joanna is naturally bony. She will always be skinny.'

I looked accusingly at Alia. *I hated her!*

Tears spilled out, but no one seemed to notice. Fortunately, Hady was so caught up in the conversation that he was oblivious to me. He dragged a chair from the table, advising his nephew, 'Consider my suggestion, Sarbast. First you finish college. Then, if there is still no peace, you can fight. But if there is an acceptable treaty with Baghdad, and no longer a good reason to wage war, at least you'll have a profession. Think about it.' He lifted both shoulders in a shrug. 'You'll be better prepared to help build up Kurdistan.'

Sarbast turned his attention back to his uncle and slapped him on the back. 'You old men have given up the fight,' he said loudly, though affectionately.

Hady laughed merrily, glancing at Alia. 'Wife, there is no wild beast like an angry young man.'

For once in their married life, Alia ignored her husband. Instead, she gazed at me, then at Sarbast and back. She drew me close with a hug, wiping my tears with the back of her hand. 'Come, Joanna.'

Reluctantly, I allowed my sister to settle me at the table in front of Sarbast. She softly stroked my shoulder and smiled as she turned to prepare a pot of tea. Then she arranged cookies on a platter, her hands busy but her eyes locked on me.

As for me, I could not stop staring at Sarbast. Even his hands were perfectly formed. They were resting on the table, only inches from my own. I could have touched them, if I dared. But I didn't. Instead, I listened attentively to everything that was being said.

Sarbast had grown up in Hady's small village, Qalat Diza, in northern Iraq. He was the son of one of Hady's sisters. He had graduated from high school in the spring, scoring such high marks that he had been admitted as an engineering student at Baghdad University. Yet he had declared that he would rather fight the government in the mountains with his childhood friends than sit in a classroom.

It was then that I learned the most exciting news of all: Sarbast would be moving in with my sister and her husband, and soon – within the next week. My mind raced with the possibilities that this presented to me. Alia really was too busy and needed assistance with her three young sons. I made plans to work harder at school during the week so as to maintain my grades. Mother would be pleased if I volunteered to continue to help Alia.

Wanting to get Sarbast's attention, I gathered my courage to announce that I would one day go to Kurdistan and become a freedom fighter myself. But before I could say the words, Sarbast jumped up to bid us farewell, saying that he had an assignment to finish. Before walking away he selected two of Alia's homemade cookies and slipped them in his trouser pocket. 'I'll be back in a few days, with my clothes and books,' he said with a friendly nod to Hady.

My emotions were in a whirl. I ached for him to notice me, to say goodbye to me, yet I was thinking that it would be best if he did not look too closely when I felt so untidy, even ugly.

But he surprised me by turning back at the doorway and glancing first at me and then at Alia. 'She's a child, now,' he announced, 'but she'll prove to be a splendid woman.' Grinning, he winked at me and then jauntily walked out of the door, vanishing like a marvellous mirage. Tiny prickles erupted over the entire surface of my flesh.

Hady walked rapidly after his nephew, continuing their conversation.

I jumped up from the table and whirled giddily. 'Splendid! Splendid! One day I'll be splendid!'

Alia shook her head and laughed. 'What is going on, Joanna?'

I continued dancing and twirling, refusing to confirm what my sister had already guessed. I had fallen in love.

Fortunately Alia was a loyal sister. As far as I know, she never told anyone my secret, not even Hady.

Over the next two days I cross-examined Alia and she willingly told me everything she knew of Sarbast.

He was one of twelve children. The reason he was so passionately devoted to the Kurdish cause was that his family had suffered terribly for being Kurds. They had even lived in exile, in Iran, for several years, after the Baghdad government had napalmed their village. Most importantly, he was not engaged. I was comforted to hear that Sarbast's family had not yet begun the match-making process, a routine procedure in our Kurdish culture once a man graduates from high school; it had been decided that Sarbast should concentrate on his studies first. I also learned that he was very artistic. He sketched portraits and composed poems.

He was perfect.

The remaining days dragged by. The image of Sarbast hovered in my mind. How I wished he would make a return visit before I left to go home and resume school!

I was desperate to look my best in case he made an appearance. So I made a point of getting up early, putting on my best clothes, arranging my hair and biting my lips to keep them pink. When alone, I walked into my sister's bedroom and examined my image in the mirror. Admittedly, I was too skinny, but for the first time I happily noted that there was a hint of breasts rising under my blouse. Soon I would be a woman.

I made a discovery about romantic love: it was a disturbing passion. One moment I was limp and miserable with a sense of hopelessness, believing that Sarbast would never see me as a beautiful woman and that in his eyes I would forever be Alia's little sister. The next moment I would be energized by hopeful certainty that one day I would develop into a beauty, and that when that happy day arrived, Sarbast would pursue me to be his bride. It must happen.

I became so irritable and unpredictable that one day Alia teased me, 'Joanna, watch out or your condition will be fatal. If you don't win Sarbast, you will die of grief. If you do win Sarbast, you will die of happiness.'

Not realizing that Muna was busy tidying the pots and pans in the nearby pantry, I brashly made a bold confession. 'Alia, I will be what I have to be, and I will do what I have to do, to capture Sarbast's love.'

Metal pots and pans crashed to the floor. Muna's face was distorted in astonishment, her eyes wide and wild as she looked first at Alia and then at me. She cried out, 'What? What?'

Alia chuckled. I smiled, too. It was clear that Muna believed that her younger sister had gone quite mad. But then Muna had never been in love, so how could she understand?

I pinched her flushed cheek, teasing her, 'Love is surely wonderful, Muna,' before prancing out of the room.

Love was wonderful, but it was not easy, for I was in love with a man who didn't love me in return.

Although my helping Alia with her boys meant that Sarbast and I often saw each other at my sister's home, he always treated me as a child, despite my efforts to appear older than my fifteen years. I even tried to butt into his political discussions with Hady, determined to alert him to the fact that my young mind was as stubborn and determined as his own.

If I was not with him, I was daydreaming about him, reflecting endlessly on his handsome face and powerful personality. He had an intensity that often created unpleasant scenes, for Sarbast never ran out of reasons for a good political argument. I even saw him shake his fists in anger at Hady, a man who would never even raise his voice. I found his political passions very appealing.

But to him, I was nothing more than Alia's little sister. Knowing that I would never love another man but Sarbast, it was painful to realize that Sarbast might never love me in return. My only consolation came from the fact that he never referred to marriage with another woman. Despite that, an imaginary clock was ticking loudly in my mind. Sarbast was of the age when his family would soon insist that he agree to marry. Our culture demanded marriage and children of its sons and daughters.

There was some small hope, though. The mirror was promising physical change. Even Mother offered encouragement. When I complained about my skinny body, she confided that several aunts had recently mentioned that I was growing out of my gangly stage. They thought I was becoming very pretty. Perhaps I would soon be beautiful like Mother, Alia and Muna, and when that happened, Sarbast was sure to take an interest in me, as I had noticed that he was attentive to beautiful women.

I resolved to use a different tactic with Sarbast. I would act as if I was indifferent.

The next time I was at Alia's home, I faked disinterest when Sarbast entered a room. I yawned and excused myself when Sarbast and Hady became involved in one of their customary debates regarding the maddening discrimination faced by Iraqi Kurds. My studied apathy took the strongest resolve.

After several days, Sarbast made an unexpected request. He began a conversation with Alia, looking first at her and then at me. 'Alia, have you noticed that Joanna has an unusually interesting face?' He paused, and then said, 'I would like to sketch her. With your permission, of course.'

I stood quietly, secretly astonished. My ploy had been successful! I hummed happily. Perhaps dreams do come true.

One unforgettable day a few weeks later, Sarbast collected his notebook and sketching pencils and placed a stool in front of a blank wall. He told me to sit on it. He was going to sketch my portrait. I did as I was told.

For the first time, Sarbast concentrated solely on me.

It felt like heaven. Never before had I held this man's full attention. I relished every moment. There were long silences, broken only when I slightly moved my head and shoulders and Sarbast chided me with soft words that I have never forgotten. 'Joanna, be very still.' He cleared his throat and smiled. 'Youth doesn't come twice, you know.'

I found that he was a talented artist. As I looked upon a likeness that I found difficult to believe was me, my shoulder accidentally brushed him. I smiled my approval while gazing into his intense eyes. He grinned, but his smile was brother-friendly. Still, I was consumed with the greatest happiness.

But that happiness was quickly dissipated when word came from relatives in the north that there was renewed upheaval in Kurdistan. Sarbast began to speak of leaving his studies and going into the mountains to fight for Kurdistan. I was plunged into a deep depression. Living in a land torn by continuous war was not easy. Experiencing love in a torn land was doubly challenging.

9

War

Baghdad
October 1980

The worst had happened. Baghdad was being bombed by Iran.

It was October 1980, and I was less than a year away from starting my first year at the University of Baghdad in the college of agricultural engineering. I was looking round the university when the bombing started. Panicking, I unwisely tried to make my way home to Mother, but the jostling crowds made my passage across the city like street fighting. Every block was jammed by surging crowds, with dense masses of people pressing from the front and from the back. The Baghdad police tried to control the crowd, but then gave up and fled from the scene. So unconcerned were they about the people they were supposed to protect that one of them trampled on me, his heavy boot crushing my toes.

When I finally arrived at our front door, limping, my hair was hanging with sweat and my face was streaked with dirt and soot. To my dismay, I discovered that I had lost one of my shoes.

Breathless, I told Mother, 'I was caught out in the open. There were many Iranian planes.' I pointed at my feet. 'I was trampled!'

Mother was in shock. She began to speak incoherently. 'Joanna, I tell you: these days no one in Iraq should go out without cleaning their house.'

I looked at my mother and laughed nervously. The country was in the greatest turmoil and Mother was talking about housecleaning. What was going on? Had her nerves shattered?

The country had been at war since September, but never did we expect our capital city to be bombed. Yet it did not take a genius to realize that we were on a risky path. We were fighting against a country with three times our population, a country governed by fanatic mullahs who would like nothing better than to die as martyrs.

I was puzzled by and angry with our government. I felt in my heart that Saddam Hussein, who had replaced Al-Bakir as president the year before, had fired the first shot, despite the fact that the propaganda claimed otherwise, with our media caricaturing the Iranian leader Ayatollah Khomeini in a grotesque manner. But I did not dare express my ideas or opinions to anyone outside our family circle. Any Iraqi heard speaking against the war was summarily executed. Already there were rumours of Iraqi parents being put to death after cursing the government for sending their sons to die at the front.

There were many other problems with the war. The Iranians were a Shiite nation, but Iraq's army was also mainly manned by Shiite Muslims. During the past few years in Iraq tensions had risen to an all-time high between the Baathist government, dominated by a Sunni minority, and the Shiite clerics. A religious edict had even been issued against the Baathist government by Ayatollah Sadr, the most popular Shiite cleric in Iraq. Saddam had then banned the Shiite Al-Dawa party and many of its members were executed during the early months of 1980. So what motive did any Shiite have to fight for Saddam? There were rumours that, in the early days of the fighting, Shiite conscripts in the Iraqi army had turned their weapons against their superiors. If this continued, we would lose the war.

And there was the Kurdish situation. All Iraqis had reasons to worry during that dark time, and Kurds more than most. Many times in the past, Iraqi Kurds had looked to Iran for protection from the government in Baghdad. Kurdish villages and cities were mainly located on the Iranian border. Sulaimaniya, where Grandmother and our aunts and cousins lived, was only a few miles from the border, as was Halabja, where Auntie Aisha lived. With Baghdad now fighting Tehran, and two huge armies stalking each other in the region, Kurdish civilians were in acute danger.

Once again I heard the loud noise of the planes dropping bombs. I seized Mother's hand and we ran into our small bathroom to find Muna cowering on the floor, her face in her hands, muffling her screams. We joined her, sitting on each side of her. I grabbed Muna's soft little hands in my own to reassure her. There were no shelters in our area and our small house gave us only modest protection.

My thoughts drifted to Sa'ad, who had already been sent to the front and who was in an area where there was heavy fighting. He was in the oil-rich Iranian province of Khuzistan, where his division was laying siege to Ahvaz. He was specially trained to provide wind speed and locations to the Iraqi artillery divisions, who we heard were pounding Iranian territory. Undoubtedly, my brother's life was in danger at every moment.

Had I been told a year ago that I would be mumbling constant prayers for Sa'ad's safety, I would not have believed it possible. Since I had been a teenager, Sa'ad and I had not enjoyed an easy relationship. Sa'ad was a young man who was simple in his habits and moderate in his desires, yet he made it his sacred duty to watch over the honour of women. Like so many Iraqi men, my conservative brother was very controlling when it came to the females of his family. Since I often refused to obey his orders, we had often clashed.

For years Sa'ad had strictly controlled what I wore. He would measure the length of my dresses, and force me to cover my arms and wear a black scarf over my long hair. But he couldn't watch me every moment. I dressed as conservative Joanna when at home, but I was liberal Joanna at school. I would leave the house with a scarf on my head and my skirt pulled right down, but the moment I was out of his sight, I would snatch off the scarf and roll my skirt up from the waistline until it was a fashionable length.

Only a few months before he was called up, we had clashed seriously. The incident occurred when I won a high honour at school, coming second in the whole of Iraq in the French language. The Iraqi government and the French Ministry of Education awarded the first- and second-place winners an all-expenses-paid trip to France. Never had I been so excited. I had never travelled outside Iraq. But Sa'ad forbade it, saying, 'No, Joanna is too young. No females should travel without a guardian.' I could not believe Sa'ad's decision. I was furious. I yelled and cried and created a commotion.

I had worked hard for years to achieve high grades. I deserved my award.

Mother felt so badly for me that, finally, she and Alia conspired to let me go after all. Sa'ad would be told I was at Alia's house. So I left for France. Thinking I was at Alia's, Sa'ad didn't question my absence.

I loved everything about France: the beauty of the country, the people, the history, the language. The pleasure of that journey will forever be etched on my mind and heart.

But my lie was revealed to Sa'ad in the most bizarre manner. The winners had been told to pack an ethnic costume. While in Paris, I was photographed in my Kurdish traditional dress. As fate would have it, the photograph was reproduced on the front page of several Iraqi newspapers on the very day I arrived back in Baghdad. I knew that, like most Iraqis, Sa'ad rarely read the newspapers, for nothing was as boring as newspapers forced to print government propaganda. So I prayed for the best. Mother, Muna and other family members and friends were forewarned and asked to hide that particular edition from Sa'ad's view.

But it was as if God Himself was conspiring against me. That day, Sa'ad went for his usual afternoon swim in the Tigris, and then lay on the bank for a brief rest. Somehow, the front page of the paper came spinning down the street in the wind and came to rest on his face. He nonchalantly lifted the paper off his face and opened his eyes, and what did he see on the front page? His younger sister, Joanna, proudly displaying her Kurdish traditional dress, in Paris, France.

Sa'ad jumped to his feet, so agitated that he forgot to put on his trousers, and startled bystanders by racing home in his swimming trunks. He roared into the house, banging the front door and waving the newspaper.

I had arrived home only hours earlier. I froze, staring in terror at the expression on his face. I had the good sense to flee, calling out for Mother, who was in the kitchen. Sa'ad raced after me.

Mother and Muna came to my rescue and intervened, the two of them leaping between the two of us, trying to stop Sa'ad from committing an act he might later regret.

There was bedlam. Sa'ad was trying to strike me, I was screaming,

Muna was crying and Mother was screeching for Sa'ad to leave me alone. I was surprised that neighbours didn't call the police.

Mother yelled, 'Joanna! Run! Go to Alia!'

While they held back Sa'ad, I dashed to catch a bus and made my way to my sister's house.

Fortunately, Ra'ad had a more modern attitude towards women. When confronted with the problem, he took my side, and Sa'ad finally calmed down, at least on the exterior, because he would never go against his elder brother.

Now, only a short time later, Sa'ad was in a trench, facing an army of warriors wanting to kill him, and all our arguments were forgotten. I loved my brother, and would accept his infuriating bossiness if only he would come back to us alive.

When the Iranian planes finally departed from Baghdad airspace, we turned on the television to see grim-faced news broadcasters. 'The criminals have been chased from Iraqi airspace but, we promise, every Iraqi will make sacrifices to bury our enemies.'

As I listened to their senseless war babble, I knew that Iran was not the enemy I feared most. From its first day in power our Baathist government had been so brutal that it was a spiritually dead movement, but no one yet dared acknowledge that truth, other than the Kurds. I believe that history will one day show that no group in Iraq fought more stubbornly against the Baathists than the Kurds. We never gave up.

In that moment, however, my main concern was for us all to survive. I knew that Ra'ad was at risk of having to join his brother in the trenches. Ra'ad had graduated as an engineer from Baghdad University of Technology. He was twenty-six years old, and not yet married, and he was running a prosperous business. He could be conscripted any day. Alia's husband Hady was forty-three years old and the father of three young sons, but he too would be considered young enough to fight.

And Sarbast? He was twenty-two years old, with only one more year of engineering school. His family had persuaded him to pursue his degree, telling him that one war or another would always be waiting for him in Kurdistan. So Sarbast had remained in Baghdad. Although the government had assured its citizens that the war would last no longer than another month, and that college students would be allowed to graduate, no one could be sure that the policy would not change. I knew in my heart what Sarbast's reaction would be to a military call-up. He was a man who would fight to the last for his own ideals, but he hated the Baathists too much to go to war on their behalf. If pushed to join the Iraqi military, he would take to the mountains at the first opportunity and join the *peshmerga*.

Exhausted by the day's trauma, we soon retired, but I could not sleep. My thoughts were dominated by Sarbast, despite the fact that nothing had changed between us. Although I could not match my mother or my sisters in beauty, I had finally left childhood behind. I was eighteen years old and had developed into a woman whom many people found attractive. I was tall and slim with thick black hair, and an interesting face that Sarbast still found beautiful to sketch. Even after years of unrequited love, I still felt the same about him. Despite my physical changes, though, he remained distantly friendly and had never once broached the topic of love. Sadly, I could never tell him of my feelings. Although I struggled against many things in my conservative culture, I could never make the first move. Such an action on my part would ruin my reputation for ever.

And so I waited.

I did have some memories to cherish. It was true that Sarbast once told Alia that I 'motivated him', and that my pretty face and lively manner tempted him to pick up his sketching pen. It was true that Sarbast often drew me into political discussions, finally understanding that I shared his love of Kurdistan. It was true that we spent treasured moments together discussing books on various topics, for at his behest I had become an avid reader. It was true that I witnessed a flash of pleasure in his eyes when he learned that I had been accepted for and had enrolled in agricultural engineering school, for he knew that I really favoured English literature.

Yet Alia believed the situation to be hopeless, admonishing me, 'Joanna! You have marked yourself as a woman with a heart to be broken. No good can come from this.'

It was easy for her to say. My lucky sister was married to a man who worshipped her.

10

The Trenches

Spring
1981

Ghastly screams woke me in the middle of the night. I was so startled that it took me a few moments to comprehend that the screams were coming from my sister Muna.

Muna's mental health had been noticeably deteriorating since the start of the war the previous year. She had depressions that rarely left her in those days.

I jumped up from bed and went to Muna's bedside, where I met Mother.

Mother pulled Muna's head into her arms to soothe her, but my sister could not stop shrieking, calling out for her twin, 'Sa'ad!' Her hysteria increased. 'Sa'ad can't breathe! Sa'ad is suffocating!'

A chill ran through me. Mother was visibly shaken. She cautioned Muna, '*Na! Na!* You had a bad dream, Muna. *Na! Na!* Sa'ad is not suffocating.'

Nothing calmed my sister. She trembled. She wept. She repeatedly called out, 'Sa'ad! Sa'ad!' Her hysteria continued throughout the night until I began to think she was going insane from grief.

Muna had an uncanny connection to her brother. She had always felt his joys and sorrows as strongly as if they were her own. Since Sa'ad had gone to war, Muna had suffered so dreadfully that I often reflected that she might go to the front and climb into the trenches with him. I felt so sorry for her.

Morning finally came and Muna slept at last. I paced back and forth from my room to Muna's bedside, watching her chest rise and fall and reassuring myself that she was still breathing. I stood beside her quietly, lifting a few locks of her loosely spread hair and letting them slip through my fingers, thinking about her and admiring her beauty. At twenty-three years old, Muna was a delicate beauty with a doll-like sweetness. Although her skin was pale like porcelain, it glowed softly, with just a hint of pink on her cheeks and lips. Yet she was so fragile in spirit that I had been obsessed about her wellbeing since I was a young girl.

In our culture, Muna was considered old to be unmarried, yet she was so pretty and sweet that she had received more marriage proposals than most. She was also known to be submissive, and our culture greatly valued obedient wives. No proposals had been accepted because Muna was shy of marriage and wanted to remain living with Mother. Yet relatives and neighbours were beginning to talk, saying that if Muna did not marry soon, she would be a spinster, and eventually dependent upon her siblings. Even Mother expressed doubt about the wisdom of allowing Muna to postpone marriage. But I was of the opinion that Muna should never marry. From what I knew, most Iraqi men were loving and kind during their courtship but often became selfish and difficult, or even abusive, soon after marriage. I did not want such an arrangement for our darling Muna. No one could love, protect and pamper her as we did.

There was so much to worry about.

Later that day we received a terrible shock. We heard that there had been an atrocious battle at Ahvaz with thousands of casualties.

My heart skipped a beat. The last letter we had received from Sa'ad had come from that place. In a state of panic, Mother and I stared at each other. Mother's eyes told me that she and I were thinking the same thing. Had Muna's dream been a warning, a premonition? Was it true that Sa'ad had been suffocating?

We scrambled to discover all we could about the battle at Ahvaz. Built on the River Karun, Ahvaz was part of the oil-rich borderlands along the Shatt Al-Arab. That strip of territory had been contested between Iran and Iraq since Iraq was first formed as a country. On the first day of the war, six Iraqi army divisions had crossed the border and attacked Ahvaz and other cities in the area, quickly driving inland and occupying over 1,000 kilometres of Iranian territory. After those first few victorious days for Iraq, though, there had been a stalemate. Neither side had been able to achieve a decisive military breakthrough.

That was why Sa'ad lived in a trench. Thousands upon thousands of young Iranian and Iraqi men were crouching in parallel trenches, waiting to kill each other.

Human life had become cheap to our government. Families were 'paid off' for their dead and Saddam had decreed that a life was worth two months' salary and a pension, as well as a plot of free land and a television set. Later, as the war continued, Saddam increased the death benefit to include a Toyota and a $15,000 payment. Poor as we were, we had no desire for any of those benefits. We only wanted our Sa'ad back.

Had his luck now run out? He had survived that mud hell for six months, but many of his friends had perished before his eyes. Sa'ad was a frequent letter writer, but lately all communication from him had ceased. We had not received a letter for several weeks. His silence, followed by Muna's vivid nightmare and the news of the terrible battle, alarmed everyone in our family.

When Ra'ad was summoned to the Al-Rasheed Military Hospital, where military casualties were taken, I nearly collapsed.

The family gathered at Alia's house to wait nervously.

After a miserably long interval, Ra'ad returned with bad news, good news and amazing news. The bad news was that Sa'ad was a patient at the hospital and was in a serious condition, having nearly died in the trenches. The good news was that he would live. The amazing news was that Muna's dream had been, in fact, telepathy.

As Ra'ad related Sa'ad's story to us, his smooth pale hands moved from side to side. 'The front-line battle at Ahvaz became so intense that Sa'ad could not abandon his trench, not even for a call of nature. His boots, soaked from the muddy trenches, began dissolving on his feet. His toilet was a metal milk box. His food supply was depleted. During one intense bombing, his good friend, squatting only inches away from him, received a direct hit and was decapitated. The shells were falling so heavily that no one in the trench could risk raising their heads to shove the dead body from the trench. Sa'ad lived shoulder to shoulder with a decomposing corpse for several days.

'After nearly a week of this horror, everyone in the trench was dead except Sa'ad. He alone was alive. There was no holding the Iranian soldiers back. Sa'ad was startled to hear Farsi being spoken by enemy soldiers close to his position. One of the Iranian officers ordered his men, "Kill everyone you see. We never want to meet these men again." Sa'ad realized that he was cut off, having been accidentally left behind the lines of the enemy – an enemy who had resolved not to take prisoners.

'Sa'ad closed his eyes and crumpled into a distorted position, tricking his Iranian enemies into believing him dead. Luckily, the Iranian soldiers gave his trench only a cursory glance before rushing past in pursuit of fleeing Iraqi soldiers. He jumped from his trench in order to escape, but then saw human movement at his back. He realized that escape was impossible. There was no option but to hide. Tall pyramids of dead bodies caught his attention. Slain Iraqi soldiers had been piled into heaps. Sa'ad made a quick decision to take cover under the decomposing bodies.'

My thoughts flashed back to Muna screaming that Sa'ad could not breathe.

'I told Sa'ad something of Muna's nightmare. Sa'ad confirmed that he had fought for breath, fearing he was going to suffocate.'

At his words, Mother and I cried out simultaneously. I gasped, holding my hand to my throat, feeling myself suffocating as well.

'Sa'ad said he would have died there, underneath those corpses, and we would never have known his exact fate but for our soldiers fighting desperately to retake the territory they had just lost. By the time Iraqis reached his position, Sa'ad was so weakened that he was unable to make his presence known. However, after a time, bodies were pulled from the mound to be buried and an alert Iraqi soldier noticed a slight movement. It was Sa'ad, struggling to breathe. He was pulled free, seconds away from being dumped into a mass grave. An ambulance transported him from the battlefield to the Al-Rasheed Hospital.'

We learned from the doctors that Sa'ad's health had been severely compromised. Upon receipt of Sa'ad's medical report, the Iraqi army released him from further duty. While relieved that Sa'ad would not be returning to the trenches, we now had the worry that he might die young.

Before we could fully absorb that troubling information, further bad news broke.

Now Ra'ad was our centre of concern. He had received orders to report for a military physical examination.

11

Ra'ad Leaves Us

Baghdad
1982–1983

My hands trembled as I packed my suitcase. Ra'ad, Mother, Muna and I were leaving Baghdad for Europe. Our forthcoming trip could prove to be our undoing.

The rising tempo of the war with Iran had increased Iraq's internal instability. Iraqis were forbidden to travel outside the country, but the country was so corrupt that a generous bribe paid to the appropriate official temporarily loosened the restriction for us. Most Iraqis wanted to flee from our dangerous land but could not, so our approaching 'holiday' created envy and suspicion in the minds of our neighbours and friends. Our sceptical neighbours and friends were right. Indeed, we were not going on holiday as we had claimed during our interview with the men at the security office. We were travelling for an illegal purpose. And, if our plan was discovered, and we were apprehended while leaving the country, we could be executed.

Ra'ad was fleeing from Iraq, possibly never to return. He had made plans to seek a new life in Europe. That new life required a certain amount of money. Iraqi law allowed each family member to take out the equivalent of $1,500. With four travellers, Ra'ad would have $6,000 to live on until he could find work or gain permission to begin training.

There was to be nothing pleasurable about our nerve-racking voyage. We would endure a tiring flight, disembark in Europe, pass Ra'ad the cash we were transporting and then return to Iraq to face potential problems with Iraqi security. How would we explain our abrupt return without one of our party? Yet despite the danger, we were all willing to take the chance to help Ra'ad escape Iraq.

There were two good reasons my brother was fleeing from Iraq. The most urgent was to do with the war. When Ra'ad had reported to the military, he had made known his desire to be a pilot. He had heard enough about the trenches from Sa'ad to wish to avoid being a foot soldier. During his medical examination, however, a problem with his spine was discovered. He received a medical exemption, which distressed him, although his family rejoiced.

But the danger had not passed. As the war ground on, soldiers became scarce. Young men previously considered unfit for service were called up. We knew that soon our fastidious Ra'ad, unable to qualify as a pilot, would be sent to the front to live in a muddy dugout in order to face hordes of enemy soldiers.

Imagine our surprise to learn that many of our Iranian enemies were extremely young and advanced into battle without firearms. Their only weapons were of a spiritual kind: keys to paradise draped around their slender necks. Even we felt sorry for these pretend soldiers, some as young as nine years old, children who had been wrenched from their mother's arms to be recklessly thrown at the battlefront. There they were gutted by machine-gun fire or marched through minefields, their small bodies used as cannon fodder and shredded into raw meat. Cruel as our government was, at least it did not stoop so low as to send young children into battle.

The second reason Ra'ad wanted to leave was his business. After graduating he had taught at the university for a year. He then went into partnership with four former college mates and set up a cable company in Ramadi, a city in central Iraq, about 100 kilometres west of Baghdad. Ra'ad had learned his organizational skills from our father, who was European trained, and impressed his partners by winning many contracts. It was rare for anyone to succeed in Iraq without the influence of one of Saddam's cronies, but my brother and his partners accomplished the impossible, at least in the beginning.

However, when his four partners were drafted and sent off to the front, their fathers became involved in the business and proved themselves unworthy of their honest sons. Soon they began plotting to steal Ra'ad's shares. When Ra'ad refused to relinquish what was his, his new partners went to Saddam's notorious uncle Khairullah Tulfah. Since Saddam had risen to his high position, Khairullah had been using it as protection to allow him to rob and murder Iraqis. He instructed Ra'ad to sign over his shares or have them taken by force. Ra'ad was made to understand that to refuse would gain him a prison sentence or even execution.

I would never forget the day when Ra'ad came home in despair, wondering how he could save what was rightfully his. He paced along the banks of the Tigris, the place he loved best in Baghdad, and found that he had lost his belief in his country. Iraq was no longer a place for a principled man. He made the heartbreaking decision to leave Iraq, possibly for ever.

After losing my father, and nearly losing Sa'ad, I did not want to lose Ra'ad too. I feared it was my destiny to lose all the men I loved.

Even Sarbast was gone. I had not seen him for over a year, since he had fled north, to Kurdistan. As I had feared, after he had graduated he had been summoned for a military medical examination, at which he was found to be in perfect health; there would be no medical exemption for Sarbast. While he was unable to avoid doing his military training, however, nothing could force him to join the ranks of his hated enemies on the battlefield. He slipped away from his army unit and fled to Kurdistan. There he joined the Patriotic Union of Kurdistan (PUK), an organization formed by Jalal Talabani, a former member of the Kurdistan Democratic Party (KDP), the first political organization for Kurdish *peshmerga*.

But Sarbast had left me with one sweet memory that sustained me during the forlorn days of his absence. Before departing from Baghdad, he startled me with a request. Passing me in Alia's hallway, he called me aside. The usually solemn Sarbast was surprisingly jovial, as though he didn't have a care in the world, despite the fact that he would soon be a fugitive from the government in Baghdad and putting himself and his family in danger. His brave family encouraged Sarbast, as well as his brothers, to do battle against Saddam: they were willing to lose everything to further the Kurdish cause.

'Joanna,' he murmured softly, 'I must leave, very soon. Before I go, though, I must attend to some business at the university. Would you come with me?'

His eyes were shining, large and dark, and he had a playful smile on his face. His dark hair was long for a man, and his winsome curls looked wild, as though he had just run through a strong wind.

I stared for a time without answering, one hand guarding the other to keep it from pulling on those curls. This was too good to be true, I thought, as a shiver of anticipation shot from my head to my toes. I was certain that Sarbast was finally going to broach the topic of marriage.

'Yes! Yes, of course,' I agreed.

That day was the first time we had been together and alone after my years of girlish longing. At first, it unfolded as the fantasy I had dreamed about for many years. We laughed as we ran for one of the many buses. As we rode to the university, he bent forward, peering from the bus windows and making sharp observations, opening my eyes to the vitality of Baghdad street life and the gallery of Baghdad characters: portly street merchants hiding their money, harried housewives shrieking at their disobedient children, young boys balancing their fat bundles, shy lovers giving discreet signals, old women with astonishingly round bodies and elderly men sitting in the heat, opening and closing their mouths like gasping *masgouf*, the fish that were such a delicacy at Baghdad riverbank cafés. He made me laugh until tears rolled down my face, and our mirth created a camaraderie with strangers on the bus, who gazed at us with affection, thinking that we must be newlyweds just returned from our honeymoon. His every action made me joyful, and I was smiling even as I waited alone while he tended to his final business at the university.

On our way back to Alia's house we were both looking to prolong the day, so we slipped into a bookstore. As we paused in the fiction section, my fingers lightly brushing the spines of books, my eyes on him, his voice was so seductive and sweet that when he disclosed that he liked my hair long and loose I believed for a breathtaking moment that he had fallen in love with me.

Baghdad was not a place where one could speak openly, so he drew close and whispered, his face so near that I had never seen it so clearly, his gaze thoughtful and the full fire of the life in his eyes directed at me. I heard him whisper that he had no fear of dying, yet he wanted to live, to work, to have a comfortable home, to know what it was to marry a beautiful woman and to hold a son in his arms.

If such a thing as complete happiness exists, I was living it.

Breathless, I leaned in closer, waiting to hear words that I was sure were forthcoming. Surely he was about to say that he could not live without me? Of course my answer would be yes. Already in my imagination I was packing a small bag, saying goodbye and fleeing from Baghdad with him to Kurdistan. I would go with him to live in a fighters' village. I would support this man in whatever it was he needed to do.

I smiled so widely that he paused, but I encouraged him. 'Go on. Go on.'

Admittedly, this was not the usual method for becoming engaged in our culture. But our family connections, I believed, made everything less complicated. Unlike most women, I had years of knowing Sarbast behind me. I had already discovered that I loved him. I kept waiting for the magic words.

I waited.

And I waited.

Finally Sarbast seemed to grow weary of talking. He nodded towards the door to the street and said, 'We must go. It is getting late.'

As if in a state of mild insanity I followed him from the shop, unsure what had just happened. I had almost blurted that I loved him, that I could not bear him to leave Baghdad without me, that I wanted to marry him. But I could say nothing. To keep my honour intact, I knew that I must restrain myself. Although Kurdish girls can be bold in many things, when it comes to love we cannot push ourselves forward.

I had done all I could do to let Sarbast know my feelings. I had spent the day with him. I had listened intently to every word he had said. I had smiled. I had laughed. A Kurdish girl could do no more.

My thoughts were swirling. In a last desperate hope, I concluded that Sarbast was planning to abduct me instead, a not uncommon method to speed up the process of marriage. My spirit soared anew. I considered telling Sarbast that he did not have to go to the trouble of abducting me: I would go willingly, if only he would ask. But I didn't, and he didn't.

Instead, his mood was subdued, almost surly, on the return bus trip. Nothing I could say or do could shake his altered mood. He stared at everything but me.

What had happened? What was he thinking? Had he believed himself in love but during our outing concluded that he did not love me after all and that I was less worthy than he had first believed?

I slumped forward, my chin in my hand, in uncertain agony. My thoughts tumbled over one another. He was leaving the following day. I might never see him again. He *must* ask me to marry him. He *must*! But he didn't.

In the silent hours of the night my anxious heart drove away sleep.

The next morning Sarbast left Baghdad after saying a breezy, unfeeling goodbye.

I had not seen him since. I had not even received any letters from him. During that time there had been sporadic but vicious fighting between the *peshmerga* and the Iraqi army. I had no way of knowing if Sarbast was alive or dead. Nevertheless, my love for him never waned.

12

The End of Hope

Baghdad
1984

None of us was arrested on our return from Europe without Ra'ad. Iraq was in such turmoil after four years of war that our risky escapade was unobserved. We were lucky, for one of the few times in our lives.

After only one short year, Ra'ad was prospering in Switzerland, employed by a prestigious company and on his way to attaining Swiss residency. His meticulousness, so like our father's, perfectly suited the Swiss, who are famous for their precision.

Although I missed Ra'ad, I realized that it had been best for him to leave our mangled country. The continuing military stalemate meant that no one knew for certain who would be the ultimate victor. The Americans had supported Saddam within the first year of the war, mostly because of US outrage and bitterness over the taking of American hostages in Iran. Many Iraqis took comfort from their belief that the Americans would never allow the Iranians to win. But the war raged on.

I was still in college, and even after more than a year of not seeing Sarbast, I had never stopped mourning his absence. During my college years my family received more than one marriage proposal on my behalf. The men were handsome and pleasant enough, and pledged prosperous futures, but to the alarm of my family, I turned each suitor down. Everyone but Alia and Muna was mystified by my stubborn refusals. Only my two sisters were privy to my secret: that it was impossible for me to marry one man while I was in love with another. Defying the marriage customs of my culture, I spent my college years waiting.

Then one afternoon I arrived at Alia's house and there he was.

It was clear from his physical appearance that life in the mountains had been challenging. He was as handsome as I remembered, though too thin, with deep lines around his eyes and mouth. But I was so happy to see him that I couldn't stop smiling. My attraction to him was as strong as ever.

I quickly noted that Sarbast had undergone other changes. His personality was more subdued. He was friendly enough, but a little distant, vaguely claiming that he was in Baghdad for political reasons.

Trying to find a settlement with the Kurds to prevent them from allying themselves with the Iranians, Saddam had authorized a rare ceasefire with the Kurds in late 1983 that lasted through most of 1984. During that ceasefire *peshmerga* fighters received an amnesty, which meant that they could leave the mountains and travel to the cities. That was why Sarbast was able to visit.

Despite his offhand manner, I was certain that Sarbast had travelled to Baghdad for only one purpose: to come for me. Obsessed with wringing a marriage proposal out of him, I made my plans. I would not allow Sarbast to leave Baghdad without a serious conversation about our future. I was nearly twenty-two years old and set to graduate from university. I was ready to marry, but only if my husband could be one particular man. Of the 4,770,104,443 people living in the world in 1984, of which nearly half were men, only he would do.

First I tried to draw him into conversation, asking to hear about his fighting adventures, but he remained oddly remote. I explained away his reluctance to speak by assuming that his fighter's life was so harsh that he could not speak of it.

One afternoon when he settled at Alia's table with a cup of tea, I saw my opportunity. I joined him, without an invitation, and probed. 'Sarbast, if this peace process fails, will you go back to the north?'

In a reserved way, he responded, 'Yes.'

There was a long silence.

He drank his tea and stared at his hands, which to my worry looked grimy, with numerous scratches. What kind of work had he been doing with those beautiful hands? Looking away, I reminded myself not to get distracted.

I took a deep breath. The moment had come. I would say anything to get what I wanted.

'I want to go, too. I can fight,' I said. 'I want to fight.' Although I knew that throughout Kurdish history only Turkish women had fought side by side with their men, not Iraqi *peshmerga* women, I had decided that if given the chance, I would learn to shoot a firearm and I would volunteer to carry messages; I would make myself useful.

Sarbast threw back his head and laughed, his curls lifting lightly. Then, seeing that I was serious, he gestured with his index finger and warned me, 'You don't know what you are saying, Joanna. It is a dangerous life. Every moment we are running to a fight, evading soldiers or hiding from the *jahsh*. Death is all around us. Already I have lost good friends.'

The *jahsh* were Kurdish turncoats, men who, in order to avoid Iraqi military service, accepted bribes from Baghdad to spy on their Kurdish brothers. They were the most contemptible Kurds, as they caused the capture and deaths of many of our fighters as well as civilian sympathizers.

I refused to give up. 'Sarbast, ever since I was a little girl I have known that I would one day support the *peshmerga*.'

His words were edged with irritation: '*Na. Na*, Joanna. It is not a fit life for you. You are a city girl, accustomed to all this.' He lightly gestured at the modern trappings in Alia's Baghdad home. 'The mountain life means nothing but sacrifice. Listen,' he said, 'I eat the same food every day. Bad food, I might add. I often sleep in the open, in the cold, without a blanket. Planes drop bombs every day. Always there is shelling. We are often wounded. Doctors have been forbidden to treat us. Many people die from treatable injuries, because we have so few doctors.'

He leaned closer to make his point, and it took all my strength to keep my hands steady on the table as I fought a desire to caress his face.

'Joanna,' he admonished, his voice rising to nearly a shout, 'this is the simple truth: joining the *peshmerga* means that many bad men will do everything in their power to kill you.'

'I do not care,' I retorted stubbornly, sensing that I was losing the argument, and that soon he would be gone and once again I would go back to that yawning void of unbearable waiting. 'I do not care!' I repeated, banging my fist on the table.

'*Na*,' he said. 'Enough!' Thrusting his chair back, he stomped to the sink and flung the last drops of tea into it. He set the cup down so vigorously that it cracked.

Then he left the room without even glancing back at me.

As I had feared, the ceasefire fell through. The Kurds felt that they were dealing with a leader so beset with problems that he would soon be unseated. There was no reason to give in to Saddam's demands: he would soon be gone. Confident of Saddam's removal, Kurdish leaders tucked their victory plans into their pockets and waited.

Sarbast left Baghdad to return to the fighting. He failed to bid me goodbye.

I returned home to Mother. My love for Sarbast was a form of madness. Despite his hurtful behaviour, I didn't know how to stop loving him.

Three days later, Alia left her three sons in the care of a trusted neighbour and travelled across the city by bus to see me. I was alone, for Mother was at the vegetable market and Muna was visiting a friend.

The television was blaring in the background as I ironed a dress for a college class the following day, but I was not concentrating on the broadcast. Baghdad television was unbearably repetitive in those days, for all the programmes focused only on the war and Saddam Hussein. I recall, though, that the show was a repeat of a speech by Saddam calling for Iraqi soldiers to 'cut off the heads of the Iranians'. He was sternly advising our soldiers to strike as powerfully as they could because the necks they were striking were collaborators with 'the lunatic Khomeini'. He called our boys 'Allah's swords on earth'.

I glanced up at the television screen to see Saddam sitting behind a desk. How I hated that man. He was the reason Ra'ad was no longer with us. He was the reason Sa'ad still suffered from health problems. He was the reason Sarbast was living the *peshmerga* life, so far away from me.

Many times I prayed for Saddam's death. I stopped ironing to study his image for a few moments. Unfortunately he looked a picture of perfect health.

That's when Alia came into the house without knocking.

The grim expression on my sister's face gave me a fright. Worst-case scenarios flashed through my mind. Sarbast! It must be Sarbast.

'Joanna, sit,' Alia said, giving me a gentle push.

I sat.

'Joanna, Sarbast . . .' My sister was finding it difficult to deliver the message.

I couldn't take the uncertainty another moment longer. I shrieked, 'Is Sarbast dead?'

'Dead? No. Oh, no. He is alive.' Alia paused, looking thoughtfully at me. 'Very much alive, in fact.'

'Is he injured, then?'

'No, Joanna.' Alia bent forward and, grabbing my upper arms, looked straight at me. 'Joanna, listen to me. Sarbast has asked some-one else to marry him.'

I tilted my head to the side. Surely I had misheard. 'What did you say?'

'That is the reason Sarbast came to Baghdad. He came to ask another woman to marry him.'

'What?'

'Sarbast wants to get married, Joanna, but not to *you!*'

I stuttered, 'Who?'

'You do not know her, darling. She was with him in class, at the university.'

'Her name?'

'Joanna, I do not know her name. I only know that he has asked a former classmate, a Kurdish girl, to marry him.'

My mind was in such a whirl that I could hardly comprehend what Alia was telling me.

'Joanna? Are you all right?'

I was not all right! I tried to get up, but my legs appeared to be tangled.

Alia hugged me with feeling, saying, 'Perhaps this is best. From the moment you met him, Sarbast has been a torment. Now you know it was not God's plan for you two to be together. You can choose another now.'

I muttered, 'Sarbast is dead, in a way.'

Anxiously, Alia pulled back to look at me. 'You are very beautiful, Joanna. How many marriage proposals have you turned down now? Five? Ten?'

Tears were falling one after the other, blurring my sight. But I found the strength to pull myself to a standing position, swinging my shoulders, shaking Alia until she let go. I ran out the front door and down the street.

I stopped running when I reached the banks of the Tigris. I threw myself down on the grassy knoll. Without bothering to wipe away my tears, I stared at the rippling green waters of the Tigris, making its tortuous way through a tortured city.

A group of young teenage boys were out for their daily swim. When they looked at me with curiosity, I turned away.

Sarbast was going to marry another. He did not want to marry me. He had never wanted to marry me. I meant nothing to him. I had never meant anything to him. That's why he was so distant when he was last in Baghdad. He was involved with her even as I was pushing myself at him. Remembering that day in the kitchen when I had practically asked him to marry me, I cringed in shame.

Who was this woman he loved? How did she capture his heart? Why had he fallen in love with her, when he could have had me? I felt a flash of anger. He was supposed to be studying while at university. Now I knew he had really gone there to meet potential brides. I was filled with the wildest jealousy. Who was she? Who was she? Who was she? Did she love him, too?

I knew one thing for certain. Whoever she was, she would never love Sarbast as I loved him. She would never know him as I knew him. Over the years I had studied him, his every mood, his every dream. Sometimes when he started a sentence, I silently finished it. He was a man memorized, by me.

I slumped forward, my head on my knees, and groaned. He didn't love me. He loved another.

I sat up, utterly still, destroyed. I felt overwhelming loneliness, even with the bustle of city life around me.

An old woman shuffled by with a puckered face. She glared at me in disapproval, and I could read her mind: a young woman alone on the riverbank, surely looking for mischief. I glared back, my palms itching with the desire to jump up and slap her for her unfounded suspicions. Young men walked past the river, their white *dishdashas* or robes flapping in the breeze. I was furious that they were not at the front, while others were risking their lives. Donkey drivers noisily urged on their overloaded beasts. I wanted them arrested for mis-treating those poor animals. A group of schoolgirls filed past like ducklings, their school uniforms still fresh even after a day of school. They glanced shyly at the boys in the river, but turned their heads and giggled when the boys took an interest. Those young girls were fools, just like me. I hated everyone in my sight.

Only when total dark threatened and the Tigris reflected the yellow of the moon did I have the strength to move. I wearily pushed myself up from the bank and slowly retraced my steps. Walking into the house, I found Mother, Alia and Muna waiting anxiously.

Alia had informed Mother, I assumed. She had told Mother that her youngest daughter had been in love with a man who did not love her in return. I was a woman scorned.

I glanced at the three women who loved me most in the world. 'I cannot discuss this matter today,' I whispered as I glided past, holding my finger to my lips. Ignoring Alia's disappointed cries and Mother's objections, I retired to my room, closing the door and bracing it with a heavy metal trunk. I stood staring at my reflection in the mirror.

I looked extremely pale, as white as Muna – something I had always yearned for. But while her porcelain white face was lovely, my white face had a mottled, unhealthy appearance. There was nothing of beauty reflected in that mirror.

As I stared at my pitiful image, I knew that everything was lost. My hopes and dreams of winning Sarbast's love had been the driving force of my life since I was fifteen years old, seven years ago. I could lose nothing more. The irrefutable fact was that Sarbast had asked another woman to marry him. I had no choice: I must bear the unbearable.

13

Secret Police

Baghdad
1985–1986

For two years my life was a misery.

Although I was a young woman of twenty-three in excellent health, had graduated from university and was the focus of attention of a number of young eligible bachelors, nothing gave me happiness. In fact, I was so melancholy during those two years that there were times when I prayed for death.

The hellish war with Iran was unending. With each passing day, it grew worse. Our young men died in such shocking numbers that it seemed the entire country was saturated with coffins.

One of my favourite cousins from my father's side of the family, Uncle Othman's son Sadik Osman, was missing in action. We feared he was a prisoner-of-war, or worse.

Iran claimed to have over 50,000 of our young men imprisoned in their dungeons, while we held fewer than 10,000 of their men. It was whispered that the figures were so unbalanced because the Iranian soldiers refused to surrender, smiling ecstatically as they charged their tanks with empty hands held to heaven, seeking certain death.

Hatred of Saddam Hussein inspired so many enemies at home that attempts on his life became commonplace, motivating Iraqi internal security to turn the whole of Iraq into one tyrannical gulag.

Nearly every Iraqi lived in terror of the government.

And in March 1985, Iran and Iraq unleashed the War of the Cities on civilians. Baghdad, Kirkuk, Basra and corresponding cities Tehran and Ahvaz in Iran were hit by bombing raids and surface-to-surface missiles. Retaliation was the order of the day and we innocent civilians were trapped under angry skies raining death.

As for Sarbast, I was full of disappointment and anger. I knew that no woman could ever love him as I loved him.

I had, by the sheerest chance, seen the object of his desire, which added torment to my misery. This happened on an afternoon when I was at the university with one of my cousins. She did not know about my love for Sarbast, but, knowing of Sarbast's connection to my sister Alia, while we were walking through the canteen she suddenly nudged my shoulder and motioned with her head, saying, 'There, Joanna, is the girl Sarbast has asked to marry him.'

I snapped to attention. My rival was a great beauty. She had lovely fair skin and beautiful long blonde hair, which was rare in our part of the world. I felt a rush of hatred.

I edged closer and was startled to hear her speak. Her voice was so gruff and deep that my jaw dropped.

I had always heard that God does not bestow every blessing on one person, and that woman's grating voice was proof. Despite her blonde beauty, all her feminine appeal vanished at that moment. My jealousy was replaced with wonder that Sarbast would find a woman with such an annoying voice attractive.

After all that, some time later I heard that Sarbast's marriage proposal had been rebuffed. The blonde beauty had refused to marry him unless certain conditions were met. She had some unexpected demands for a Kurd. She had insisted that he give up the life of a *peshmerga*. She had also demanded that he turn his back on Kurdistan. Lastly, he must gain permission to leave Iraq and seek citizenship in a European country. Otherwise, her answer would be no.

I was not surprised that Sarbast refused her selfish ultimatums, for I knew that he would never turn his back on the Kurdish cause. The man I loved would never leave Kurdistan voluntarily.

Although my mood was lifted by the news, for I never pretended to wish them wedded bliss, his failed proposal did not revive my hopes of a life together. In fact, I was determined to push Sarbast for ever from my mind. Finally I understood that Sarbast did not love me, and that he had never loved me.

Never again would I humiliate myself.

Rather than go for a job in my field of agricultural engineering, I had accepted a position at a travel agency. The work was sociable, suited my gregarious personality and paid well. I earned double the salary of an engineer. For the first time in my life I had money of my own, although each payday I gave most of my pay to my mother for household expenses. With war raging, goods were not only scarce but extremely costly.

My job was the sole pleasure in my life, at least for a time. With the war on, tourist travel was non-existent. Iraqis were still forbidden to leave the country unless they were on official government business. Our offices were responsible for making travel arrangements for expatriate workers who came to Iraq to fill jobs vacated by our men, who were busy making war.

But too soon I received a frightening summons.

Arriving at work one day in early 1986, my boss met me at the door, visibly shaken. He motioned for me to enter his office, closed the door and whispered, 'Joanna, you had visitors. From internal security. You are to go to the Sadoun Security Headquarters. Tomorrow.' He stood in silence with his hand over his heart, shaking his head with worry. Finally he asked, 'Do you have any idea what this is about?'

I lifted my shoulders in a shrug. 'No. I do not.'

I was speaking the truth. I had committed no crime. I did my job. I went home. I visited family. Occasionally I visited a girlfriend. Very occasionally I went with my family to the cinema.

I had not even been to Kurdistan for the past two summers. The northern area of Iraq had become a dangerous war zone. There were roadblocks at every corner, and we had heard that innocent Iraqis were being hauled off to prison even for travelling into the area. Kurdistan was out of bounds.

However, the summons from the secret police gave me a jolt. I was half-Kurd. Before the war with Iran, I had spent much time in the Kurdish north, an area considered the den of the government's most hated enemy. My brother had left the country to live in Europe, never to return. Through my sister Alia, I was connected to Sarbast, a man considered the most heinous criminal, a *peshmerga*. All these things would look suspicious if held under a magnifying glass by the secret police.

I shuddered with foreboding, wanting to run away. But there was nowhere to hide. There was nothing to do but appear the next day as summoned.

My poor boss was solicitous and so anxious for my safety that he volunteered to accompany me – something few Iraqis would do. Although he was a Baathist, I knew he was a member for the same reason so many other Iraqis belonged to the party: they had no choice. I would never allow him to put himself at risk on my behalf.

'No. I will be fine,' I assured him, although I was not convinced.

I warned Alia and Hady of my unexpected summons in case I failed to return. Wanting to avoid worrying Mother, I told her nothing. If I were imprisoned, there would be ample time for her to become involved.

That night I could not sleep, suffering dark imaginings about what the morning would bring. Despite my Kurdish connections, so far I had avoided any problems with security, but perhaps my luck was now out. Perhaps it was the last night I would enjoy the comforts of my own bed. After all, there were many Iraqis just as innocent as I, rotting in one of the many prisons scattered throughout the country. Everyone living in Iraq had heard horror stories of Saddam's prisons. There were prisons where Iraqis were confined to holes in the ground, such as the one Ra'ad and Hady had experienced. There were the dreaded coffin prisons, where prisoners were locked in coffins with a single air hole, allowed out for only one hour out of twenty-four. There were dank dungeons where prisoners never saw the sun.

There were no good prisons in Iraq. Even ordinary prisons without bizarre confinements were a horror because of overcrowding. At best, I would be in a narrow cell crammed together with too many other women. There would not be enough room to extend my arms or to stand up straight. I would be forced to sleep on a damp cement floor without bedding. Perhaps there would be a single toilet, or perhaps not, in which case the toilet would be wherever I might find a space.

I lingered on the variety of tortures I might undergo. I had heard of electrical shocks and hanging hooks and yanked-out fingernails. There were whispers of mirrored rooms where women were violated while their male relatives were forced to observe.

I shivered. What was going to happen to me? What had I done to draw the attention of the security officers? I relived everything of my life during the past few months and I could think of nothing. I had not visited Kurdistan. I had received no communication from anyone in the north.

Morning came too quickly and, with a heavy heart, I took a taxi and dutifully appeared at the Sadoun Security Headquarters.

My taxi driver was middle-aged, with a kindly face. His eyes squinting with worry, he expressed concern for my safety and asked if he might wait for me. He said that he had three daughters and would not allow any of them to go alone into that building.

I asked him to return in two hours, if possible. If I failed to appear, he agreed to go to Alia and Hady and tell them that I had been taken. That sweet man watched me until I was inside the security doors, his consideration reminding me that there were still decent Iraqis.

The stench of old sweat rose from the building like a vapour. It was the odour of fear, I supposed, wrung from the bodies of the innocent tortured.

Upon entering, I gave my name to a clerk who was sitting behind a large metal desk. He scrawled my name on a piece of lined paper held by an old clipboard. When he lowered his head, I peeked at the list. There were many names above mine, yet I was the only person in the waiting area. Where had everyone else gone?

The clerk busied himself with a ringing phone, grunting, pointing at a group of six wooden chairs and telling me to sit.

I did as I was told.

The recessed waiting area was grimy. In fact the entire interior was shabby. This in a country that had the second largest known oil reserves in the world. Making war for six years had depleted Iraq's treasury. All the oil money was being spent on tanks, planes and bombs.

I sighed, looking around for anything of interest. Nothing surrounding me was attractive. The dark brown plaster on the walls was peeling. The light blue plastic on the chairs was splitting, and nasty tufts of stuffing were spiking out. There was a small wooden table with one chipped ashtray, spilling over with cigarette butts. Practically everyone in Baghdad smoked. Who could think of a reason to quit while living in a country where death already beckoned from every direction? Not me.

I longed for a smoke. I had begun the habit shortly after Sarbast asked another woman to marry him. But it was a secret habit. No one in my family knew, although Alia and Mother sometimes accused me of smoking after sniffing my long hair, which unfortunately, attracted the smell of tobacco. But it was not acceptable in Iraq for a respectable woman to smoke in a public place, so I had nothing to soothe my nerves.

I only hoped I would not break down under questioning. I must not!

My interrogators would be bullies, ruling by fear. From all the stories I had heard from Ra'ad, Hady, Sarbast and my Kurdish relatives, I knew that their greatest pleasure came from terrifying innocent people. I promised myself that no matter what they did or said, I would hang on to my composure. I was worried, though: I had always had problems controlling my sarcastic tongue. While friends and family joked about my sharp-wittedness, I knew that the men in this building would gleefully snap my skinny neck.

I turned my thoughts to the reception clerk, wondering how he justified to himself working in such a place, trying to imagine whether his family were pleased with his station. He was interesting to watch, with his air of self-importance. He was far too absorbed in his clerical duties to give a visitor a reassuring look – a kind act that would have cost him nothing.

Just then a small round man in a rumpled security uniform came into the room and called out my name. I took a deep cleansing breath, straightened my back and followed him without a quiver, so anxious to get out of that dismal place that I was suddenly eager to get the process started.

I was ushered into a small, dimly lit room where two overweight men were perched side by side in chairs so close that I thought they might be welded together. There was a single chair in front of them. They didn't invite me to sit, but, afraid that my trembling legs would give me away, I literally fell into the chair.

The security officers were strikingly different from each other. The moustache on the man on the left was long and thick, while the hair on the other man's lip was sparse. The man with the bushy moustache was bald, while the other showed off a healthy, full head of black greased hair, fashioned in a rather elaborate pompadour style reminiscent of Elvis Presley. Under different circumstances I would have asked him about that wild hair.

Judging by their brutish façades and place of work, I expected them to be ill-mannered, but they were soft-spoken and polite.

The bald man opened the conversation haltingly. 'Welcome. We know you are an Al-Askari. Welcome.'

Trying in vain to control my trembling lips, I smiled widely, as though my life was not in mortal danger and I was a friendly acquaintance dropping by to invite their families to a celebration.

The man I had secretly named Elvis courteously asked, 'How are you today?'

'I am well.'

'Is your work satisfactory?'

'Yes, of course.'

Elvis opened a file he was holding in his hand. 'Miss Askari, we have a report on you.'

Sitting so rigidly straight against the hard chair had made my back begin to ache. I shifted, crossing one leg over the other.

'This file says that you are working in tourism.'

'Yes. That is true.'

'But it says here that your speciality is engineering. You are a graduate in agricultural engineering.'

'Yes. That is true.'

'It says here that you were an acceptable student.'

'Yes. That is true.'

'It says here that you are not working in your field of study. Is that true?'

'Yes. That is true.'

'Tell us, Miss Askari, is there some reason you choose to work at a job where you routinely meet foreigners? We are curious. Why would you spend years studying and then abandon your field?'

An image of Sarbast's face flashed in my mind. I could not tell these men the truth: that I made a stupid decision because I had fallen in love with a man who was now a *peshmerga*. Surely I would be arrested and held as a hostage until Sarbast reported for an exchange. Then they would execute Sarbast. I was angry at him, but not that angry.

I could not even confess a second truth: that soon after going to university I had discovered that I hated my choice of subject. I preferred literature to agricultural engineering. But in Iraq, once a decision was made there was no turning back.

Knowing that they were taping the interview, I willed myself to clear my mind, to think quickly and, most importantly, not to show my fear. 'It was a simple matter of salary. The pay in tourism is better. My father died when I was a teenager. My mother does not work. I contribute to our household.'

'I see.' Elvis thumbed through my file. 'It says here that you have a brother, Sa'ad Al-Askari, who supports the family. Is this true?'

'It is true that my brother is still at home. And it is true that he helps us. But he has serious medical problems. And he has a wife. He also has other responsibilities. I am an adult. I must help out.'

'Hmm. You were born on 13 May 1962. Is that correct?'

'Yes. That is correct.'

'So, you are twenty-three years old, soon to be twenty-four. Is that correct?'

'Yes. That is true.'

'Tell us, Miss Askari, we are curious. Why are you still unmarried at your age?'

'I do not know.'

Elvis exchanged a look of disbelief with his partner. 'You do not know?'

'Yes. No. Yes. That is true. I do not know why I am not married.'

Elvis squinted and stared me down.

I cleared my throat and lowered my head, pretending to examine my skirt and taking a swipe at an imaginary speck on it.

'Are you a Kurd, Miss Askari?'

'My mother is a Kurd. My father was an Arab.'

'Do you feel yourself to be a Kurd? Do you feel yourself to be an Arab? Or do you feel yourself to be both?'

Here we go, I thought. Having any Kurdish blood puts a person under total suspicion.

'Yes. That is true.'

'What is true?'

I lied. I have always felt myself to be a Kurd, but I knew the danger of truth in this particular case.

'I feel myself to be both.'

'Tell us, Miss Askari, why is it you never joined the Baathist party?'

Ah! Elvis was smooth, slipping in one of the most vital questions of the day as though it was insignificant. But I had prepared my response, knowing that any question about party membership would be crucial.

'I was too busy at home. My father was dead. My mother was struggling. My sister was ill. My brother was at the front at the time when the war had gone to the trenches. I had no time for anything but school and home. I did not want to be a lazy party member, unable to participate fully. I would have been of no advantage to the party.'

'It says here, Miss Askari, that your best friend at university, a young lady by the name of Jenan, was a very active party member. Is that true?'

'Yes. That is true.'

Of course I couldn't tell them that Jenan had loathed the Baathist party, and that she had only joined because she was unlucky enough to be pressurized to do so on a day when she didn't have a good excuse on the tip of her tongue. My dear friend was trapped and ended up becoming one of the thousands of reluctant card-carrying members. Jenan and I had giggled about the Baathists, their silly 'Baathist speech', their self-importance, their suspicious minds, their stiff mannerisms, their arrogant certainty that they had the right to hassle other students.

When the Baathist students assigned a member to bully me into joining, Jenan volunteered. Many afternoons after lectures she would catch me in the hallway and whisper, 'Let's go for a coffee, Joanna. I'm supposed to bully you today.'

And we would go for our coffee. We would discuss clothes and marriage and relatives, with our faces posed in serious expressions, knowing that somewhere in that coffee shop there was an informer, another member appointed to watch Jenan to make certain that she had indeed spent ample time recruiting me. At the next Baathist meeting, Jenan would dutifully report that I had two sick family members and had to go straight home from class to work in the garden to grow vegetables until dark and afterwards only had time for my college work. I wanted nothing more than to join the Baathist party and would do so at the first opportunity.

And so our game persisted all the way through university. Thanks to Jenan, I never did have to join those unpleasant Baathists.

'Miss Askari, you are working in a sensitive field with visitors to our country. You must join the party.'

'But my mother?'

'Your mother will be fine, Miss Askari. She will be proud that her daughter is a party member.'

The bald official leaned forward. 'Unless she believes the party not worthy?'

Elvis's black eyebrows shot up. His pompadour wobbled. He whispered, 'Is your mother *against* the party, Miss Askari?'

Baldy chimed in, his voice rising in excitement. 'If so, it is your duty as a loyal Iraqi to report her, even if she is your mother.'

I could feel sweat dribbling down my back. Their little game was becoming dangerous. I must look sharp.

'No, no. My mother is not against the party. The President is a member of the party. She respects the President and the party. But she needs me at home. She is old and sick.'

'Your sister lives at home. Is that true, Miss Askari?'

'Yes. That is true.'

'Surely your sister can take care of your elderly mother?'

My interrogators were shrewd. They were masters at entrapment, their every question a calculation, a form of trickery. And how did they know Muna was living back at home?

'It is true that my sister now lives at home. But it is not true that she can help my mother. My sister Muna is in many ways practically an invalid.'

'Your sister is an invalid?' There was a rustle of papers as Elvis sorted through the file. His voice sounded an alarm. 'There is no mention of this in your file.'

'It is absolutely true. My sister is unwell. She cannot take care of herself. And she has a toddler. Mother is their caretaker while I am at my classes, with the help of my brother's wife. But, being elderly,

Mother cannot be the caretaker for twenty-four hours a day. I assume responsibility when I return in the afternoon.'

Elvis slapped my file down on the desk, hastily picked up a pen and began scribbling in the margins.

Oh dear. Muna's condition was now a matter of police records. I shifted uneasily.

Poor Muna. She had been ill-omened since she had been in the womb with her twin, Sa'ad, and the past two years had been the worst of her life.

Although I had spoken against marriage for Muna, there was nothing I could do. My culture pushes marriage on everyone, even those for whom the institution would be unsuitable, such as Muna, who had been crippled by serious depressions since she was a young girl. People believed that 'girls must marry', and that it was a great humiliation for a woman to forgo the opportunity to be a wife and mother and remain a spinster. And so Muna was married, and she moved away to live in the home of her husband's family.

The marriage was questionable for reasons other than Muna's fragile health. Muna's husband was too old. Her mother-in-law was cruel. These two tyrants passed themselves off as ordinary people and then exploited my compliant sister as a slave.

Muna became pregnant within a few weeks, suffering a difficult pregnancy that produced a beautiful baby daughter named Nadia. After the birth, the marriage quickly collapsed. Although she had a new baby and her husband to care for, her sadistic mother-in-law insisted that Muna continue doing the heaviest housework. When she was unable to perform all the duties to her satisfaction, mother-in-law and son began to beat her.

Muna was a gentle girl who had never been subjected to angry voices or raised hands. One day while trying to avoid their physical blows, she ran out of the house and made her way home. Mother would not force Muna to return to that place. But Muna had left Nadia behind because she had been so frightened and confused. Her husband's family claimed they had the right to keep her, as in Iraq fathers have custody of children. But when Mother appeared at their door, she somehow convinced them to give her Muna's baby.

Although Muna was now back home with her child, and would never again be mistreated, the painful episode had taken its toll on her. She had withdrawn almost completely, except when playing sweetly with her darling Nadia.

My incomplete file seemed to have thrown Elvis. Its imperfect status appeared to work in my favour, for he abruptly sprang to his feet and sent me away with an ominous warning. 'Miss Askari, you have a few months to get your affairs in order. Then you will join the Baathist party and become an active member. You cannot work in the tourist sector otherwise.' Politeness forgotten, he barked, 'You are dismissed.'

I nodded, saying, 'Thank you for your kindness,' and then moved as quickly as possible away from those shady characters, out of that dark room, through the gloomy hallway and into the sunshine, clearing the sinister Baathist air out of my lungs.

I had not been arrested. I was not going to prison, at least not that day. I felt like dancing.

I spotted the taxi driver waiting in his car on the other side of the road. He looked as relieved as I was happy. Although we Iraqis had learned to be guarded when talking to strangers, I knew that this man was not one of 'them', and while he drove, I shared something of my frightening experience, confiding that they had given me only a few months before I must join the Baathist party, or else face dire consequences.

With his mouth open wide and stained teeth visible, he gaily said, 'Do not worry. Anything can happen in three months.' He turned his head to look me in the eye, asking, 'Do you remember the story of the king who offered fabulous riches to anyone who could teach his donkey to talk?'

I had to admit that I did not.

'I will tell you,' he said eagerly, one hand on the wheel and the other held triumphantly in the air. 'The king offered advance payment to anyone willing to take on the job. Teach his donkey to speak and keep the money. But at the end of the year, if the donkey was still braying rather than talking, the volunteer would pay with his life.

'A man said to be the wisest man in the kingdom accepted the king's offer, pocketing the money and saying yes, he would teach the donkey to talk. His friends cautioned him and wondered if he had lost his mind, because there was no evidence that a donkey could ever be taught to speak. But he was an optimistic man. In his opinion, many things might happen in a year. The king might die. He might die. The donkey might die. Or perhaps there would be a miracle and the donkey would learn to speak.'

I giggled.

The driver glanced at me in his mirror, his face bright with a knowing smile. He winked slyly and lowered his voice to a whisper. 'Who knows? The President might die. Those two officials might die. The Iranians might fight their way into Baghdad. The Sadoun Security Headquarters might burn down. Your family might move away. Anything can happen in three months.'

Later I would remember every word of that conversation.

But at the time, I had no way of knowing that everything in my life was set to change. And most inexplicably of all, my fate would be linked to a donkey.

On the very day that I was riding through the busy streets of Baghdad in that taxi, a donkey was making its long steep climb over the foothills of mountainous Kurdistan, its final destination Sulaimaniya. That donkey was transporting heavy bags and bundles. Tucked carefully into one of the bags was a letter addressed to Joanna Al-Askari of Baghdad, written months before. The unexpected communication would put me on a different path, changing my life for ever.

14

Love Letters

Baghdad and Sulaimaniyah
1986 and 1987

The New Year

My darling Joanna,
With the arrival of a new year, I feel a certain melancholy in the air. We had a small party here in the mountains, and afterwards I returned to my pen, to greet the New Year. I had dreamed of welcoming the New Year while having accomplished a cherished wish, to begin my life with you.
You are the world to me.
Please accept my proposal.
Please be my wife. Make me complete . . .
Sarbast

'What?' I said aloud, tightening my lips as I sceptically rotated the single thin sheet in my hands, examining first the flipside of the letter and afterwards the plain brown envelope, front and back. I could not find even the slightest indication of a postmark.

A short time earlier Alia had darted in through the front door, loudly exclaiming, 'Joanna! A letter! A letter for you! From Kurdistan!'

A warning bell went off. Sarbast had been killed and someone was writing to tell me. But why would I care? Nevertheless I held my hand out and ordered, 'Give it to me!'

As I was ripping open the envelope, Alia kept interrupting. 'It must be from Sarbast, Joanna. It was hand-delivered, this morning, by one of Hady's cousins from Sulaimaniya. The cousin told Hady that this letter was brought to his home by a mysterious woman he did not know. He heard a tapping on the door. He opened the door. There she was. She looked rough, he said, as though she had been hiking through the mountains. Without a word, she passed him this one letter. She then walked away. He didn't have a chance to question her. Can you believe she never spoke? Is it from Sarbast?'

'Alia, please! Give me a moment.' My sister was giving me a headache.

Alia had been concerned for some time about my well-being. Nothing I said convinced her that I had successfully pushed Sarbast from my mind. She was certain that I would never be happy with any man but Sarbast, and I knew that she was secretly hoping we would make our way back to one another.

I read the letter again. Was it some kind of joke?

I could not believe it was from Sarbast, although the flowery style of writing implied it could be him, for he was a poet. But the last time I had seen Sarbast his heart had been closed to me while open wide to another. That man would not have written this letter. Never!

After my interrogation by the security officals, I had become mistrustful. Perhaps Elvis and his bald partner had sent this letter. Perhaps our home was under surveillance. If I replied, perhaps I would be arrested and given a long prison sentence for communicating with Iraq's enemies, the *peshmerga*. I held the letter at arm's length. Perhaps it had been rolled in a toxic substance. Nothing would surprise me in Saddam's Iraq.

Still holding the letter far away from me, I read the words one more time. I had to admit that the writing looked very similar to Sarbast's handwriting.

But Sarbast had scorned me for another. And now, without a meeting, without any previous communication, he wanted to marry me? No, I didn't think so.

If not Sarbast, who, then, was trying to bring further shame on me?

Who hated me enough to want me to reply to a fraudulent marriage proposal? The letter was making me very angry.

I glared at Alia, feeling an unreasonable spark of fury. I felt the need to scold somebody. 'What is going on here?'

Alia looked chastened and shrugged. 'I know nothing other than what I've told you, Joanna. The letter was brought to us by Hady's cousin, who arrived yesterday from Sulaimaniya.' She eased the letter from my hand. 'The handwriting does resemble Sarbast's, Joanna.' She studied it more carefully, holding the page before the light, drawing it near her eyes and then away. 'I don't see any hidden messages. It must be from Sarbast. Look,' she said, indicating his signature, 'he signed his name. Why would anyone else take such a risk, Joanna?'

I dropped down into a chair at the table, positioning the letter and envelope on the table, considering the complicated journey the letter must have made in order to arrive in my hands, if it was indeed from Sarbast.

An active underground existed in Kurdistan, with smugglers constantly on the move, transporting money, post, food and military equipment. Without the underground, the *peshmerga* couldn't survive a month.

With the continued face-off between the Iraqi army and the Iranian army, and with the PUK allied with the Iranians, Kurdistan had turned into a particularly vicious battleground. Although the PUK had recently gained a lot of rural territory – a cause for celebration – there were still plenty of urban areas that were held by the Iraqi army. In those regions, roadblocks had proliferated until it was almost impossible for any Kurd to make the shortest journey without risking life and limb. We had heard that Saddam was so enraged by the joint Kurdish and Iranian victories that he planned to move strong reinforcements from the south to the north. If that happened, Kurdistan was doomed.

To receive a letter from a *peshmerga* in Kurdistan was equivalent to receiving a valuable gift. No *peshmerga* would risk the life of any smuggler over a mere letter in the present conditions unless the content was felt to be very important. Should any contraband, such as *peshmerga* mail or fighting supplies, or even food, be detected at a checkpoint, the smuggler would pay with his life. His or her family would not be informed and would be made to endure the special kind of agony of never knowing.

Was this letter from Sarbast, then? If so, what had changed to make him believe he loved me now? And even so, I cruelly reminded myself, I was second choice. I must never forget it.

Still, I was curious. I lightly brushed the page with my fingertips, thinking. I knew that the letter in my hand, if authentic, had gone on quite a journey. It would have left Sarbast's hand months before and been concealed in the load on the back of a smuggler's donkey. Smugglers were most often men, but on occasion women transported mail, for their sex had proved to be a believable cover. Iraqi soldiers, accustomed to the Arab tradition of keeping women away from the front lines, did not understand that Kurdish women routinely imperilled their lives to assist the cause. The smuggler and donkey would have made their way through the mountains, past the checkpoints and into the cities, the dangerous undertaking requiring nerves of steel. Once in the city, the smuggler would have sought out a chosen *peshmerga* family, who would have somehow arranged to deliver the letter to the addressee by another arduous process.

Certainly if grime was the test for authenticity, the letter was from Sarbast. The page was filthy with dust in the creases. I lifted the envelope to my nose. 'Whew!' It stank of a fetid pack animal. I had been in the company of a few donkeys and mules when visiting Kurdistan and found them to be very smelly, at least to my city nose.

I mulled over the letter for so long that Alia finally left, saying she had to get home to her boys. 'Let me know if it is from Sarbast,' she said as she closed the door behind her.

I clutched the letter in my hand and went into the garden, settling in a chair to read it a third time.

When Mother, Muna, Sa'ad and his wife came home, I tucked the letter in my pocket, telling them nothing.

At bedtime, I retrieved the letter, reading it several more times before I slipped on my nightgown. I sprawled across the mattress, but I couldn't sleep. If the letter was from Sarbast, where was his explanation for that magical day at the university? Our hearts had met that day. What had happened? Why hadn't he asked me to marry him then? Where was his explanation for his coldness on the day when I made it clear that I wanted to return with him to Kurdistan? Where was his explanation for asking another to marry him?

He offered no explanations, only a declaration of love.

I finally accepted that the letter was from Sarbast. I knew his hand-writing too well. But I felt incredibly sad. At another time, Sarbast's letter would have made me the happiest woman in Baghdad. But I could not forget that I was second best in Sarbast's eyes. Had his blonde said yes to his proposal, Sarbast would have been married, and perhaps a father by now. I swallowed my pain, but I found it impossible to swallow my pride.

I ignored the letter and did not reply.

Several months later a poem came to me via a similar route. This time, Sarbast did not address me; nor did he sign it.

> *I might have wronged you.*
> *I might have taken the decision too late.*
> *I had my doubts*
> *And now I know how wrong I was*
> *What I am sure of is my love for you.*
> *My love has no boundaries.*
> *And you are crushing my heart with your silence.*
> *Don't be silent.*
> *Don't be cruel.*
> *You are in every page I turn*
> *In every word I write*
> *All the birds here chant your name.*
> *I am nothing without you.*

Now the birds were chanting my name?

This was becoming very interesting. Yet despite Sarbast's heartfelt pleas, I felt stubborn, unwilling to meet him even halfway. When I glanced into the mirror I was surprised to see stern features reflected there. I was sad to acknowledge that I was a new person, no longer the joyful Joanna I had always been.

I slipped the poem away in a secret place, along with his first letter. I did not respond.

★

Several months later, a third communication arrived, again carrying the smell of the donkey express.

> *Dearest Joanna,*
> *If sadness had sizes, I would wake up every day to a mountain of sadness. If yearning had a language and tunes, you would hear symphonies. I know no geography except that towards the south. From the mountain top my vision is as clear as that of Zarqa Al-Yamama, and it pierces the distances towards Baghdad's gates to your window.*
> *The north asks the south about you, the mountain tops ask Baghdad's buildings about you, the pecan trees ask the palm trees about you, but there is no answer. I cover distances, I go over mountains looking for one word of you, but words are missing, and the distances are killing me.*
> *Tell me how to reach the road to your heart, give me a sign, and I will be there. I am ready to travel to you; only give me a sign, and I will come to you. I do not want to lie to you, but I mean it when I say I will sacrifice my life for you.*
> *Sarbast*

I laughed aloud. If the mountain tops and trees were beginning to discuss me, this was becoming a very serious situation.

By this time everyone in my family knew something of my quandary, for such a secret could not be kept for long in such close living quarters. But I provided them with few details. Only Alia and Hady knew the urgency of Sarbast's love campaign.

Alia told me to be happy that I was being pursued, yet I could take no satisfaction from the fact that our situations were now reversed – for years Sarbast had been casual about me, while I had been desperate to win his love, and now, it seemed, he had fallen in love with me, while I was the hesitant party. I felt he had squandered our chance for happiness. And a great misery hung over me as I remembered the grief and pain that attaches itself to romantic love. I willed myself to be strong and not to return to that wounding place.

Then a fourth letter arrived.

Do not declare your war on me
In this case
I am a weary stranger in this town
Do not torture me
From there afar, thousands are persecuting me
Your war on me is not heroic
Stay with me and make me happy
For I only have your eyes to make me happy
Nothing is heard save the beat of my heart
The mountains and the trees
Have ceased talking to me
As they used to before
The sun has set
Another day is demolished by my loneliness
I am sad and weary in these mountain tops
And together with silent nature
I am in mourning.

Suddenly Sarbast's dashing image came to me, and I was swept away with memories of why I had fallen in love with him in the first place.

I began to weep quietly.

Mother slipped into the room and sat beside me on my bed. My hair was piled on my head and she took out the pins and let my long hair fall down my back, lifting strands with her fingers, pulling them to her nose, sniffing their scent. Then she kissed my cheek before raising my chin with one finger and pulling me to face her, saying, 'Daughter, you look so sad.'

Leaning my head against Mother's shoulder, I began to sob.

I felt Muna's presence in the room, but my darling sister stood quietly, saying nothing.

Mother and Muna had been watching me closely for several weeks. In fact, everyone in my family was suffering with me.

My wounds were reopening. Sarbast's letters and poems were getting to me. My entire body felt raw, crushed. I had become impossible, irritable. Sa'ad and his wife had begun to avoid me. My colleagues believed there was a family crisis.

Since the day Sarbast had disregarded me, unhappiness had been

walking with me, but I had put that unhappiness in a locked com-
partment, and now his letters were letting it out. Remembering the
agony of love's rejection, I feared its return.

The following morning, Mother asked me to sit with her for a
while. We sipped tea, talking about mundane matters.

Then, with a firm look, Mother reminded me, 'Daughter, there are
people risking their lives to deliver these unanswered letters. It would
be a pity for some brave man or woman to be killed because of them.'

I cringed. I had not considered the dangers for others.

Mother patted my knee. 'Joanna, write to him with a yes. Or write
to him with a no.' She kissed me. 'Joanna, I do not want you to marry
this man and live the fighter's life. But if you love him, and that is
what will bring you happiness, I will support your decision.'

I stared at Mother, loving her even more for her offer of sacrifice.
In the current climate, few families would allow their daughters to
marry a fighter, even Kurdish families supporting the cause. Kurds
were losing many of their sons; they didn't want to lose their
daughters too. If I travelled to the north and lived the *peshmerga* life,
my mother would exist in a fog of endless worry, never knowing if
her youngest child had been captured, was being tortured, or was
dead or alive.

I began to tremble. I felt a true yearning for Sarbast. I finally made
up my mind.

I threw myself into her arms. 'Mother!'

I had my answer.

III Love and Tragedy in Kurdistan

15

Love and Marriage

Baghdad to Sulaimaniya to Serwan
May to June 1987

Mine was a wedding without a groom. Everything normal was denied me.

When I leant my head against Mother's shoulder and whispered my disappointment, she reminded me that I should be happy that I was having a wedding at all.

It was true that weeks of uncertainty lay behind us. Much had taken place since the day I had tearfully confessed to Mother that I had never stopped loving Sarbast, despite my resolve to pull out the roots of the love planted ten years before. I had caught the fever of his letters and poems, and his confessed love for me had become overwhelming, regenerating my love for him. I grew passionate to become the woman of my childhood fantasies, a woman who marries her handsome *peshmerga* hero and lives out her life as a freedom fighter in the mountains of Kurdistan.

Taking Mother's advice, I had finally answered Sarbast's communications. However, my message was not the love letter he was hoping to receive. Instead, I poured out my heart, telling him of my feelings, my frustrations, my slow-burning anger. I vented my resentment of the woman he had asked to marry him, writing hateful words, telling him that in his stupidity and blindness he had chosen an incompatible woman with selfish demands, a woman who sounded like a man. I spitefully added that had she said yes, he would have found a rasping shrew in his marriage bed. With that letter Sarbast understood that there was a new aspect to his happy and sweet Joanna, indeed a new persona that he had created, for it was pain caused by his actions that had created my bitterness.

Despite my anger, he was not discouraged. In fact, he became even more forceful in his efforts to persuade me to say yes.

Unbeknownst to me, Alia slipped a brief note in with mine, disclosing that other men were seeking my hand in marriage. I no longer had to endure lengthy silences from Sarbast. Tortured by the idea of other suitors, he wrote another letter which arrived in record time from the distant mountains. It said that I must say yes or else he would not survive.

I had nearly forgotten the intensity of Sarbast's passions for everything he loved, whether country, cause or family. And now those passions were directed at me. It was splendid to be loved by the man I had vainly loved for so many years.

All ended as it was meant to be. I finally said yes, I would marry him, and I would leave Baghdad life behind me to join him in the mountains, even if it meant becoming a fugitive in the process.

I was not frightened. I was excited, for with one decision two dreams were fulfilled. I was going to be a *peshmerga* wife, a freedom fighter supporting her husband and her beautiful country.

I set about leaving Baghdad for ever. I informed my boss at the tourist office that I would be leaving as I was to be married. I did not advise him of the full truth: that I was marrying a *peshmerga*. I bade trusted girlfriends secret goodbyes, friends who so loved me that they were horrified to learn that I was going to marry a PUK *peshmerga*. Even in Baghdad we had heard that Saddam's soldiers no longer made distinctions between *peshmerga* men and their wives. When captured, all were slaughtered. I told other, more casual friends that I was moving to Sulaimaniya to be with my mother's family.

A worried Sarbast sent an urgent message that I must leave Baghdad quickly, as everything in Kurdistan was changing for the worse. The fires of war were roaring out of control.

Only the year before, in 1986, the PUK had allied itself with the Iranians to fight Saddam as the common enemy. The Iraqi President became savage with rage, screeching that PUK leader Talabani and his fighters were 'agents of Iran', and vowing to destroy all members of the PUK. Sarbast was PUK and very soon I too would be considered PUK in the eyes of our enemies.

While the Iraqi military occupied all the cities in Kurdistan, the PUK *peshmerga* remained strong in the outlying areas, and with new support from the Iranians they had begun assaulting the occupying Iraqi army forces in the northern city of Kirkuk. Kirkuk was a city coveted by all, as it was blessed with enormous oil resources.

Baghdad's answer to the PUK's new military offensive was extreme. On 29 March 1987, the Revolutionary Command Council issued decree number 160, which granted Ali Hassan Al-Majid, the head of the Northern Bureau, the power to proceed with the Kurdish final solution. A particularly brutish man, Ali Al-Majid would see that the Kurds all died.

Two weeks later he began the campaign of genocide that would earn him the infamous title Chemical Ali. On 15 April, he dropped poisonous gases on the PUK headquarters in Sergalou and the PUK communication centre in Bergalou. While there was some loss of life, most of the fighters survived, because the chemicals had been mixed incorrectly. Then when the chemicals were dropped the wind was not blowing in the right direction. But with chemical warfare now a reality, there was a new urgency for the need to defeat Saddam.

The *peshmerga* could not win against the invisible weapons sarin and mustard gas, for there were few gas masks available for the fighters and none for the civilians. Saddam had made it illegal for Kurds to own gas masks. The ruling had sparked an ill-omened implication: with the PUK unable to offer protection to civilians, villagers would be forced to flee. If the villages were abandoned, the *peshmerga* would lose access to their secret mountain hideaways. If the mountains were overrun, the *peshmerga* and Kurdistan would be finished. An old Kurdish saying came to mind: flatten the mountains and Kurdistan will not last one day.

I fretted about the new turn the war had taken, eager to be there and to share with Sarbast the escalating danger.

Three days before I was to leave Baghdad, I was jolted by another summons from Baldy and Elvis. I was commanded to return to their offices within a week to report on my membership of the Baathist party. Amidst all the excitement of my engagement, I had forgotten Elvis and Baldy, but they had not forgotten me.

It had been some time since those men had given me a few months to join the Baathist party. I had expected the summons earlier, but obviously they had been busy with other, more important matters than a young woman working in a tourist office. Now my time was up.

While the earlier summons had terrified me, I found the second less unnerving. I even smiled a little, recalling the kindly taxi driver's prediction that 'anything could happen'. 'Anything' had happened. I was leaving Baghdad, fleeing to the mountains where Elvis and Baldy would be the hunted ones, should they be so stupid as to try to pursue me there. I would be living in the forbidden area where only Kurdish fighters and villagers walked the land, out of reach of routine police surveillance.

Or so I thought.

I ignored the summons and prepared a letter that my boss volunteered to deliver to Elvis and his partner once I had left for the north, informing them that rather than pursue a career, I had married and moved away from Baghdad. I assumed that their interest in me would fade upon receipt of my letter.

'Cheerio, Elvis!' I gaily called out several times a day, causing bewildered expressions on the faces of friends and family, who became concerned for my sanity.

My last night in Baghdad would be 5 May 1987. Mother and I would travel the following day to Sulaimaniya, where we would be welcomed by Sarbast's family and have a week to organize the wedding. As the head of our family, Sa'ad would follow, arriving in Sulaimaniya in time for the marriage contract to be formalized.

Not having seen Sarbast for three long years, and desiring to be beautiful for him, I foolishly spent more money than I should in the finest shops located in the Mansour district and the Al-Nahir souq. My closest girlfriends helped me to select the latest fashions, the highest heels and the sexiest nightgowns, as well as extra supplies of make-up and perfumes. Who knew how long I would be living in a mountain village without access to anything of normal life? With blissful anticipation, I carefully packed my girlish treasures into a large bag.

I was ready.

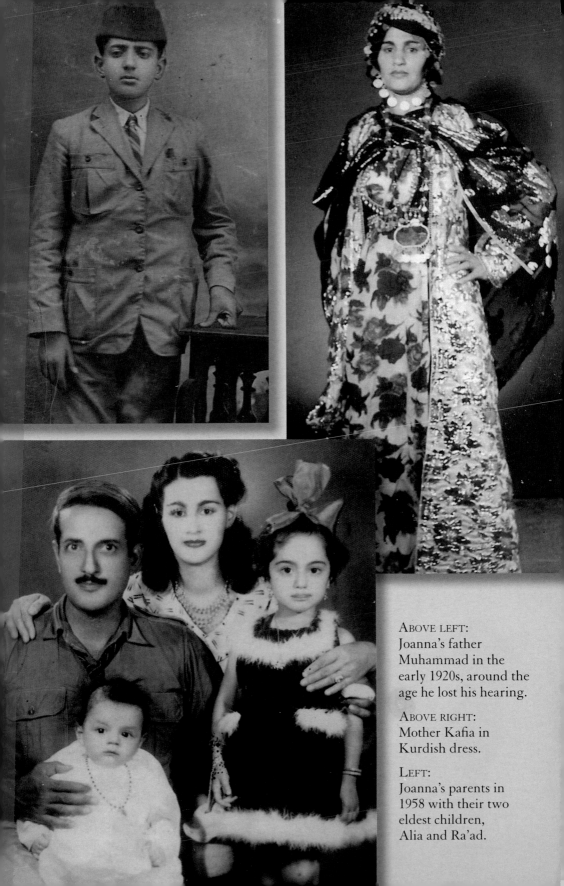

LEFT:
Baby Joanna with Hady, who later married her sister Alia.

BELOW:
Kurdish dancers.

BOTTOM LEFT:
Joanna (left front) with family members on a summer holiday visit to Kurdistan.

LEFT:
Twins Sa'ad and Muna in the garden of the family home in Baghdad.

BOTTOM MIDDLE:
Joanna in the garden, 1970.

BOTTOM RIGHT:
Teenage Joanna wearing conservative Islamic dress at brother Sa'ad's command.

ABOVE:
Joanna as a student (second from left), attending a lecture at Baghdad University.

RIGHT:
Joanna's first job at Baghdad travel agency, shortly before Sarbast proposed.

BELOW:
Brother Sa'ad as a soldier in the trenches during the war against Iran, early 1980s.

ABOVE:
The wedding without a groom:
left to right, Joanna's father-in-law,
brother-in-law, Joanna, Sa'ad, sister-
in-law (Auntie Aisha's daughter).

LEFT:
Joanna and Sarbast on their honeymoon in Serwan.

BELOW:
Newlywed bliss.

ABOVE:
Joanna and Sarbast huddled up against the cold in the Kurdish mountains.

RIGHT:
Sarbast (left) with fighter friends under canvas.

BELOW:
Ashti, Joanna's fellow *peshmerga* wife and friend.

ABOVE:
PUK radio tower in the mountains above Bergalou.

RIGHT:
Joanna's beloved Auntie Aisha, murdered in the chemical attacks of 1988.

BELOW:
Destruction after Saddam's army's bombardment.

TOP LEFT:
Joanna and Sarbast in exile in the village of Al-Wattan, Iran, after their escape from Iraq.

TOP RIGHT:
A pregnant Joanna with Shamsa, the Iranian woman who became her second mother.

ABOVE:
Passport photo of Joanna, Sarbast and their son Kosha, seeking asylum status in the UK.

LEFT:
Safe and free in England with son Kosha.

*

Alone at home the day before my departure, I went round the house selecting favoured spots and treasured objects to wish a fond farewell to, for something inside me cautioned that I might never return to my childhood home.

Many family treasures sparked happy memories, but none more than my mother's clothes chest, still full of fine clothes from the early days, before the 1958 revolution, when she and my father had enjoyed prosperity and received formal invitations to the palace. I was such a lively child that my exhausted mother had often encouraged me to dig around in that chest and pull out ballgowns and high-heeled shoes. I would put on a fancy gown and slip into red heels with toes so pointed that I could, and did, inflict dents or marks on the walls with them. After dabbing my lips with Mother's brightest red lipstick, I would hang a small beaded evening bag on my arm and prance around the house, making believe I was at a fancy ball where there were kings and queens and young princes and princesses.

I went to sit in my father's fine walnut desk chair, a simple but elegant piece that he had designed and made with his elaborately carved desk at his beloved furniture factory, the factory I had never had the pleasure of visiting but had heard described by Ra'ad and Mother so many times that I felt I had worked there myself. Many were the occasions I had watched my poor overworked father sitting upright at that desk, his broad back erect against the chair, his elbows propped atop the desk, as he busily examined documents, adding and subtracting long rows of figures, in a vain search for money to feed our large family for one more day. Those two pieces of furniture were the only items my father had salvaged from the fire that destroyed the factory during the 1958 revolution. Even an untrained eye would guess that the walnut desk and chair had been crafted by a talented furniture designer.

The pain of my father's loss felt unbearable even after eleven years. I left the house and drifted out into the garden, to the largest palm tree, my favourite refuge, where I had so often escaped as a child. I settled easily in a familiar spot, a furrow worn into the ground from many years' use, leaned my head against the solid trunk and looked up into the brilliant blue sky. 'Goodbye, palm trees. Goodbye, Baghdad sky.'

I bid farewell to twenty-five bittersweet years. 'Cheerio!'

I was happier than I had ever been, a young woman fulfilling an enduring dream.

When the day came for Mother and me to depart, all our family gathered to say goodbye, the women weeping, the men quiet and solemn, as if they had just received word of my funeral.

I laughed away their fears. It was a happy occasion!

Had I known the mayhem soon to face me, or how long it would be before I would see them all again, no doubt my courage would have failed me and I could not have left them, even to run into the arms of the man I loved.

I comforted a sad Alia. 'Just remember, with every end comes a new beginning. I am ready for this new beginning.'

Alia smiled her knowing smile. Only Alia had been there at the beginning of my journey of love. Only Alia could fully comprehend the years of anguish that lurked behind my happy ending with Sarbast.

I wasn't sorry to see the last of the dust of Baghdad, despite the fact that we were travelling into unknown danger.

After several years of seclusion in Baghdad we were not prepared for the stark changes in the north. The land we loved was being assaulted from the air and from the ground. Too many helicopters to count roamed like angry bees overhead. Military checkpoints were dotted along the main highway from Baghdad to Kirkuk to Sulaimaniya, making sure supplies and communications did not get through to the *peshmerga* fighters or the Kurdish villagers. Saddam wanted to starve us.

Mother and I endured the strange horror of waiting at checkpoints, for every visitor to the area was deemed a spy. We sat watching helplessly as several Kurdish men were pulled from their cars and taken away. Those poor men were doomed. It was rumoured that Kurds were being murdered indiscriminately. But at each checkpoint, we were two women alone with our papers in order, with many relatives in Sulaimaniya, so during routine questioning we were able to convince them that we were just visiting those relatives, and we were waved through.

As we sat on the bus Mother clicked her prayer beads so loudly that I peered into her worried eyes and asked, 'Are you trying to create a special tune with those beads, Mother?'

She whispered anxiously, 'This day will seem a picnic compared to your new life, Joanna.'

True. But I would not have wanted it any other way.

After my wedding I would be going with Sarbast to live in a vital guerrilla hideaway for the PUK, the village of Bergalou, nestled in the narrow Jafati valley, a long strip of difficult terrain in north-eastern Iraqi Kurdistan. Bergalou was a temporary village, inhabited by fighters, which housed the PUK radio station and a field hospital. Bergalou's importance to the Kurdish resistance made it a tempting target for the Iraqi army. The village was routinely bombed and shelled.

Strangely enough, I felt wholly unconcerned for my own well-being. I stared out the window and thought about Sarbast, eager to begin our married life, impatient to play some small role in support-ing Kurdish freedom.

A heartfelt Kurdish welcome awaited us at the house of Sarbast's brother, Osman, who lived in Sarchnar, a residential district of Sulaimaniya. Mother and I felt at home for another reason: Osman was married to my mother's niece, Nawbahar, who was the daughter of my favourite aunt, Aisha.

I was taken by surprise when Sarbast's family presented me with a lovely wedding gift of four gold bracelets.

Gold is greatly valued by the Kurds, and the groom's family traditionally offers expensive presents to the bride, usually items of gold that will always belong to her even if she is widowed or her husband asks for a divorce. In the event of such tragedies, many women have found that their wedding gold kept them and their children from starving. Yet I had been expecting nothing. After I had accepted Sarbast's marriage proposal, he had written to ask what I wanted for a dowry. I had replied, 'Other than a plain gold wedding ring, I will accept nothing.' I knew that his family had made many financial sacrifices for the Kurdish cause, and that because the Iraqi army had retaliated against the family for having two sons who were *peshmerga*, they had lost their family home.

We would begin our marriage on equal footing. Neither of us

would possess anything of value. We would build our future together. After Kurdistan was free, we were sure to prosper. Sarbast claimed to be the luckiest man alive, understanding that I was marrying him for true love.

Although those gold bracelets were only a token, I was delighted, for I knew that the gift was a way for Sarbast's family to notify me of their pleasure that I was joining their family.

The ladies of the house were inquisitive when I unpacked my large suitcase. They gathered round me in a friendly, jostling circle as I proudly showed off my expensive new wardrobe.

I was baffled by the peals of laughter that greeted every item.

'What? What?' I looked at the women, my hands held aloft, my eyes wide in puzzlement. Sarbast's mother was such a sweet-faced lady that I loved her already, but when her expression grew grave, I became confused.

She guided me by my shoulders to the edge of the bed, and pushed me to sit. 'My dear girl, Bergalou will not be a party. You are going to the mountains to live the *peshmerga* life. Your clothes must protect you in those harsh mountains.' She lifted the edge of one of my satin dresses, a bright shade of red. 'This dress should be declared a murder weapon! You'll sparkle like a beacon.' She shook her head. 'The Iraqi army will love it if you wear this dress, Joanna. You will make their surveillance very easy. Everyone on that mountain will go straight to Allah if you wear this.' She threw both hands in the air. 'Boom! And this!' She pointed at a lightweight beige blouse and lacy skirt, one of the latest fashions from Paris. 'Joanna, you will freeze. And these? Is my son marrying Cinderella?' Everyone laughed when she prodded my impossibly high black Italian stilettos with a gold streak.

I was mortified. I had been so keen to excite Sarbast and look my best for him that I had temporarily lost all common sense. I bit my lip and looked around, wishing that the lot of them would evaporate.

The moment grew worse when one of Sarbast's younger sisters pulled out my most beautiful sheer nightgown and a pair of matching panties and began to dance. I gasped and snatched them from her, the blood rushing to my face. By that time I was the only woman in the room who was not bent double laughing.

After catching her breath, Sarbast's mother appeared sympathetic. She hugged me, and then became serious. 'Joanna, what you will need is heavy trousers, boots and sensible jackets. You can leave your silks and satins here, for the future, when everything settles down.'

My face fell in disappointment.

She shrugged, patting me on my shoulder. 'Every war ends, eventually.'

That afternoon we all crowded into a dilapidated taxi and went to the local souq. The women assisted me in selecting sensible mountain clothes, which, to my dismay, meant menswear.

I purchased several pairs of the smallest men's trousers available, the baggy-legged trousers so popular in Kurdistan. They were so wide in the waist that they drooped. I'd tie them up with string, perhaps, I thought glumly, beginning to realize that I had been wrong to think I would not miss anything of my former life. I was not accustomed to dressing so shabbily. Every young bride wants to look beautiful for her husband and I was no exception.

A future sister-in-law noticed my gloomy face and teased, 'These trousers will be invaluable, Joanna. You will be able to ride donkeys, climb tall mountains, and,' she added with a hearty laugh, 'leap as high as my head in them. And look,' she explained, 'look at these long pockets. You can transport whole loaves of bread in these.' Indeed the pockets ran the length of the trouser leg.

I despondently folded my lovely clothes and repacked my suitcase. However, I refused to leave behind my beautiful new pink bedding, despite warnings that I would be travelling by donkey at some point during my trek to Bergalou, and that such elegant bedding had no place in the mountains. I even got into a physical struggle with one of my future sisters-in-law over it, but I refused to turn over my quilt or my pillow, determined that I would have something of beauty in my new mountain home.

Later we made a second trip, this time to the gold souq, to purchase wedding rings. Everyone chuckled when I pulled a twig from my handbag, telling the shop owner, 'My fiancé sent me this. His ring finger is this exact size.' What fun I had sliding various styles of men's wedding rings down that twig while a mesmerized crowd gathered in excited curiosity!

There were several more hurdles to overcome before I could marry Sarbast. Saddam had made it a crime for any woman to marry a *peshmerga*. No government officials anywhere in Sulaimaniya would risk their necks to provide us with the proper papers. Few Kurdish mullahs were brave enough to officiate at our union ceremony.

Just as I was beginning to believe that our marriage would not take place, and I would be forced to admit bitter failure and return to Baghdad, Sarbast's brother solved the problem. He arranged the paperwork and he knew a brave Kurdish mullah, Ibrahim Salih, who agreed to conduct the ceremony.

With that problem solved, yet another arose, making me wonder if God Himself was against my marriage. A message came that Sarbast was unable to make the journey from the mountains to Sulaimaniya. I felt the bitterest pang and my knees buckled. As with all *peshmerga*, there was a bounty on his head. Furthermore, Baghdad had just intensified its offensive in the area. It was impossible for any *peshmerga* to leave the mountains, cross the forbidden zones, clear all the checkpoints and enter an occupied city. Such a trip might cost Sarbast his life.

In mute desolation I sat and brooded. But I felt better when reminded that our traditions do not demand that the bride and groom attend the marriage ceremony together. In fact, in many Muslim countries, men and women are separated during the ceremony. The mullah could solemnize the marriage first with Sarbast and then with me. Once the marriage was consummated, we would be considered man and wife.

I was amazed and forever grateful when that brave mullah volunteered to make the perilous journey into the mountains to Sarbast. I was heartbroken, though, that Sarbast could not attend our wedding. I tried to remain stoic in front of Sarbast's family, but failed to restrain tears of disappointment.

Finally the anticipated day arrived. Swinging between hope and despair that at the last minute Sarbast would unexpectedly show up, I had spent the two days before in Sulaimaniya beauty salons having my long black hair styled, and undergoing facials, waxings, manicures and pedicures.

But Sarbast was nowhere to be seen.

My brother Sa'ad arrived a few hours before the ceremony, reporting that he had experienced no problems at the checkpoints, which was an enormous relief. With Ra'ad living in Switzerland, Sa'ad would be the one to formally agree to my marriage to Sarbast.

Finally realizing that Sarbast would not be surprising me at the last minute, I chose not to wear the beautiful pink dress I had purchased for my special day. Instead, I wore a sensible pink and grey suit. I pulled my long black hair back with a barrette. I put on minimum make-up.

Sarbast's absence dulled the day for me. I could not believe that after so many years of anticipation my wedding would be without a groom. But it was.

Everyone gathered in Osman's sitting room. It was a warm and pleasant room, with red fabric on the walls and a wooden floor strewn with handmade carpets. There was a painting of wild horses hanging behind the sofa and other interesting knick-knacks scattered about.

In celebration, my cousin had made some sweets. But I was too edgy to eat, worried that something else would happen to derail the ceremony. Perhaps the mullah had been shot at a checkpoint. Such tragedies occurred on a daily basis in Kurdistan. But that dreadful scenario did not happen and finally Mullah Ibrahim Salih arrived. I couldn't help noticing that his thin lips were closed tight, as though he found it difficult to smile. Being a Kurdish mullah had become a dangerous calling.

Sarbast's father and brother rushed to thank him. I smiled at him gratefully.

Mullah Ibrahim said little of his mountain adventure, other than to admit that it had been harrowing. He proudly displayed a document with Sarbast's signature that confirmed his permission to conduct the ceremony in his absence. He glanced in my direction and, with a smile, told me that Sarbast wished me a safe trip into the mountains.

I took this to mean: bride, get here as rapidly as you can.

Just then Sa'ad noticed that my head was uncovered, which was more than he could bear in the presence of a mullah. He made a bit of a fuss until someone tossed me a white scarf. I threw the thin scarf loosely over my head.

Sa'ad grunted in irritation but managed not to speak his true thoughts.

I glanced at Sa'ad and smiled. I loved him. My brother was a handsome man and incredibly sweet, at least in all things but his opinion of how women should dress.

He nodded and smiled back, looking happier than I had seen him for a long time.

I had a quick thought that my brother was probably thrilled that I was finally getting married. At the age of twenty-five, I was old for a Kurdish bride. After the wedding, I would no longer be his problem.

The ceremony began.

My religious ignorance soon became apparent.

Mullah Ibrahim read the required passages from the Koran in formal Kurdish and I was told to repeat the words after him. I had enormous difficulty understanding them, for I was fluent only in colloquial Kurdish. In a daze, I stumbled over every phrase.

Sa'ad and Mother both shifted in their seats, looking uncomfortable.

Generally the clerics I knew were stiff with dignity, but this cleric proved to be a lovely, less formal man. He repeated each phrase several times, shortening them and trying to ease the embarrassing situation for me. I was hopeless. I tried to suppress my giggles, knowing that Sa'ad would never recover if I laughed aloud during my own marriage ceremony. I was so pathetic that even Sarbast's sweet relatives looked at one another aghast. Sa'ad glared at me. He knew the Koran by heart and was appalled by my lack of religious knowledge.

My pink and grey suit was damp with sweat when the ceremony finally ended. What should have been the happiest day of my life had turned into an embarrassing fiasco. And I feared I had failed the test. What if the cleric ruled that I had spoiled my chance to marry? But Mullah Ibrahim obviously regarded my performance as passable, for he said nothing negative as he presented some documents for signature.

My marriage was official. Sarbast was my husband. Finally.

Although a groom might not be a requirement for a Kurdish wedding, a groom is crucial for a successful honeymoon. I was in a hurry to leave Sulaimaniya and find my groom. But I could not make the trip alone: guides would be necessary all the way. My fate would be in the hands of people I did not yet know.

After the ceremony, everyone enjoyed a lovely lunch, although we were unable to confide in any visitors who might pop in that we were celebrating my wedding. We could not be too careful: a careless word spoken might lead to the discovery that the mullah had broken one of Saddam's laws by performing a *peshmerga* marriage. If that happened, everyone would be punished.

Late that evening word rushed through Sulaimaniya that Saddam's army was preparing for a big attack against the *peshmerga*. I bade a hasty farewell to my new in-laws and to Sa'ad early the next morning.

Mother and one of Sarbast's sisters accompanied me from Sulaimaniya to the village of Qalat Diza, where I would be passed like a parcel into the hands of a female guide. We were to be driven by a male driver, for women in that area do not normally travel on the roads without male protection.

The fertile plains surrounding Qalat Diza soon came into view. Despite the current tensions, Kurdish farmers in baggy trousers were cultivating fields of wheat. Kandil mountain rose majestically behind the village, its rocky vaults still covered with snow and its beautifully wooded slopes framing the village.

Qalat Diza was one of Kurdistan's most beautiful villages. It was of particular interest to me for it was where Sarbast had spent much of his childhood and his life had been dramatically altered there. Kurdistan had always been a hotbed of rebellions and massacres and in 1974–5 the unrest simmered yet again. Without a word of warning, the Iraqi government dropped napalm on the civilians of Qalat Diza, and hundreds died. Sarbast was a youthful witness to the chaos of sudden death. He had once described to me his anguish as he attempted to save neighbours and friends. After the attack, Sarbast's family fled to Iran and lived in a refugee camp for nearly two years. By the time they returned from exile, Sarbast had formed a life-long hatred for the government in Baghdad, a hatred that would lead to his becoming a *peshmerga*.

Arriving safely in Qalat Diza I discovered that my guide was someone very special. She was Zakia Khan, Sarbast's cousin, and the wife of a high-ranking PUK *peshmerga* Qadir, a Kurdish warlord, considered royalty by Kurds. Zakia had courageously volunteered for the risky mission of helping me cross into the forbidden area of Kurdistan controlled by the *peshmerga*.

At Qalat Diza I bade my mother goodbye. It was a most emotional farewell for us both, for the seriousness of the situation in Kurdistan was now clear to us. Perhaps we would never see each other again. However, although saddened by the parting, I was in a rush to begin the precarious trek to the forbidden zone. I must get to Sarbast.

During the journey I found Zakia to be a brave and resourceful woman. While I quaked with fright, she skilfully manoeuvred us through some very dodgy situations at checkpoints.

I was horrified to discover that some of the checkpoints were manned by the *jahsh*, the Kurdish traitors who should have been fighting on the side of their Kurdish brothers but were in fact betraying brave *peshmerga*. The *jahsh* were in many ways more dangerous to us than Saddam's soldiers, as being of our kind they were difficult to distinguish and easily slipped into *peshmerga* ranks as spies. These shameful collaborators sold out Kurdistan and the Kurds for a government that would happily murder them once they were of no more use.

The perilous trip was grinding and tense, but finally, once under the protection of the high mountains and the canopy of the trees, I felt free and unafraid for the first time in days. I looked at the beauty around me, the mountains rising in lofty peaks, the luxuriant creepers that covered the limbs of gigantic trees, and the rushing streams swollen by the melting of the snow. The breathtaking vista helped me forget the hostile forces we had left behind.

At last, after a six-hour drive over rocky unpaved roads, so bumpy that the top of my head constantly bashed against the ceiling of the jeep, we arrived at the small village of Merge.

This extremely poor Kurdish village was divided in two by a main road, lined by simple houses built of concrete blocks. None of the tourist wealth that had once flowed to its close-by neighbour, Dokan Lake, a well-known holiday region in northern Kurdistan famed for its vineyards, figs and pomegranates, had benefited Merge.

I knew that Sarbast was there, somewhere, in one of these homes, waiting for me.

My husband.

I wondered how on earth we would find each other. Impatient, I began anxiously searching the doorway of each house we passed. Suddenly there was a flash of movement and Sarbast appeared from one of the houses. When his eyes met mine he began running as quickly as he could, his long hair flowing, his eyes flashing, trying to catch the jeep.

I screamed at the jeep driver to stop. I reached out with my hands through the open side, wanting Sarbast to pull me from the jeep and into his arms. For some unexplained reason the driver sped up. I peered out helplessly. I had never realized that Sarbast was such a fast runner. He was gaining on the jeep.

Fearing that the driver was going to race through the entire village without slowing down, I decided to leap from the jeep into Sarbast's outstretched arms. I braced myself, preparing to jump. When the driver saw me, he finally pulled to the side of the dirt road. I was out of that jeep before the man could turn off the ignition.

Sarbast grabbed me in his arms and started spinning round and round, twirling me in the air.

I laughed out loud. I had survived a thousand tribulations to reach that moment.

I opened my eyes and looked past Sarbast's shoulder to see many smiling faces. A small crowd had gathered. It's not every day that a *peshmerga* marries a girl from Baghdad.

One *peshmerga* embarrassed Sarbast by revealing that for the entire time I had been travelling, Sarbast had been so anxious that he could not eat or sleep. He had sat up watching the road all night, dashing out to check on each vehicle that passed through the village. His comrades had added to his torture by calling out false alarms every few hours, telling him that the jeep with his bride had passed through the village without stopping.

And that is nearly what had happened. I turned to look at the driver, wondering what on earth he had been thinking. When I saw him laughing heartily, I realized that he, too, had been in on the joke. But all had ended well, so I smiled happily at him.

Zakia climbed out of the jeep to stand proudly beside us, nodding at her cousin Sarbast and accepting his heartfelt thanks for bringing me safely to him.

I laughed, more excited and happy than I had ever been in my life. I knew in my heart that I belonged with those good people. I had come home.

I could barely take my eyes off Sarbast. To me, he was still the most handsome man in the world. But he looked different, no longer the dashing young man with whom I had fallen in love. He seemed to be in need of a good night's sleep. He had grown a full beard. His hair was even longer, and those curls of his were completely tangled. I felt a rush of anticipation as I thought that soon I would be free to tousle those curls with my hand. I had wanted to pull on those curls for ten years.

Then I remembered my own shabby appearance. Although I had planned on looking as pretty as possible, when Zakia spotted my large suitcase she had firmly snapped her fingers and ordered that it be taken away, saying that such a piece of luggage would create dangerous curiosity at the checkpoints. I was told that I could carry only one change of clothing, one plain nightgown and a comb, which were put into a worn and torn plastic bag. The rest of my belongings would come to me on a mule within the next few weeks.

A further blow came when I was told to wash my face clean of all make-up and to pull my long hair into a bun. Zakia held my hands for a few minutes, admiring my beautiful nails, which were polished and painted to perfection, and said that while she had never seen such elegant fingernails in her life, they must be cut off. 'Joanna, if one soldier at a checkpoint spots these stylish nails, he will instantly know that you are not a mountain girl.' I could hardly bear to watch as those long nails were clipped and tossed into a bag of rubbish.

The worst was yet to come. Zakia furnished me with a plain navy-blue dress, a black robe and a dark scarf. I was ordered to slip on a worn pair of plain flat slippers. It was imperative, I was told, for me to look the part of a poor village girl. Never had I dreamed that I would have to wear the veil and cloak again in my life. I was only glad that Sa'ad was not there to witness my humiliation. I struggled not to weep. I did not want to greet my new husband in such attire, but Zakia was unmoving on these points. She was not willing to risk her own life if I were so foolish as to flaunt my Baghdad sophistication. I saw her point.

Now I looked at Sarbast and whispered, 'I'm sorry your bride had to come to you,' and I looked down at my dress and slippers, 'in this. I am ashamed of how I look.'

Sarbast's dark eyes glittered with the purest happiness. 'You are beautiful, Joanna.' He tossed back his head, laughing, and I saw a flash of his perfect white teeth, thankfully all still intact. 'Do I look like the groom of your dreams?' He shrugged and arched his eyebrows as he ran his hands over his threadbare shirt and trousers, and fingered the thick beard on his face.

'Yes, you do, you are the groom of my dreams,' I admitted. Consumed with happiness, I lightly touched his beard with one finger. 'I will shave it off for you,' I said, with a smile of promise.

Everyone circling us was watching and listening in delight. Rarely do we Kurds show any affection in public, but our traditional society excuses the affections of a young couple in love, a bride and groom just married. For Sarbast's friends our breathless reaction to each other was as entertaining as a rare visit to the cinema.

Zakia modestly interrupted. 'It is time to go now. Say goodbye to your friends, Sarbast. You will see them again in a month.'

On the trip I had been elated to be told that Sarbast and I would not go to Bergalou immediately, as Sarbast's *peshmerga* bosses had rewarded him with a month's break from the fighting and he and I were to have a month's honeymoon at the house of Zakia and her husband, Qadir Agha.

I very nearly shouted out my joy, but fortunately did not embarrass myself further in front of the others. I was eager to leave, though. From what Zakia had told me, I expected that she and her husband lived in mountain splendour, in a huge home, in the village of Serwan, not far from Merge. They were so generous to invite us to spend our honeymoon there, saying that we deserved some happy, carefree days before reporting for duty in Bergalou. Never had I dreamed I would have a real honeymoon in the mountains.

I was living in a fairytale where all dreams came true, for after years of hesitation, I could see that Sarbast finally did love me. I suffered one quick moment of doubt. Why had his feelings of friendship changed to love? By showing him the tenderness of my heart, had I won his? I brushed all such questions aside. There would be plenty of time in our future for me to find out the answers.

In the jeep Sarbast and I sat as closely as possible, our arms lightly touching.

When Zakia leaned forward to speak to our driver, Sarbast glanced to make certain no one was looking and then surprised me with a quick kiss on my lips.

I felt a delicious tingling, revelling in the sensation his kiss created.

Since that first night long ago when I had fallen in love with Sarbast, I had spent endless hours daydreaming of the moment he would be my husband. But never could I have imagined the joy I would experience in simply sitting by his side. And that kiss! It had been tantalizing.

I was tempted to kiss him in return, in full view of Zakia and the driver, but I clasped my hands in my lap, turning to stare out of the jeep and think of something else — anything else! That's when I noticed the magnificent woods all around. The meandering road was shadowed by groves of chestnut and pistachio trees. Colourful wild flowers dotted the sloping mountains.

Kurdistan was simply heaven on earth.

Soon we arrived. Zakia's home seemed untouched by time, set back from the road, and shaded by trees so huge that I assumed they were ancient. The house was very large and filled with children. I immediately felt at ease. Fortunately, because I needed a good bath, their home was equipped with an intricate pipe system that brought spring water from the mountains.

Zakia took us round and out to the back, where there was a huge vegetable and fruit garden. I saw a barn almost as large as their home, with many cows, horses, donkeys, chickens and ducks. The family could easily be self-sufficient.

I blushed crimson when Zakia showed me the room where Sarbast and I would spend our honeymoon. I was grateful to see that our bedroom was the most private bedroom, well away from the central area of the house where the family congregated.

Qadir Agha Al-Pishderi, Zakia's husband, was a man of almost irresistible power. His title of Agha indicated that he was the owner of vast amounts of land, as well as the head of his tribe. Although he had jeopardized everything he owned when he joined the PUK, his eyes were calm with confidence, as though he didn't have a care in the world.

I was quickly in awe of him, impressed by his serenity and his cheerfulness. I had expected such an important man to be different, grave and pompous perhaps. But he showed an interest in all, was solicitous and kind to his wife, laughed easily with his guests, and joked and played with his seven children.

The youngest of his offspring was very mischievous and grabbed his father's precious binoculars. Binoculars were rare and difficult to obtain, for Saddam had made it an automatic death sentence for a Kurd to own a pair.

When the boy handled the binoculars like a toy, I became anxious, and thought they should be put on a safe high shelf, but the Agha laughed easily, saying, 'My children are the owners of everything in this house, including their father.'

I envied those children their relationship with him, remembering how my own father's disability had kept him at a distance from us.

Dinner was light because the mistress of the house had been away, and I was so tired that Zakia suggested that Sarbast and I retire early. I blushed when we left our hosts, despite the fact they had done everything to make me feel at ease.

Finally Sarbast and I were alone.

Becoming his wife was more wonderful than I could have ever imagined. Even after the passing of many years, when my children are grown up and grandchildren are running at my feet, when I am so old that the hair on my head is glistening and white, I will remember the magic of my wedding night.

16

Under the Bergalou Sky

Bergalou
June 1987

I awoke to see a strange quivering. My mind was too hazy to know exactly what I was seeing, but as I fluttered my eyes open, the roof over our little hut – a primitive roof that was in reality a mesh of small logs and twigs – seemed to be trembling. Narrowing my eyes for a more careful look revealed that indeed the ceiling was moving.

Sarbast was sleeping soundly by my side.

I inched closer to him, whispering, 'Sarbast, wake up. Wake up!'

Sarbast opened one groggy eye. 'What?'

'Look,' I whispered. 'Look. The roof is moving.'

His voice was tired and sluggish. 'No, Joanna, the roof is not moving.'

'It is!' I was fully awake by then. Although our small kerosene lantern spread only the dimmest light, I could see well enough to know that two sides of the roof line were being stirred by something.

'Sarbast!'

Bleary-eyed, he tossed back the pink coverlet, swivelled his neck and grudgingly studied the ceiling.

'See!' I said, my excitement mounting. 'There! The ceiling is moving!'

Without speaking, Sarbast got up and walked to the front door.

Grabbing one of his plastic slippers, he stood on his tiptoes and used the slipper to beat the wall where it met the ceiling.

Several gigantic scorpions fell to the floor.

I nearly screamed, gasping and cupping both hands over my mouth.

Sarbast slapped them until they no longer moved.

'Scorpions?' I murmured with dread. Glancing upwards, I realized the explanation of the mystery of the quivering ceiling. The entire roof was swarming with scorpions!

My voice was shaky. 'Oh, no, Sarbast. Oh, no. I can't sleep under nests of scorpions.' I repeated, 'No, no!'

Sarbast dropped heavily beside me, his arm draped loosely around my back. 'Darling, scorpions would rather retreat than fight. They won't bother you if you don't bother them.'

I then understood what the other fighters had been hinting at when Sarbast bade them good night. Several men had chuckled, while one muttered, 'Happy hunting.'

I had only been in Bergalou for a few hours, and I had already been chased out of our toilet by a snake. Now scorpions dangled over my head. I might as well sleep in the woods.

Sarbast kissed me lightly on the lips and fell back on to the cotton mattress. He pulled the coverlet up under his armpits. 'Go back to sleep. Forget about the scorpions.'

I gaped. 'Forget? Forget those scorpions? Never!'

A daring child always, nothing much truly frightened me in life, other than snakes and scorpions. When I was six years old, a Kurdish cousin in Sulaimaniya had chased me with a wiggling snake. He had dangled it by the tail, the snake's face curving close to my own, fangs threatening, causing an eternal snake phobia.

Since that incident, I had remained on guard for serpents when in Kurdistan.

Then several years later during another summer holiday, while admiring Grandmother Ameena's flower garden, I had un-intentionally tracked the path of a large scorpion. Hearing my screams, Grandmother ran out. When I tearfully pointed out the hairy-legged creature, she enthusiastically detailed the dangers of a scorpion bite. She pointed out the six pairs of legs, describing how handy they were: one set could grasp a toe, she said, while a second set could rip it. Then the deadly creature could suck the juices right out of your body. My grandmother said that she loved me and wanted to keep me safe. But she gave me a lifelong horror of scorpions.

Before marrying Sarbast, I had contemplated the threat of shells and enemy soldiers, and remained serene and undaunted. Scorpions and snakes had not been a worry. But our uninvited guests reminded me that Bergalou was surrounded by mountains and forests. I was intruding on territory inhabited by wild things and they were letting me know it.

I tossed and turned, and to get my mind on other matters, started thinking about our beautiful honeymoon. Sarbast and I had just spent thirty wonderful days honeymooning in Serwan, with the delightful Zakia Khan and her husband Qadir Agha. Relatives and visitors living near the region had flocked to deliver small gifts and give us their blessing. Happily, there were plenty of opportunities for me to wear make-up and arrange my long hair in elaborate fashions as well as don my beautiful pink wedding dress. I was delighted that Sarbast had the chance to admire his bride at last.

Yet there was some quiet time too in which we were able to renew our joy in each other, plan our future and discover all that occurred in the years after he left me in Baghdad.

There was excitement as well, as the war didn't cease just because we were newlyweds. I learned a lot from Zakia Khan regarding the duties of a *peshmerga* wife.

I learned to pluck a chicken. I learned to milk a cow. I learned to identify Iraqi planes as the enemy. I learned that the first thing I should do at any new mountain location was to locate the nearest bomb shelter. I learned that sharing a common enemy creates an instant camaraderie between people, even if they are different ages and from contrasting backgrounds. I learned that *peshmerga* wives are never idle, and that a true *peshmerga* woman toils persistently to support her husband and the cause. I learned that I would be leading a primitive lifestyle.

I learned that I had made the best decision of my life when I accepted Sarbast's marriage proposal and joined him in Kurdistan to share the freedom fighter life. Finally I was in a position to fulfil my lifelong goal of supporting the Kurdish cause. As a single woman, it would have been unrealistic to live in Bergalou. It was a fighter's village, essentially for men, although there were a few courageous unmarried women as well who had a brother or father who was *peshmerga*. I would not have been accepted before, but now that I was married to Sarbast I would be warmly welcomed.

Sarbast accidentally pulled my pink bed cover off me when he rolled over, already in a sound sleep. How could he sleep? Then I reminded myself that Sarbast had been living the *peshmerga* life for over five years. The reality was that it was much more dangerous and demanding than I had expected.

But I would learn, and I would make a difference. I was determined.

My eyelids felt heavy. I should sleep, as tomorrow I would meet Sarbast's *peshmerga* friends and acquaint myself with Bergalou. There had been no time to do so today, as we had arrived shortly after dark, trembling with fatigue after our long trek through the mountains.

I closed my eyes, and then blinked them open again, keeping a steady eye on the writhing scorpions and wondering what on earth there was in those twigs that kept them so busily occupied. I turned to sleep on my stomach, pulling the bedding over my head as a shield. I would prefer a scorpion on my back than on my face. I must learn to bear it. I might well live in this hut for years.

While waiting for sleep, reflections of the past month flickered in my mind.

While in Serwan, I had made the distressing discovery that I was woefully ill-prepared for the most ordinary challenges of *peshmerga* life. While I possessed the brave heart of a freedom fighter, I didn't have the necessary skills or the adept hands. Pampered always by my mother and siblings, I was embarrassingly inept when it came to cooking and cleaning. I had already humiliated myself on two occasions.

One morning a few guests arrived unexpectedly for lunch. I volunteered to help cook, insisting that Zakia assign me a duty.

Zakia made a quick gesture to the back garden, saying, 'Joanna, yes, please catch eight chickens and prepare them.'

I stood helplessly, having never touched a live chicken in my life. But I was too self-conscious to admit the truth to Zakia. Anyhow, she had already dashed out of the room to complete other pressing tasks.

Sarbast had gone on a small errand, so he was not around to help. I was on my own.

I sauntered outside. The back garden was full of plump chickens, busily walking about, pecking at worms, kicking up dust with their feet. How hard could it be? I asked myself as I purposefully marched towards them.

Five minutes later I was sprawled flat on the ground, without a chicken in hand, although feathers were fluttering. At least I was an amusing distraction, as the ruckus had got the attention of a small crowd of Zakia's guests.

I'm certain Zakia was flabbergasted at my domestic ignorance, but that kindly lady patiently instructed me in everything I needed to know about killing chickens. Soon I was standing beside her confidently plucking a chicken.

Several days later while assisting with chickens a second time, having volunteered for the worst part of the job in hope of reclaiming my dignity, I was standing over a pot of boiling water, dipping chickens into it to soften the roots of the feathers, when suddenly everyone around me dashed in the direction of the barn.

Zakia seized the chicken from my hands, threw it into the pot and grabbed me by my wrist, shouting, 'Run! Run for the shelter!'

I ran.

Seconds later, as Zakia pushed me into a small earthen shelter beside the barn, I heard a tremendous roar.

The ground was suddenly rocked by an explosion. We were being bombed.

Although while living in Baghdad I had suffered Iranian bomb attacks many times, I had not expected our mountain paradise to be found so easily.

I looked at Zakia. 'I had no idea the Iranians were bombing Kurdish villages. There was no warning roar. And how did you know that wasn't a passenger aeroplane, anyway?'

Everyone sharing the shelter laughed loudly. One gleeful woman even slapped her thigh as she doubled over. I blushed crimson, the naive city girl from Baghdad.

Zakia gently explained. 'Joanna, that plane was not Iranian. It was Iraqi. And passenger planes don't fly low in these mountains. If you hear any aeroplane, it is an enemy plane. In these mountains, our enemy hails from Baghdad, not from Tehran.'

'Oh.' I knew that the Iranians had allied with the Kurds to fight Saddam, and it wasn't as if I hadn't heard before leaving Baghdad that the Iraqi military had begun targeting solitary mountain villages with increased enthusiasm, but I had been so accustomed to being a target for the Iranians that the switch would take some getting used to. I was so embarrassed that I wanted to cry.

Zakia patted my shoulder. 'Joanna, remember this: when we work, eat or do anything, we give only half our attention to the task at hand. The other half is listening to the sounds of the sky. You'll soon learn, for in Bergalou it will be the same. Before long, you'll identify the distant roar of a plane even before the birds hear it.'

My heart skipped several beats when she whispered, 'We hear that Saddam has begun testing chemicals.' She glanced around to make certain her children were out of earshot. 'Who knows what that madman will do.' She pulled me close to her for a brief hug, warning, 'Be careful, child. Always be alert. We are entering a dangerous period.'

Yes, my time in Serwan had taught me several good lessons. I had much more to learn, but I would tread carefully, watching and listening, not wishing to be a source of Bergalou jokes.

During our honeymoon Sarbast had excited me with his stories of life in Bergalou, despite the fact that he had lost several good friends on the battlefield and he had suffered many close calls himself.

The following day I would explore my new home and meet the brave fighters Sarbast had told me so much about. I was anxious to meet the women of Bergalou, although I had been disappointed when Sarbast reported that with the several hundred fighters there were only a few women and two children living in the village. It was too unsafe for most women, he said.

Bergalou was one of a chain of small villages tucked away in the Jafati valley. The villages accommodated the most important infrastructure of the PUK. While Bergalou was home to the radio station and main field hospital, Sergalou, a twin village near by, housed the regional command. Other adjacent villages contained equally important PUK facilities.

Over the years, I had heard Kurdish patriots ask why the PUK didn't locate their command centre in Sulaimaniya, which was a 100 per cent Kurdish city. Now I understood the PUK leadership's logic.

Sulaimaniya was a large city filled with civilians, who could not be easily protected. On the other hand, the Jafati valley was protected by tall mountains, separated from the rest of Kurdistan by extremely difficult terrain. The location made it nearly impossible for Saddam's soldiers to reach us.

To help me realize the importance of Bergalou and the other PUK fighter villages in the Jafati valley, Sarbast had simplified the situation for me by saying, 'Joanna, think of it like this. Baghdad is the capital of Iraq. Baghdad is where the central command of the Iraqi military is located. The Jafati valley is the centre of command for the PUK. Bergalou, Sergalou, Haladin, Yehksemar, Maluma and Zewa are just as important to us, the PUK, as Baghdad is to Saddam. The Jafati valley is our PUK capital, the nerve centre.'

Happy to be a part of such an important movement, I finally drifted off into a night of peaceful sleep. Thankfully, I did not sustain a deadly scorpion bite during the night.

The following morning Sarbast woke me with a low laugh and a sweet kiss. 'Wake up, wake up, Joanna. Welcome to your new home.'

I stretched contentedly, pushing myself upright. Remembering what was hanging overhead, I glanced at the ceiling.

Reading my mind, Sarbast said, 'Don't worry. The scorpions are generally quiet during the day. They like the warmth of the sun hitting the roof and they sleep.' He laughed. 'Just don't move around at night. That's when they get busy.'

I shivered nervously, asking, 'Have you ever been bitten?'

'Never.'

Taking a deep breath, I decided at that moment that there was nothing to do but to make the best of it. Never again would I concern myself with scorpions. They could stay in their place and I would stay in mine.

It was a good day, I reminded myself. While few sensible people would choose to leave a comfortable home in Baghdad and live in a fighter's village surrounded by deadly enemies, for me Bergalou was a dream come true, the fulfilment of my fondest fantasy.

A memory flashed before my mind of three beautiful faces from seventeen years past: the beautiful Kurdish sisters selling jewellery at the bazaar in Sulaimaniya. The brutal regime in Baghdad had taken their future from them, dashing their dreams of marrying men they loved and living the *peshmerga* life, fighting for Kurdistan. While those three sisters had probably died at the hands of their jailers, they had never left my mind. As a girl I had so envied those young women. Now I was living their dream, and my own. In some way, I believed my existence kept them alive.

With tears in my eyes, I prepared myself for the first day of a new life.

I decided to inspect my new home before eating breakfast and unpacking. When I insisted that my husband show me around, I watched his face fall in worry as he warned me, 'Darling, you know that revolutions are never comfortable?'

'You are correct, husband,' I replied, as I clung to his strong arm, swinging along beside him, so happy that nothing could discourage me.

'We can take our meals here.' Sarbast gestured with his hand at the small sitting room.

I looked at the meagre furnishings, wondering what I might do to brighten the place. A low Japanese-style table stood in the middle of the room, with two worn cushions stashed underneath, along with Sarbast's weapons, a Kalashnikov rifle and a pistol. Even in Serwan, Sarbast had kept his weapons within reach. He told me that the first lesson for a freedom fighter was to always keep loaded weapons to hand. Most battles struck with lightning speed. Sarbast had refused to teach me to use weapons while on our honeymoon, saying that it could wait until we were in Bergalou.

Now he was reading my mind again. 'Tomorrow. Tomorrow I'll teach you how to protect yourself.'

I nodded. But for the moment I was thinking about our home. There was nowhere to store our belongings, a few books and photographs in addition to our clothes. We were surrounded by forest. My mind raced with possibilities. Surely I could have a bookcase and some small tables built from one of those thousands of trees?

An unexpected sight caught my attention. A television set was pushed up against the wall.

'Oh! Does it work?'

'It's difficult to get reception here. Sometimes I can get one station. And the TV is very old, as well.'

Hmmm. I would see about that. It would be lovely to watch any kind of transmission, but in any case I would keep it. Its mere presence was a reminder of normal life.

Our little dwelling had been built for survival, not for luxury. The walls were unpainted cinderblocks, enfolding two miniature rooms for living and a tiny area converted into a make-believe kitchen, equipped with a refrigerator that Sarbast was using as a cupboard. There was also a hot plate. Only occasionally would we have electricity, when the generators were working, so neither could be used routinely.

The floors were rough concrete with perceptible ridges. I would need pads on my feet to walk comfortably over the floor.

Our two windows were covered with razor wire. Few homes in Kurdish areas were equipped with glass windows. The flying glass caused by the recurring bombardments would have been a constant hazard.

'At least the water is pure and sweet,' Sarbast proclaimed proudly. 'It's spring water, brought directly into our homes through hoses.'

My dear husband was worried that I found our home lacking.

'This is a doll's house,' I pronounced loyally, in that moment adjusting fully to my environment and giving in completely to the cause. 'There is no need to show me the toilet,' I reminded him. I was recalling the night before and the dismal state of that bleak hole of a room, and the snake coiled in a corner, its jittery eyes focused on me, an intruder. I had fled, with my clothes dragging on the floor, and Sarbast had run in to investigate. He came out with a red face and jutting chin to report that I had mistaken a looped twig he kept inside to kill bugs for a snake. I pretended to believe him, but thought that my husband just wanted to protect my peace of mind; I suspected that he had killed the snake and tossed it in the grass.

Remembering my close call with the bombs in Serwan, I insisted on inspecting our bomb shelter and Sarbast obliged. He told me that there was a large concrete shelter in the village centre which was more comfortable, but with bombing and shelling attacks on the rise, rarely was there enough time to dash down the hill, as our little home was at the greatest distance from the village centre.

Our personal shelter edged the house, concealed under the lip of a tufted ridge of packed dirt. I knelt low to peer inside, catching a scent of dank air that smelled like the den of a fetid animal. It was a very small space, casting doubt in my mind as to whether Sarbast and I could both fit into it. For once in my life I was glad of my slim build. Perhaps there would be enough space if I lay flat. I silently questioned how Sarbast might edge his bulky frame into that hole, however.

I could think of nothing favourable to say about the shelter so I said nothing at all.

We walked back into the house.

'I love it here,' I said to my husband, as I began unpacking my case, carefully laying my comb, brush, hand mirror, lipstick, soap and lotion on top of my pink bedding. I had fought to be allowed to keep the bedding all the way from Baghdad, through Qalat Diza to Serwan and to Bergalou. Everyone who saw it cautioned against it. It was too bulky. It was too luxurious. Even Sarbast questioned it, claiming that a fighter's hideout was not a place for such extravagance, but I had insisted and won, saying that surely a fighter deserved some comfort. Ironically, he slept most contentedly under it.

'We will make it a fine home,' I said with a glad heart and a confident smile.

Relieved that his bride was truly content, Sarbast grinned, lifting me into the air and holding me there, and then pulling me down beside him.

Several hours later Sarbast introduced me to Bergalou.

While our little hut was less than perfection, I could not say the same about our surroundings. Bergalou was one of the most secluded spots in all Kurdistan, situated in a beautiful green valley surrounded by a natural fortress of mountains. It made a perfect protected setting for a guerrilla stronghold.

Sarbast informed me that there were numerous caves in those high mountains, caves that would make ideal hideouts for the fighters should the day ever come when our enemies succeeded in their quest to invade the valley.

I felt completely safe in that mountain refuge as I paused to look around. The mountains ringing us were topped with peaks so high they appeared to touch the sky. How could any army invade over them? I naively believed it impossible.

The myriad chirpings of a multitude of birds entertained us as we hiked along a rocky mountain path down to the village. I peered with curiosity at the chain of small huts, similar to our own, wondering about the lives being lived in them. These modest homes had been constructed for the *peshmerga* fighter families along the perimeter of the village with our neighbourhood extending out to the base of the mountains. Most of the dwellings were constructed with their back walls braced against hills. On one side of each home, at least, the earth provided some protection from bombs.

Although I had walked through those mountains on the way into Bergalou the previous day, I was so weary after a full day – spent alternately walking and riding on a donkey for the first time in my life, and a particularly disagreeable donkey at that, who tried to fling me from his back on more than one occasion – that I had not noticed the beauty of the valley.

Before it was in Bergalou, the PUK radio station had been in a village called Nowzang, but following the onset of the Iran–Iraq war the two mighty armies met there in battle in 1983, and the PUK fighters had to find a new location for their headquarters. The fighters had moved to a village called Sarshew, but soon that village became engulfed by the war as well. That was when the PUK came to Bergalou. It was then an abandoned village that had once been an important base for guerrilla fighters for the PUK rival, the KDP. The PUK had repaired the vacated buildings and added more. There were now over sixty buildings in Bergalou, housing nearly two hundred *peshmerga*. Additionally, other *peshmerga* living elsewhere in the valley often used the village as a temporary stop-over when going back and forth to the fighting front. The village square had a medical clinic, a communal kitchen and a large shelter. These collective dwellings were roughly constructed of concrete blocks topped with thatched roofs – buildings easily erected yet easily destroyed.

After settling in Bergalou, the fighters built their radio station in the mountains, anchoring the antenna in the hard rock at the summit of the highest mountain, a twenty-minute hike from the village. The radio station was a powerful PUK propaganda tool, which recruited Kurds to the cause, called for Saddam's downfall and alerted Kurdish villagers to the location of Saddam's army.

Sarbast would be walking to that place every day, to work. Women did not work at the station, as it was considered particularly dangerous because Saddam's airmen were always on the prowl trying to make direct hits on it. I would help him in his work from home.

Sarbast was one of several people who broadcast from the clandestine PUK radio station, 'the voice of the freedom fighters'. I knew from his letters that he was a talented writer, although I had not yet read or heard any of his political writings. The PUK radio station had won the open hatred of Saddam, so all the broadcasters took pen names to protect their identity. Sarbast was known as Nabaz, meaning invincible.

I was immensely proud of my husband.

On my first full day in Bergalou, I saw *peshmergas* everywhere, busily dashing to and fro.

Sarbast looked around uneasily. 'The village is even more active than it was when I left to meet you in Merge.' He hesitated, adding, 'Something major is happening.'

'What? What do you think?'

'We'll find out soon enough. The front line is located around the Duban mountains, not so far from here. Fighters have always passed through here to go to the front, but it's been a lot busier since the beginning of the year.' Then he focused on me with his most serious expression. 'They know we are here, Joanna. Saddam hates us Kurds more than all his other enemies combined. Right now, he has many painful boils to lance, but the Kurdish boil is his most painful. We broadcast his misdeeds. We encourage others to rebel. He knows exactly where we are.' He clicked with his tongue. 'He intends to kill us all. The instant he swirls his signature on a peace agreement with Iran, he will come to lance the Kurdish boil. That's when we start to worry.'

I was quiet, thinking. I had been praying for the war with Iran to end since the first day it started. But if what Sarbast was saying was true, I was wrong to do so. At the moment, Saddam could spare only minimum troops to man the checkpoints and to drop bombs on us. When the war with Iran ceased, and there was talk that it seemed to be moving to a finale, he would have a huge land army at his disposal, armed for battle and, most frighteningly, not far from where we were living, for most of Kurdistan was close to the Iranian border where the war raged.

Sarbast coughed, clearing his throat, and said, 'Even now the pressure is building. Every day we are under bombardment from aeroplanes and rockets.' He glanced at his watch. 'I'm surprised they haven't started already. Be prepared to run with me.'

Just then we stepped into the communal kitchen. Although there were assigned cooks, Sarbast whispered that none of them was accomplished. He had confided while in Serwan that one of the most unpleasant aspects of a fighter's life was the lack of appetizing food. With Saddam's armies blocking most of the known roads into the mountains, it was nearly impossible to get supplies through. Smugglers mainly concentrated on transporting military equipment and ammunition, leaving fighters and their families to eat very bland rations. What I pity, I thought, for Kurdish food was the best in the world.

Sarbast looked mischievous as he whispered, 'The delicacies of Baghdad are not to be found here.'

I chuckled, so happy to be sharing everything with him, even bad food.

And it was bad. We were served a bland meal of white rice and flat beans simmered in tomato sauce. After filling our plates we settled at a communal table to eat the tasteless fare. Sarbast was greeted warmly by his friends and introductions were made.

Some fighters expressed stunned surprise when told that I had left Baghdad to come to Bergalou.

I truthfully replied, 'I have a stake in this fight, too.'

Before we could finish our lunch someone dashed inside to shout that missiles were coming in. There was a mad scramble for the air-raid shelter. Sarbast and I sprinted.

I heard a piercing crack just as Sarbast pushed me into the shelter, a rather large room that had been partially built into the earth. Compared to the cramped earth burrow behind our hut, it was pure luxury. I felt a small stab of desire, wishing that our home was closer to the centre of the village. I'd never make it to the central shelter from that distance. More often than not, it would be the earth lair for me.

Obviously other villagers had no time to get to the communal shelter either, for I was the only woman among a large number of fighters. During the attack, everyone sat without talking. Heads were propped against the walls, hands in laps, as we listened to the dull thuds of the incoming shells. Most looked worried and I thought I knew why, for during our time in Serwan, Sarbast had told me that some of the conventional bombs were so large that nothing could protect against them. A direct hit on the shelter would kill everyone inside.

I refused to consider the possibility. Surely I could not be so unlucky – at least not so soon?

The attack grew even louder. Sarbast had mentioned that the government troops routinely dropped cluster bombs, which caused grievous injuries. My thoughts focused on the human beings and animals caught out in the open.

Sarbast reassured me with his arm around my shoulder, tapping me on the arm, but I was truly unafraid, thinking that being under bombardment under the Bergalou sky was not as frightening as being bombarded under the Baghdad sky. On many occasions I had huddled with Mother, Muna, little Nadia, Sa'ad and his wife, all of us crammed into our tiny bathroom, a pitifully unsuitable bomb shelter, waiting for the deadly Iranian cargo to find us there. Here I was again, hiding from danger raining from the sky. Some things just never changed.

When the bombardment ended, everyone filed out, looking around to see the destruction. Surprisingly, there was little structural damage, although I saw that two small storage buildings had been hit. It appeared that most of the bombs had missed their targets. Sarbast told me that our enemies were notoriously inaccurate when directing their firepower. Although there were casualties at Bergalou, there were fewer than one might have expected.

Everyone in Bergalou then carried on as though nothing out of the ordinary had occurred. Human beings can adjust to almost anything, I decided.

Sarbast walked me home before looping back to Bergalou and then on to the radio station. He would return for dinner, and afterwards, he promised, I would meet the other women.

Sarbast forgot to warn me of one very important fact: that it was a daily ritual for the Iraqi army to end each day by lobbing three shells into the village. The Iraqi soldiers kept to their routine on my first full day in Bergalou.

I was alone at home when these shells burst. Wondering if they were the beginning of a serious offensive, I huddled in a corner, holding my hands over my head, in what I thought was a safe position.

Then Sarbast ran in through the door, looking worried. He was surprised to see that I was calm. He gathered me in his arms. 'You are such a brave *peshmerga*, darling,' he whispered. Then, laughing, he said, 'Now your dreams have finally come true. Welcome to the real world of the Kurds, Joanna.'

Dinner was congealed leftovers we had brought back from lunch.

Sarbast said that after dark we would join other *peshmerga* gathered on the hillside. Once the Iraqi soldiers had sent in their final three shells, the villagers often gathered to dance or tell stories, to celebrate living through another day.

The evening promised to be all that I had dreamed of.

While some fighters remained on duty, guarding the village, many other Bergalou residents congregated on the green grass. Although it was June, there was a slight breeze, dipping down from the high mountains. The moon was nearly full, its rays brightening the gathering.

I spotted three women sitting among all the men, and I felt their eyes follow me. Sarbast mentioned that there was a fourth wife living in the village, but she was not there that evening. I was living in a village of hundreds of men and only five women. I looked closer at the three women and my eyes settled on a young woman holding a small boy on her lap. She was whistling and cooing to him. I was intrigued by her and her beautiful boy, wondering about her story, for every *peshmerga* had a story.

I felt strangely shy in the midst of all those heroes, and sat quietly beside Sarbast, a new and inexperienced bride. But when a group of the men jumped up, forming a line to begin dancing in their guerrilla uniforms, I started to relax. Someone brought out a tambura to tap out the beat of the dance. Several of the dancers used sticks to depict a mock battle scene.

Sarbast leapt up to join them.

I clapped along with the crowd, sharing a smile with those welcoming me. Several dancers began to sing a popular song in our Sorani dialect. I felt my emotions building and fought back tears of joy. I was doing exactly what I had always dreamed of, exactly where I had always wanted to be. I was home. Home in Kurdistan.

17

Good Kurd, Bad Kurd

Bergalou
July 1987

Wednesday 22 July 1987

My dear Mother,

Kisses and greetings to you. I hope you and the rest of the family are all right. I must admit that I miss my nephews terribly, particularly little Ranj, for I know that I am missing his precious babyhood. I cannot believe that he was born nearly a year ago. Please tell Alia to never let her boys forget me.

This letter is a bit late, but you know the situation and why it is difficult for me to correspond regularly. I have no way of knowing if you will receive this letter, as it will leave my hand to go to another hand and travel hand to hand all the way from me to you.

Dear Mother, I have been living in this village long enough to know that I have taken the correct path. I have no regrets about choosing Sarbast and this peshmerga life. He is the man I want for my partner. He has a strong will and attitudes that suit me. He has chosen a life full of adventure, risk and danger, but it is a good life that makes me proud because he has sacrificed his life for a cause he believes in. I feel honoured to be the wife of this struggler and to share his hardships, because his cause is my cause.

But of course my life has changed very much. I barely remember the young woman I was in Baghdad who ate delicious food, shopped for pretty clothes, drank tea and coffee, and visited friends and family. That girl is no more.

The new Joanna is experiencing each day a very hard, merciless war. In Baghdad we heard stories of the cruelties against our brothers and sisters in Kurdistan, but the reality is worse than we ever imagined. Such a savage war is being waged against our people, who are struggling to live free in this land, yet we all feel happy because of a strong determination to win.

Your little Joanna is sure of her decision, so should I make the ultimate sacrifice, let there be peace in your heart that I died doing what I wanted to do. Do not destroy your life with mourning, Mother.

I want to tell you all that has happened since we parted.

From Qalat Diza I travelled with Zakia to Merge, where I met up with my darling Sarbast. There were enemy roadblocks at various locations, but after the peshmerga Karbala-Ten offensive of 27 April (which we hear caused nearly five thousand enemy casualties in the Iraqi Fifth Army) some areas were held by our fighters in conjunction with the Iranian troops. As you might have heard, there was another important offensive, Nasr (meaning victory), that targeted Sulaimaniya province. I hear that many land gains were made and for that I am glad. Perhaps life will become easier for those we love in that area. We heard a radio broadcast from Tehran, where their president, Rafsanjani, claimed that 'Sulaimaniya is a gate of entrance to the rest of Iraq', so we assume that the Iranians are going to concentrate their forces in that important area, which may or may not ease our situation here in the Jafati valley.

After meeting Sarbast in Merge, together we travelled on to Serwan with Zakia, and spent our honeymoon days in her home and in the surrounding area.

For now I want to tell you about my life here. Sarbast is on an important mission, which means I am alone today, a rare time of complete solitude that I will spend talking to you through the pages of this letter.

I will hide nothing from you. I will always be honest. There is nothing of normal life here. I am living in a tiny hut in a primitive village. Yet it is more precious to me than a palace in Baghdad. Our modest home is plain and simple, with the barest of furnishings. We share our home with many mice, who are quite cute when they pop out and sit on the floor on their little haunches, their little eyes watching my every move, their small paws poised as though waiting for a meal. I give them breadcrumbs, and sometimes bits of cheese — despite Sarbast's objections that word is getting around in the mouse community that a tender heart lives in this house. But the mice can do us no real harm, as I keep our food in a refrigerator. The refrigerator does not function, but it makes a handy storage cupboard.

Although the mice are harmless, I cannot say the same about the other creatures, especially the snakes, which keep me alert with each step I take. Yes, there are snakes. And there are scorpions.

As for the quality of our food, it is best that I say nothing. The roadblocks are a deterrent to our smugglers, so little food gets past our enemy. Like a prisoner on a diet of dry bread and water, I often dream of your Kurdish dishes. But I am thankful that we do not starve.

At least ours is a home filled with love. Few married couples can match our happiness. Even my girlhood dreams fail to measure up to the joy I know living the peshmerga life alongside my husband. This despite the fact that we are under constant bombardment in our little village.

Let me tell you about the bombing. The warnings I received never prepared me for the level of the attacks on Bergalou. My ears and my eyes are now finely tuned to the danger. Finally I understand what Zakia meant when she warned me in Serwan that whatever one might be doing here, half the mind will be focusing not on the task at hand but on the sounds and sights from the sky. When I am preparing breakfast, my hands are busy with the task, but my ears are listening for the shrill whistling resonance of shells, or for the noisy roar of an aeroplane or helicopter engine. It is the same when I am reading Sarbast's radio scripts, using the toilet, washing clothes, visiting other peshmerga ladies or walking to the village. Never do I let my guard down.

Although we have had sad losses, there have not been as many as the frequency of the attacks might suggest. But one particular incident haunts me. Two of the youngest peshmerga were recently lost. The two young boys were devoted friends and very young, although I do not know their exact ages. I had seen them many times in the village. I felt bad that they were not in school, but they seemed happy and focused on their peshmerga life. One day when they were manning the anti-aircraft guns they took a direct hit. Both were killed instantly. I'm sorry that I saw their crumpled bodies because now I cannot get that image out of my mind. One day they were laughing and teasing and the next day they were dead. They were put into bags and buried in the fighters' cemetery near the village. The only consolation is that their lives rested on the hope of freedom. Perhaps their sacrifice will help to bring freedom to the rest of us.

Not knowing from one minute to the next if a bomb might find you is very nerve-racking. Sarbast insists that I go to our earthen shelter each time I hear a plane, but I cannot make myself if he is not at home. Instead, I sit it out in a corner of the house, the way we used to in Baghdad during the Iranian attacks. But when Sarbast is home, he forces me into that hole in the earth.

I would rather take my chances with the bombs. If I describe the shelter you will understand. I have to be on my hands and knees in order to wriggle through the opening, with Sarbast pushing from behind. The shelter is very confining, so small that I cannot even sit up straight. I am forced to crawl to a cramped position with the crown of my head touching the earth ceiling.

Mother, did you know that every kind of insect species makes their home in Kurdistan? And did you know that most of these insects live in Bergalou? They all visit me when I am in the shelter. They particularly love to snuggle into my hair. One with long legs tried to settle in my nose.

I fidget in that shelter, unable to rest. I marvel in admiration at Sarbast, who curls in a ball and sleeps like a contented baby.

I asked Sarbast yesterday how he could have borne this for five years and he laughed, saying that it has never been so bad before; while they were bombed in the past, the attacks were infrequent. But since I arrived in Bergalou, the bombing has never ceased. Sarbast teased me, saying that I brought this upon Bergalou.

Thankfully we are snugly protected by high mountains, making it impossible for our enemies to grapple with us face to face.

I have met so many good Kurds living in this village. Their sacrifices make the troubles we have known as Kurds living in Baghdad appear insignificant. I am not the only woman here. There are four others, one the wife of a senior peshmerga who sets a good example to us all. There are also two children, a toddler girl and a baby boy.

The woman I have come to know best is the mother of the baby boy. I want to tell you a little about this woman because she has been living this life of sacrifice since she was a young girl. While I was attending university in Baghdad, she was living this violent life already. When I think about this, I wonder if I should have joined this cause at an earlier age. Although my spirit was with the Kurdish cause, I was not contributing. I could have skipped university and come to the north to take up my responsibility. When I have such thoughts, I worry that perhaps I selfishly claimed the privileges of my Arab heritage and my Kurdish heritage simultaneously.

Regarding Ashti, the woman I so admire, you would look upon her as a daughter, as she is so dear, more brave and intelligent than most men. She is a small woman but her courage matches that of a mountain lion. Her father was a well-known peshmerga, murdered years ago at the hands of a jahsh.

She was born into a fighter family. From the moment she was old enough to contribute to the cause, she did. At the young age of fifteen or sixteen, Ashti became an undercover agent working in Hawler. Just as a jahsh had killed her father, so a jahsh tried to kill the daughter. She was turned in by an informant and forced to leave her home and flee into the mountains. Because her brother Azaad was already fighting from the PUK base in Toojhala, she went there, and because she was clever, she was assigned intelligence duties, analysing political commentary broadcast from Baghdad, Tehran and the West.

I have been told that it was most unusual for a single woman to live and work in a fighter village, but her brother's presence made it acceptable. Of course, some of the unattached peshmerga men expressed interest in such a pretty, intelligent girl, but Ashti was vigilant of her reputation. She kept herself to herself, leading a life of social isolation.

But before long, one of the engineers, a highly respected peshmerga named Rebwar, fell in love with her. Since Rebwar knew Ashti's brother, he was able to go through the proper channels by talking to her brother before approaching her. There was a happy ending: Ashti and Rebwar married.

When the PUK media headquarters was moved to Bergalou, Ashti and Rebwar were among the first to arrive. I hear they lived in tents and caves in the beginning. While living as a fighter, Ashti gave birth to a precious baby son, Hema. You would love this baby. He would break your heart, as he breaks mine. He cries too much because the bombs scare him, but he brings joy and hope to all of us in this little village. Hema reminds us of what we are fighting for. Even if we die, perhaps he will survive to live a free life in Kurdistan.

Earlier in the year that poor baby endured a gas attack. You may not have heard that Bergalou was hit by poisonous gas shortly before I arrived in Serwan on my honeymoon. Fortunately the chemicals were incorrectly mixed, or perhaps the wind was blowing in the right direction for us and the wrong direction for the murderers, so the casualties were not as high as they might have been. I heard that two hundred fighters were lost, but the number could have been in the thousands had the chemicals been more effective.

I don't want to worry you, but there have been other chemical attacks in the area since then. I believe this is because Saddam has given his cousin, Ali Al-Majid, full authority to eliminate the Kurdish problem. Have you heard of this appointment? He is the most fanatical servant of Saddam.

We hear that our continued rebellion has driven Saddam into a bitter fury. For this reason, the threat of chemicals has become so serious that we have all been supplied with gas masks. So try not to worry.

One of my most thrilling experiences has been learning about weapons. As you know, peshmerga are armed at all times, but I am quite upset that our leaders have ruled that women cannot go to the battlefront. Is my life worth more than Sarbast's? I believe that our lives are equally valuable. So when he leaves on important missions, my heart skips many beats until he returns. However, although I am not allowed to go with him to battle, I must be prepared in the event of an attack. Since our home is the furthest from the centre of the village, I suppose we would be the first to confront the enemy should they emerge over the mountains and into this valley.

I have some interesting news about Kamaran Hassan. You must remember him: his mother is Nazara, sister of Sarbast's mother, Khadrja, so he is Sarbast's first cousin. He and Sarbast have lived side by side since their childhood, when they were in Qalat Diza, and for the two years after the napalm attack when they lived in the Iranian refugee camp with their families. So they have a strong bond. If you remember, Kamaran put his patriotism first, and as soon as he graduated with his economics degree, he became a member of the PUK. I am excited to know that he will be working near by. We have not been told when he will finish his current training, but we will celebrate at the sight of him. He will contribute much to the cause.

I wanted to tell you something of our work here. Although fighters are always poised to rush to the front to share in the fighting, the main work coming out of Bergalou comes from the tips of pens. There are a number of writers who produce patriotic materials about the struggle for liberation. Sarbast is a part of this effort. The writings and the broadcasts keep other fighters and civilians informed of what is happening on the battlefront, warning of areas to avoid. We transmit speeches from our leaders, such as Ma'am (Uncle) Jalal Talabani, and discussions on the demand for Kurdish freedom. We also send out other information, recruiting young men and women to the peshmerga cause.

While the government in Baghdad broadcasts its lies, we broadcast the truth.

Often I ask myself, Where is the rest of the world? Is there anyone out there who knows what is happening to the Kurds? Does anyone know, or care, that Baghdad has been murdering innocent Kurdish citizens for decades? Or that their lust for our blood is increasing? Does anyone know that Arabs are taught that Kurds are animals, or that they are encouraged to rob, beat and murder us? Does the world know that the government in Baghdad has been emptying entire villages of Kurds, taking the men away to God only knows where, and shipping the women, children and elderly men to live in refugee camps in the south? Does the world know that these Kurds are forbidden to return home? Does the world know that Arabs are moving into our homes, and appropriating our livelihoods?

If the world knew, would they care?

It's as though we Kurds are bleeding from thousands of wounds, yet no one will expose our sufferings.

Tears are falling from my eyes.

The most disappointing thing for me, Mother, was that I was forced to acknowledge that although there are good Kurds, there are also many bad Kurds. Nothing has damaged our cause more than the bad Kurds, the collaborators and informers. They join the PUK, pretending to hate Baghdad. After discovering important information they slip away and give out our positions. They cause the deaths of many fighters. It makes me believe that Kurds' loyalty to one another is disintegrating. I hope this is not the case, for our unity has always been one of our strong points.

Sarbast says that the war with Iran meant that rather than live in the trenches, as our Sa'ad did, many men would rather sell their honour, taking money from Baghdad to betray their fellow Kurds. Some men will do anything to avoid those trenches of hell, I guess. But they might as well go to hell in those trenches, for that's where they are going eventually, for spying on their Kurdish brothers. The jahsh are only postponing hell.

Living in Baghdad, hiding from these bombs, I hated the Iranians. But here in Kurdistan, they are our only friends. In Baghdad the Iranians are trying to kill you, my mother, and my brother and my sisters. In Bergalou, the Iranians are fighting to protect me and Sarbast, and all the other Kurds. My feelings regarding the Iranians are torn.

We Kurds have been fighting against Baghdad for over sixty years. Will I stay in this fighting village for another sixty years? My past motivated me, pushing me to come here. Now I am motivated by the future I envision, a future where my children can be free to speak the Kurdish language, to learn Kurdish history, to travel up and down these mountains without fear of ambush.

So we must win! We will never give up!

Never!

Mother dear, I see that the afternoon sun is moving towards the edge of the sky. Soon the enemy will send off their finale of shells, and the frogs will start up their symphony. My husband will come home, and we will eat our dinner together, and then we shall join the other fighters on the hillside or in someone's home. There we shall laugh with giddy delight at our good luck to be alive, we shall reminisce about our days of childhood and we shall share our dreams of a future blessed with freedom.

May you be safe in Baghdad,

Your little Joanna

18

Chemical Attack

Bergalou
Autumn 1987

Jalal Talabani asked for a special channel of communication. I gave him one. I went to Sulaimaniya and hit them with the special ammunition. That was my answer. I continued the deportations at the same time. I told our contacts in the Kurdish villages that I could not let their villages survive, because I will attack them with chemical weapons. They said they loved their villages. I told them: then you and your family will die. You must leave right now because I cannot tell you the same day that I am going to attack with chemical weapons.

I will kill them all with chemical weapons. Who is going to say anything? The international community? Fuck them! The international community, and those who listen to them.

Even if the war with Iran comes to an end and the Iranians withdraw from all occupied lands, I will not negotiate with Talabani and I will not stop the deportations.

This is my intention and I want you to take serious note of it. As soon as we complete the deportations, we will start attacking them everywhere according to a systematic military plan. Even their headquarters. During our attacks we will take back one-third or one-half of what is under their control. If we can try to take two-thirds, then we will surround them in a small pocket and attack them with chemical weapons. I will not attack them with chemicals just one day, I will continue to attack them with chemicals for fifteen days. Then I will announce that anyone who wishes to surrender his gun will be allowed to do so. I will publish one million copies of this leaflet and distribute it in the north in Kurdish, Badinani, Arabic and Sorani. I will not say it is from the Iraqi government. I will not let the government get involved. I will say it is from the Northern Bureau. Anyone willing to come back is welcome, and those who do not return will be attacked with destructive chemicals. I will not mention the name of the chemical because that is classified. But I will tell them they will be attacked with new weapons that will destroy them. So my threats will motivate them to surrender. Then you will see that all the vehicles of God Himself will not be enough to carry them all. I swear that we will defeat them.

I told our comrades that I need guerrilla groups in Europe to kill whomever they see from these Kurdish saboteurs. I will do it, with the help of God. I will defeat them and follow them to Iran.

> Ali Hassan Al-Majid, secretary general of the Northern Bureau
> Transcript of a tape recording at a meeting in 1987,
> exact date not known

Sarbast and I were silent and thoughtful during our lunch at home that day. Lately we had got into the habit of bringing our meals back from the communal kitchen to eat at home, enjoying some time alone together. But times were tense and it was difficult to relax. Much was happening in the area between the Iraqis, the Iranians and the Kurdish freedom fighters.

Sarbast and his colleagues at the radio station were transmitting appeals for more PUK volunteers. With the Iranians behind us and beside us, it would take only a determined push to achieve final victory over Baghdad. Or so we thought. But we needed more fighters to make this victory possible.

After Sarbast had left I rinsed the dishes clean and put them away. Then I went to visit Ashti and little Hema, one of my favourite pastimes during the few times when there were no bombardments.

When I arrived I was happy to see other *peshmerga* women there.

Pakhshan, the wife of a high-ranking *peshmerga*, was holding her small daughter, Lasik, in her lap. Bahar and Kazal were there as well, both young wives like me, without any children, although I had been suffering from persistent nausea lately, which caused me to worry that I might be pregnant. Ashti was filling a large plastic bowl with water, preparing to give Hema his bath. Although Ashti always put on a brave front, I knew that with a baby, life in Bergalou was doubly worrisome.

As I drew closer, I saw that Hema was excited, enjoying a brief time out in the sun and being surrounded by women who were giving him a lot of attention.

I picked him up and gave him a kiss. I enjoyed playing with that precious boy but I had been uneasy about his well-being from the moment I had first seen him in his mother's arms. With bombs falling, and shells erupting on almost a continuous basis, the safety of both him and Lasik was a concern. I knew that Ashti and Pakhshan fretted endlessly for their children.

It was pitiful: when Bergalou was under attack, both children were wide-eyed with fear as they listened to the bombs.

Ashti took Hema from my arms and settled him in his soapy bath. Lasik toddled over and began to splash the water with her hands. Everyone laughed.

Kazal, whose husband was the most famous broadcaster in Iraq, said, 'I was told that Sergalou will be receiving a shipment of meat tomorrow.'

There was a buzz of excitement. Meat was a delicacy. On the rare occasions when the shop in Sergalou received food shipments, a group of Bergalou residents would hike there and buy everything available. We would celebrate by having a small party and a barbecue.

My mouth watered. For the past month I had been eating beans and tomato sauce, without any meat, although Sarbast's brother had popped in for an unexpected and quick visit the day before and brought us some pastries and a few other baked items from his mother. We were planning a good meal that evening.

Holding Hema by the arms as he sat in the water and splashed, Ashti looked at me and smiled. 'When is Sarbast going to make us a cake?'

Sarbast was a wonderful baker, and when he could get his hands on some flour and sugar, he relaxed from the rigours of war by making small cakes. Ashti looked forward to them as much as I did.

'Soon, he promised,' I told her.

The visit ended prematurely when Bahar's husband sent word that the food shipment had arrived in Sergalou a day early. Someone would be leaving to make the hour's walk to Sergalou within a few minutes. Sarbast, I was told, had already contributed money to buy our share. In a rush of excitement, everyone scattered.

In no mood to return home, I decided to take a walk. Rarely did I take walks without Sarbast, as it was one of our preferred ways of relaxing; generally after the last shelling of the day, we would take a brisk walk and enjoy the pure mountain air. But today I had a lot on my mind. We had heard from Sarbast's brother that there was chilling talk that Ali Al-Majid had more chemical attacks planned. It didn't take a genius to realize that the man was planning to make Kurdistan a wasteland. Reports were rampant of the near-total destruction of Kurdish infrastructure and assets, the murder of men and boys from twelve to sixty, and the abandonment of Kurdish civilians in isolated areas. We desperately needed more PUK fighters. I hoped that Sarbast's appeals would encourage more Kurdish men to join our fight.

As I walked, I pondered what kind of arguments might motivate a good Kurd to commit to the cause. Although my mind was racing, I paused to take a few deep breaths of the brisk mountain air, knowing that before long the valley would be crusted with snow and ice. Once winter was upon us, I would no longer be strolling for pleasure.

Suddenly I was startled by the noise of incoming artillery shells. While we were always subject to attacks, our enemy was off their usual schedule. Generally we could set our watches by the afternoon and evening bombardments.

I felt a rush of confusion. But before I could decide the best action to take, the shells began to land. I was too far from our house to run for safety, so I darted off the trail, crouching, waiting for an opportunity to dash home and take cover in a corner room.

Just then I noticed something strange. These bombs were different. They fell silently, but when they landed dirty white clouds puffed up from them. My mouth dry with anxiety, I continued watching the strange spectacle, not letting myself imagine the worst scenario. Perhaps the silent canisters were harmless.

Then another strange thing occurred: birds began falling out of the sky.

I instinctively cried out, 'It's raining birds!'

The combination of silent bombs and plunging birds stirred my disbelief. I whipped my head from side to side, searching all around me. The edge of the afternoon sky was dotted with flashes of colour, as gaudy specks plummeted to earth: more birds. The poor creatures were fluttering helplessly, falling as heavily as stones – down, down, down to the ground.

I winced as I heard dreadful thumps all around me. I had always loved birds. I couldn't bear to see the pitiful sight. If birds were dropping from the sky, I knew that I should move, and move fast, to the shelter. But I was frozen in place.

I searched the trail for Sarbast. I knew my husband well. If he realized I was in danger, he would come to me. But perhaps he would think I was already in the shelter. Because of the suddenness of the attack, perhaps he would be forced to seek cover in the communal shelter in the centre of the village.

I bit my lower lip as I continued to look for Sarbast's brawny frame, feeling a rush of concern for his safety.

Just then a bird fell directly at my feet, the dull thud of its impact causing me to gasp. The creature was in great distress. Its tiny black beak scissored vigorously, and then more slowly, as it pitifully sucked at the air.

I stayed put, for the silent canisters were still dropping from the sky. I could hear my heart thumping loudly, and noticed that these strange missiles were still billowing smoky puffs that turned into a dirty brown cloud that hugged the ground.

Another bird fell near by.

I was smart enough to know that animals provide the first indication of a chemical attack. Was this the poisonous gas promised by Ali Al-Majid? With that chilling thought I threw caution to the wind, leaping to my feet and sprinting down the path home, fearing for my life.

Everything was a blur, but I caught sight of an untethered mule as it bucked into a frenzy. It hustled past me on the path, trotting so fast that it seemed to dance. Never had I seen a mule move that rapidly. I kept running, trying to avoid the splayed birds strewn in my path. Finally I dashed into the house, gasping for breath.

Safe!

Seconds later, Sarbast burst in through the open door.

Mouth open, panting, I stared at him without speaking.

He yelled, 'Joanna, upon my honour, this is a chemical attack!'

Yes! I knew it! I now recognized the unpleasant odour I had heard about from survivors of previous chemical attacks: a smell like rotten apples, onions and garlic.

Sarbast moved quickly, reaching up to a shelf above the side door. 'Joanna, put this on!' He handed me a gas mask as he pulled a second mask on to his own face and tightened the small bands that fastened it around his head.

I held my breath while I fumbled with the strap. In all the excitement, the simple task felt cumbersome. While Sarbast and I had discussed these masks several times, with Sarbast urging me to familiarize myself with the apparatus, I had stupidly failed to do so. Finally Sarbast grabbed the mask from my hands and slipped it into place over my head and face.

Hand in hand, we ran to our earth shelter and crawled down into it, as far back as possible.

Once settled, I realized that I had been holding my breath the whole way. I hungrily drew in a much-needed mouthful of air, but all I managed to do was strain my throat muscles. I could not capture a single breath.

Sarbast had no idea of my problem.

Desperate, I yanked at the mask until it slid from my face and shouted, 'I can't breathe in this thing!' Finally I had his full attention. He wriggled towards me and, grabbing my mask from my hands, examined it.

I felt as if I was about to explode and I was forced to breathe in the foul gases. I felt as if my eyes had been set on fire. The pain was so intense that hot needles probing my eyeballs could not have hurt any more. I could not stand it another moment. I started rubbing my eyes with my hands, not caring that I had been warned never to rub my eyes during a chemical attack.

'The gas is in my eyes,' I screamed, as I began to choke on the poisoned air that was fogging the shelter.

The gases were settling low over the ground, filling the shallow dugout. Sarbast moved quickly, crawling out of the shelter and then pulling me out behind him. With my mask in one hand, he grabbed me with the other and pulled me back into the house.

I thought we should run up the mountains, for I distinctly remembered Sarbast telling me that one should seek low shelter during a conventional bombing attack and climb as high as possible during a chemical attack. But first I must have a working mask.

My throat was aching, my eyes were stinging. I crumpled to the floor and Sarbast knelt beside me. A clammy fog was clotting my senses and muddling my thinking.

Well, hello death, I thought to myself.

Forced to take a breath, I inhaled more foul-smelling air. I hoped that the end would come quickly. I was terrified of prolonged suffering.

Then, to my amazement, I grew aware of a mist-shrouded presence in the room. A black-garbed woman appeared to float in front of me.

It was Auntie Aisha.

Auntie Aisha had dropped by for a visit! That was entirely unexpected, despite the fact Halabja was not far from Bergalou. She had moved there nearly ten years earlier, shortly after my father died. She was a religious woman and she said that as she aged she wanted to live near to the shrine of Al-Sheikh Ali Ababaili, a revered Islamic cleric who was buried there. Auntie Aisha had been my favourite aunt since I was a child, and I had always been in awe of her ability to soothe all my worries away. Since I had become an adult, I had also realized that she received messages in the form of dreams. Despite her devoutness, she was surprisingly light-hearted, a woman who enjoyed having many children around her, laughing easily at our silly behaviour.

But now Auntie Aisha was not laughing. She had a grim expression on her face. And what was she doing in Bergalou? It was an unfortunate time for a visit.

Still, I felt better in her presence, which made me feel with a child-like confidence that everything would sort itself out with her around.

That she was floating had me so riveted that I could think of nothing else, wondering how she had learned to hover like that. She was a magical aunt in many ways, yet I had never seen her suspended above the ground before.

Auntie Aisha bent towards me, her features only inches from my face, and with a sigh said four shocking words: 'I am dead now.'

I winced, whispering, 'Dead?' Everything was too eerie. Was this Auntie Aisha's ghost? Had her village been hit by poisonous gas at the same time as Bergalou? Was she dead?

Was I dead?

I hoped not. I was too young to die. At twenty-six, I had too many years ahead, years and years and years that I wanted to share with my beloved Sarbast, years in which we would have children of our own. With signs that I was in the earliest stages of pregnancy, despite the fact Sarbast and I had agreed we should not yet bring children into our dangerous world, life seemed more precious than ever. I had postponed telling Sarbast anything about the possibility. He had enough worries at the moment.

Everything was confusing. I held my hands over my face to protect my eyes, but I peeked out between my fingers to see what Auntie Aisha did next.

I was disappointed when she evaporated. I reasoned that she had appeared to me for one reason only: she wanted to make certain I knew about the danger of the gases. She wanted me to live. She wanted me to know she was watching over me. That idea made me feel more hopeful. Auntie Aisha was a powerful woman. How could I die with her watching over me?

I looked at Sarbast, who was pulling and probing my dysfunctional gas mask, clearly shaken that he could not discern what was wrong with it.

I began gagging. He glanced at me and then started to remove his own mask, to pass it to me, but I shook my head. 'No!' Never would I take his mask. I wouldn't want to live without him, anyhow.

I held my breath once more, squeezing tight my stinging eyes, shrouding my face in my hands and rolling forward. I buried my face in the folds of my clothing.

Just as I felt myself losing consciousness, Sarbast solved the problem by removing the small cap that activated the mask's vent. He slipped the mask over my face.

I inhaled hungrily, catching the most satisfying breath of my life. No dish had ever tasted as sweet as that welcome air, despite its rubber-scented taint.

My God! I was happy! Life!

Relief swelled throughout my body, coursing down into my legs, feet and toes. A multitude of thoughts shot through my mind. Aunt Aisha had saved me! Sarbast had saved me! I would live! I pushed aside the disturbing idea that Aunt Aisha might have died in a similar attack. I told myself she was safe at her home in Halabja.

I chuckled. My untoward jollity seemed to frighten Sarbast. We both knew that people fatally damaged by chemicals often lost their minds immediately before death. *Peshmerga* commanders had filed a report on the physical effects of previous attacks. It was said that grown men and women had giggled and danced through the chemical-soaked streets like gas-addled idiots. I hoped I would not humiliate myself in such a manner. Deep down, though, I knew that I was not going crazy. I was merely happy to be alive.

My joy was interrupted as two *peshmerga* wearing gas masks burst through our open door. Soggy towels were draped over their heads and shoulders.

One of the men pushed aside his gas mask to tell us that the attack was over, but the chemicals were still doing their deadly work. 'Get out! Gas is heavy – it will now settle in all low areas. You are not safe here,' he shouted.

As the fighters spun around to leave to warn other neighbours, the sodden towel on one man's shoulders slipped to the floor. Sarbast yanked it from the floor and tossed it over my head. He pulled me with him out of the door.

As we struggled up the mountainside, I saw everything through a murky grey colour. The entire village was in chaos. Everyone was running up the side of the valley to the mountains.

Sarbast and I pulled ourselves upwards. I moved as rapidly as possible, even though my discomfort was growing worse. I could feel a sticky burning substance ooze from both eyes and gather on my cheeks under my mask. Even more frighteningly, the gas was still blunting my ability to think or to react. Each step I took suddenly required an enormous effort. Every stone on the trail loomed as if it were a huge boulder; each small incline seemed a towering mountain face.

I thought I would never make it up the mountain.

Finally, though, we reached a rocky outcrop high enough up to offer sanctuary from the gases. My legs gave way, and I collapsed on to the damp earth.

Sarbast removed his gas mask and mine. 'You are safe, darling,' he reassured me. 'You are safe now.'

I reached out to embrace him, but he pulled away, cautioning, 'Joanna, do not touch me. Do not touch yourself. We are both contaminated.'

By then my eyes were nearly swollen shut. I stared at Sarbast through dim slits, curious as to how I might contaminate someone already contaminated. Before I could ask, we heard the roar of an Iraqi aeroplane returning to the valley. Had we been detected?

'Down!' Sarbast shouted.

Explosions erupted all around us as together we hugged the rocky mountainside. Earth and small stones were lifted into the air by shells raining down on our bodies.

Sarbast lifted me in his arms, and before I realized what he was doing, he took a high dive into the void with me, as though we were two carefree lovers springing into the waves of the surf. We tumbled down the mountain, entwined, rolling over and over, until our descent was violently halted by a large boulder that blocked our path.

Stunned by the fall, we were both silent, our bodies still loosely entangled.

My God! Sarbast could have killed us both with that jump down the mountain. I wanted to slap him, but I couldn't find the strength to move. But at least the aeroplane had flown past.

Sarbast was so close that I felt his deep breaths as intimately as I felt my own.

'Sorry, darling, sorry,' he whispered. 'Are you all right?' He pulled small twigs and clumps of earth from my hair and mouth. 'Joanna?'

Winded by the fall and by slamming into the boulder, I was struggling to speak. I wanted to berate him for his dangerous stunt, but my efforts just produced low gurgling sounds. I wondered if I was choking on my own blood. I slowly unwound my arms from Sarbast's neck and moved my hands over my body, from my neck to my knees, searching for an injury.

It was only then that I realized my world was turning hazy and dark. My tongue felt too thick, as well. I had to swallow three or four times slowly before I could croak out, 'Sarbast, something's wrong with my eyes.'

He cupped my face in his hands. 'Can you see?'

I blinked. 'A little. Only a little.'

Sarbast must have been terrified by my news, for we both knew that blindness was one of the most common side effects of poisonous gas. He was breathing deeply, but said nothing more. Instead, he picked me up in his arms and began to rock me back and forth.

It was difficult to hold back my tears. I was more frightened than I had ever been in my life. My imagination ran away with me. What if the attack was not over? I could not see. If a full assault was imminent, and the front had moved to us, there would soon be fighting – hand-to-hand combat. Sarbast would be handicapped by a blind wife. We would be left behind to be killed, and our lifeless bodies tossed into an open grave. Such things were happening to Kurds all over Kurdistan.

Sarbast was of a different opinion. 'Joanna, don't worry. We'll wash out your eyes. The bombardment has ceased. The gas will disperse, and we will return to the village.'

Sarbast was right. The planes were gone. My worst case scenario did not come to pass: the gas attack was not followed by a full armed assault. I was grateful, as I was in no position to defend myself.

My useless eyes still swollen shut, I heard the *peshmerga* villagers trudging past us, returning to Bergalou. One fighter reported that the smoke was clearing. It was safe to return. Perhaps there were survivors down there, waiting to be found.

Another fighter announced, 'We must warn all Kurdistan. They are using stronger chemicals now.'

I thought of our relatives. Between Sarbast and me, we had hundreds of relatives living in Kurdistan. In truth, they were all in danger.

Word travelled quickly up the mountain that while no one had been killed, there were a lot of injuries, similar to my own. Perhaps other gas masks had proved defective. If Sarbast had not come home, I would never have solved the problem. I would have died.

There was no time to waste. The radio station had to be manned. Without the PUK radio, many Kurdish villagers would be cut off from news of the ongoing war. They would have no advance warning that poisonous gases were being used against them.

Where were the peacekeepers? Where was the UN? Why was the entire world ignoring Saddam's attacks upon his own people? Were we Kurds considered so unworthy, so disposable? I longed to stand at the top of the mountain and shout out, Where are you, world? Where are you?

As voices streamed by I covered my burning, swollen eyes with my hands. I felt a flash of shame that my failing sight would keep me from aiding injured villagers.

Violent nausea started to wrack my body. Reacting to the gases attacking my bloodstream and my vital organs, I began to retch repeatedly.

Suddenly I realized that I still might die. And what if I were pregnant? Had the fetus been harmed? Even if it were healthy, my baby would open its little eyes on war. Could I really subject an infant to the dangerous life I had chosen? I decided then and there that I could not. My life was too dangerous. If not pregnant, I would be more careful.

I still couldn't see, and I asked Sarbast to tell me what was going on.

He described how the *peshmerga* were trekking back down the ancient pathway, returning to their homes while bearing injured comrades on their backs or in their arms. He said many were silent and empty-eyed as they drifted haphazardly down the path that was now cratered by the explosions.

Still huddled on the damp earth, I listened to the murmurs as they passed by us. Sarbast pulled me up and I held tight, confident that his sure hand would safely guide me down the mountain. Instead my beloved Sarbast lifted me up and cradled me in his arms as if I were a small child. He carried me down the mountain, whispering the sweetest words of love in my ear. 'My love, my queen, I will accept all the world's hardships, but I cannot endure your being hurt. Joanna, Joanna, I love this world because you are in it.'

I nestled my head against his shoulder, and despite my blindness, I was the happiest woman in the world.

19

Blinded!

Bergalou
1987

As Sarbast carried me down the mountain, he remained alert, observing and calculating, plotting his next move. I knew that he was absorbed with the most lethal danger that had ever faced the *peshmerga* or the radio station. Despite the fact that my eyes were swollen shut and I could see nothing, I could imagine his expression.

He made me feel safe. For once in my life I was vulnerable and I needed to depend upon another person. I was glad that person was my Sarbast.

Suddenly Sarbast said in a hoarse voice, 'Our home is still standing.'

A small cry of joy escaped my lips, my happiness as complete as if our tiny home was a palace decorated with ornate furnishings.

Sarbast added, 'The village has not been overrun.'

'Thank God for that.'

I was still worried, though. The Iraqi Fifth Army was using new tactics. Perhaps it had softened us up with the chemicals and now planned a full-scale invasion after all. For the moment we were protected by the mountains and the dark of night. But perhaps it was gathering. Would we be invaded at first light?

Back in the village, confusion reigned. The chemical attack had unsettled everyone.

Sarbast said, 'I must get you out of here. You need to see a doctor, to check your eyes.'

I could not see. I was sick to my stomach. I felt weak. I was struck by the thought that I might have spent my last night ever in our little hut, where I had experienced the happiest yet most dangerous moments of my life.

'Is anything damaged?'

'Everything is as it was,' Sarbast answered abruptly.

Relief flooded through me, and I mentally did an inventory, for I had managed to make our primitive dwelling into a real home. Our two small mattresses were stacked in the furthest corner from the door, where most of our worldly possessions were neatly arranged. I had piled my hoard of tattered paperback books and family photographs on the leaning bookcase. The television still had its spot in the corner of the sitting room. I had had two small tables made from trees in the forest. My pink quilt and pillow set was folded neatly on one of them.

Sarbast continued to stand, his breathing still laboured.

The silence between us descended heavily, just like the gas. It was as though neither of us knew what to say to the other. What was this strange stillness growing between us that felt impossible to breach, as if invisible particles were settling between us and hardening into an unseen wall neither could penetrate?

I had an unwelcome thought: what if the chemicals had caused permanent loss of sight? Would my blindness change everything? Would I become a symbol of loss to Sarbast, rather than a source of affection, companionship and strength?

When Sarbast had finally realized what I had always known, that we were perfect for each other, he had written me many love letters and poems. One came to my mind at that very moment, and instinctively I recited the verse I had most treasured and, now that I was considering my loss of sight, the most ironic. 'For me, you are the whole wide world, and my sorrows are but a sinking boat if they do not find the shore of your eyes.'

I felt Sarbast drop down next to me. 'Darling.' He placed a steady hand on my shoulder. 'Joanna, you are still my whole wide world.'

To prove his words, and despite our contamination, Sarbast gently touched my lips with his. He cupped my face with his hands and

asked, 'Can you see anything? Can you detect light or dark – an outline at least?'

Both eyes were still swollen and caked with mucus. I saw nothing
but vague shadows. I avoided telling Sarbast my worst fears. Slowly I
touched his face. I caressed the roughness of his stubbled face. Long
ago I had kept my promise and shaved off that beard, a wonderful
moment of intimacy that I would never forget. I stroked his wide
forehead and I slipped my hand upwards into his dark hair, tugging
slightly on those curls that had once exercised an almost hypnotic
spell over me and were now damp with perspiration. I softly traced
the outline of his full lips.

Sarbast cleared his throat, and then coughed a raspy gas-induced
hack that made me shudder.

'Are you all right?' I asked anxiously.

'Fine. I'm fine. So are you. Listen. Listen, darling, listen to me. Your
sight will return. This is temporary, a short-term problem.'

I didn't agree. 'Can a dead body rise and live again, Sarbast?' My
voice spun higher in tone. 'No. No. The chemicals have destroyed
my eyesight. I feel certain of it.'

Sarbast gripped my hands tightly in his own. 'Come with me.'

I followed him outside, where I could hear him handling the
coiled water hose.

Despite the fact that Sarbast and I were living in a mountain area
where cold water springs were abundant, giving us a steady supply of
fresh water, water purer than any found in Iraq's major cities, transporting that water to our hut had its complications. The village had
multiple hoses that the *peshmerga* kept connected to the nearest
mountain spring. Once a week, the chain of hoses was passed from
house to house so that residents could manually top up the water
tanks that perched on every roof. We were lucky that one of the hoses
was still in our yard.

'This is better than nothing.'

With our clothes still on, he hosed us both down, from our heads
to our feet. We shook ourselves like wet dogs to get the excess off our
face and hair. He guided me back into the house.

'Where is the medical kit?' he asked.

'In the refrigerator.'

Every *peshmerga* family had been supplied with a basic medical kit.

The clinic in the village was so low on supplies that there was no reason to go there. Recently, injured fighters had been sent to Iran for medical care.

I stood quietly while Sarbast found the kit. 'Here are the eyedrops,' he said. He carefully lifted one eyelid and then the other, squeezing a few drops into each eye. He tried to wipe away the discharge that had coagulated in both my eyes, but my eyelids still felt glued down.

'Joanna, I've read a lot about chemical blindness. Victims often regain sight, sometimes as quickly as a day after and others within a few weeks. The survivor's sight often returns to normal. There are many known cases of this.'

I said nothing.

Sarbast shifted his thoughts to the problems immediately ahead. 'I feel certain we will get orders to take out the women and children.' He paused. 'I believe that they are finally coming for us.'

I was of the same opinion. Something wicked was coming our way. I cocked my head, listening for the sound of enemy soldiers, but heard nothing. I sighed noisily.

Sarbast's voice suddenly softened. 'Are you hungry, darling?'

'No.' I had not thought of food once since the attack had started. I still felt nauseous.

Sarbast began to stroke my shoulders. 'You will get hungry. Any food not in a tin will be contaminated.'

'What about those pastries your brother brought us? They were in the refrigerator. And our bread is there as well.'

'Yes, you are right. The refrigerator is airtight. That food is likely to be safe.'

'We won't starve.'

'I must go to the village. I want to find out what is going on.' Sarbast brushed my face lightly, and reminded me, 'Then I must get you out of here.'

Forcing a lightness into my voice I did not feel, I encouraged him. 'You go. Help the others.' I smiled. 'I'll prepare our things for departure.'

'I don't like leaving you here alone,' Sarbast commented.

'You must. Now go.'

'Be careful. Listen. If you hear anything unusual, make your way to the shelter.'

'I will,' I promised, although I knew that if our enemies were so near by that I could hear them, groping my way to that shelter would be futile.

'And don't fall,' he cautioned.

'In this tiny house you presented to me as a mansion?' I forced a laugh. 'Three steps in any direction and I'll find a wall to stop me.'

There was a pause. Even though I could not see him, I could feel his strength pulsating and sense his concentration.

'Good,' Sarbast said. 'I'll be back shortly.'

'Sarbast,' I implored, 'check on Ashti and Hema.'

'Yes. Yes, I will.'

Suddenly Sarbast was gone and I could let my true feelings surface. Unwilling to let him know how devastated I was, I had kept up an optimistic façade. In reality, I was distraught by the turn our lives had taken. But I willed myself to survive. I had suffered too many close calls from the first moment of my conception to give up easily. Yet that determination became tinged with sadness when I was struck by the thought that an important segment of my life was ending, for when we left Bergalou, it was likely that I would never see it again.

I steeled myself for the challenges ahead. 'All right, Joanna, you can't park yourself like a lizard in the sun. You must move, now.' My poor father had always inspired me, and I used his image to strengthen me. Not being able to speak or hear, my father had led a sad, lonely life in so many ways. Yet he soldiered on, valiantly supporting a wife and five children. I felt him looking down on me. I could not disappoint him.

I used my hands to push myself up from the hard floor, knowing that, above all, I must not stumble out of the door and fall down the hilly path. I had enough problems without breaking a bone. I held my arms and hands straight out and moved one leg after the other. I was suddenly struck by the long-lost memory of a horror film I had seen as a small girl in Baghdad, in which a group of zombies escaped from a graveyard to terrorize an entire town, moving unbendingly, arms, hands, legs and feet stiffly extended, just as I was doing. I laughed faintly.

I easily found my small stock of clothing, packed away in a plastic container. Good, I thought, these items will not be so contaminated.

When I came across a chocolate bar in a trouser pocket, I was struck by hunger. I had been saving that bar as a special treat to share with Sarbast. But he would be happy for me to eat it. I fingered it, unsure if the plastic wrapping had protected it from the chemicals. I unwrapped it and bit into it.

I laughed at the sheer pleasure of the sugar on my tongue. I felt better.

When I raised my arm, I caught a whiff of pungent body odour.

Oh my God, I smelled! I rubbed my hands against my clothes. My trousers and shirt were covered in dirt. I brushed my hair with my fingers, finding twigs. What would Mother say? She had raised standards of cleanliness to a new high. Our home in Baghdad was always immaculate, and Mother had always insisted that we take a bath every day and, in the hot summer months, twice a day. I had never known of anyone in our family having body odour. It would have been a scandal. But it was not possible to maintain Mother's exacting standards in Bergalou. Learning to be modest in all needs was a requirement of being a *peshmerga*. So upon my arrival Sarbast and I had agreed to alternate bathing days. The day of the attack had been Sarbast's day to wash, and I had not even sponged down. I had to ignore my stench.

However, I wanted to pack our things. Concerned that I might fall, I crouched on my hands and knees and began to crawl across the room, searching systematically. While probing beneath our low table, my fingers felt Sarbast's pistol. I knew he would have taken his Kalashnikov with him, as it was rarely out of his sight. There was a pile of ammunition stacked under the table. I took the loaded pistol and left the ammunition.

I made several trips across the uneven floor, towing our belongings behind me. The sharp ridges on the ill-made floor scratched my hands and feet. I will not miss this floor, I thought grimly.

I soon heard Sarbast's hurried heavy steps. I smiled. Sarbast made normal walking into a form of war.

'Did you hear anything while I was away?' he asked.

'No. Nothing at all. They probably thought they killed us all with those chemicals. They are celebrating, waiting until it is light to come and dump bodies.'

'I don't know. They probably have plans to hit us with chemicals for a few weeks, to make certain we have no uncontaminated water or food so that we run away. Then they will come in.' Sarbast coughed loudly, a harsh gag that was beginning to concern me. I hoped his lungs had not been damaged. Choking, he said, 'I brought you some food.'

That chocolate bar had stimulated my appetite. My nausea had gone.

Sarbast was breathless. 'We found several boxes of tinned goods that were not contaminated. We divided them. I have some peas and chicken.'

As he opened one of the tins with his knife I heard the grating sound of metal on metal and I smelled chicken.

'Ashti? Is she all right? And the baby?'

'They are well. I caught a glimpse of them both. Rebwar wants them to leave as well.'

'So Rebwar is all right?'

'He was with Ashti and Hema. They all survived.'

'Did little Hema suffer ill effects from the chemicals?'

'Joanna, I really don't know. I saw them briefly. I had no time to ask questions. But they looked all right. The baby was wrapped in a blanket but he was looking around. Now I want you to eat this quickly, for our entire world is now contaminated. Open your mouth.'

I felt miserable instantly. Being spoonfed marked the dismal depth of my situation. But only my sight was affected. I was not helpless. I could feed myself.

'Come on, Joanna. Eat,' Sarbast ordered, his words almost a shout. 'Open up. Quickly, now!'

'I can feed myself, Sarbast.' I extended my right arm. 'Give me the tin.'

Sarbast talked as I ate. 'Saddam has his eye on the Jafati valley. It is becoming too dangerous to him. It will be only a matter of time before we are overrun. We have been ordered to relocate the radio station. We'll make our way first to Merge and from there to the designated station. We'll find out that location tomorrow. I believe the station will be moved closer to the border. If so, we'll get you medical attention in Iran.'

I was surprised that we were running away. Yet I knew that the radio station must not be captured. The equipment would be impossible to replace. Nothing was more important to the PUK than the communication centre.

'Merge is still safe?'

'Yes, I believe so. We are their first target. Once we leave the valley, our enemy will focus on other areas.'

So we would be returning to Merge, to the village where Sarbast and I had met before travelling on to our honeymoon in Serwan. Perhaps we would see Zakia and her family. Nothing would give me more pleasure.

Between bites I asked, 'Have you eaten anything?'

'Later, later,' he answered quickly.

'When will we leave Bergalou?'

'Tomorrow, I hope.'

'Is there any uncontaminated water we might drink?'

'No. I don't think we should drink the water. Tomorrow we will find a fresh spring, high in the mountains and out of reach of the gas. You must wait until then.'

I nodded as I swallowed, asking the question that was haunting me. 'Sarbast. Were there any casualties?'

Sarbast hesitated, and then confessed, 'There are four or five fighters who are not expected to live. Others we are not certain about. Some people were caught out in the open and didn't get to their gas masks in time. We will know more in the days to come.'

How I prayed everyone would survive! Death was claiming too many of our fighters. And Sarbast was right. Baghdad's targets now obviously included the villages in the Jafati valley. While the villages had withstood daily bombardments for the past year, even the biggest and strongest fighters could not survive if chemical attacks became routine. With gas masks, one could survive the attacks themselves, but water and food and everything else necessary for life would be contaminated. Life after a chemical attack was the real problem.

I drank the juice from the bottom of the tin; I was so thirsty that I drained it and licked out every drop.

'Do you want the peas now?'

Just then there was a loud thump.

Sarbast hissed, 'Get behind the door. Now!' He rushed out of the room.

I decided not to hide. What good would that do? Instead, my fingers caressed the pistol. If anyone grabbed me, I would defend myself.

Tense moments passed until Sarbast reappeared. 'I could find nothing.'

'Perhaps it was the thrashing of an animal?' From what little I had seen prior to the attack, all Bergalou animals must be dead or dying.

'Perhaps.' He sounded worried, I thought. 'I will take you to the shelter. You rest there while I go back to the village. I will be back soon.'

'No, no. I'll be safe here in the house.' The last place I planned to go to was that earthen shelter. It would be more terrifying than a grave, and I would be alone. No, I was not going. Handicapped by the injury to my eyes, I would be unable to keep watch for worms or any other many-legged creature intent on invading my clothing or crawling into my hair. And I couldn't forget about those snakes. Perhaps they had been knocked out by the poisonous gas. Perhaps they would wake up in a rage.

The tone of Sarbast's voice reflected his impatience. 'Joanna.'

I circled my arms around my body. 'No. I would rather die here than live there.'

'I want you safe.'

I spoke through clenched teeth. 'I will not go blind into that shelter, Sarbast.'

Sarbast was losing patience. 'Joanna, please. I'll only be gone a few minutes. I could take you with me but I want you to rest, if you can. While I am away, go to the shelter. When I return, I'll get you.'

I argued the main point. 'Perhaps there are snakes in that shelter.'

'Joanna, soldiers will kill you if they find you.'

'Snakes, Sarbast! Snakes! Have you forgotten? My eyes are sealed shut. I couldn't see a snake if it was coiled right beside me. No!'

Sarbast moved quickly. His arms went round my waist and back, tightly, and he lifted me up.

My high-pitched screams blasted through the silence, prompting Sarbast to release me hurriedly.

'Well, if our enemy is near, they now know where you are.'

With flattened palms I steadied myself against his chest and then pulled back and shouted, 'No! Sarbast, I said no! I will not go blind into that shelter. I will not.' I clenched my fists, bracing myself for a physical fight.

Although I was born stubborn and determined, Sarbast was born even more obstinate. We were like twins in that regard. But – oh happy day! – Sarbast relented.

In a voice tinged with admiration, he said, 'You surprise me, darling.' Then he chuckled. 'If our enemy appears, please do scream. Your shouts will reach every secret corner of the village, giving everyone an opportunity to run away.'

I spoke calmly and seriously. 'Yes, I will do that. I will scream a warning.'

Sarbast chuckled.

I changed the subject, telling him my plan for ensuring my safety. 'After you leave I will sleep with my body wedged against the door,' I told him. 'I will keep the pistol in my hand. When you return, call out first and I will slide away and let you in.'

He gave my arm a fleeting squeeze. Then he was off to the village centre.

Rather pleased with the outcome of our first dispute, I squatted on the floor, carefully placing the pistol at my feet. My long hair kept falling down over my face, and I mechanically flipped it back before feeling for my pink quilt. I gave the coverlet an energetic shake, trying to remove any lingering toxins, and shook the pillows. Just as I had exhausted myself with all that activity, I suddenly wondered if shaking was a mistake. Had I just released the chemicals back into the air? Were invisible poisons propelling around me, stealing into my nostrils and settling on my exposed flesh? I stood nervously, thinking. Could those same toxins burrow also into a fetus? I patted my stomach, sending loving thoughts. If I were pregnant, my baby's life was more important than my own.

Then I felt them: small painful blisters forming on the tips of my fingers. I noticed that small bumps had also begun to erupt from under my flesh everywhere my skin had been uncovered during the chemical attack: on my face and neck and ankles. I had heard about blisters being a side effect of chemicals. Something else to worry about.

I decided that there was nothing I could do but give my burning eyes and stinging skin a rest. I set about getting ready for bed.

Everything was much more difficult without being able to see. But I managed to arrange my pink quilt on the concrete floor and, after flattening the curled edges with my fingers, I fell on top of it, resting my head on the pillow and pulling half the quilt over me as a comforter. It was contaminated, for certain, but everything in Bergalou was contaminated. I patted the floor with my hand until I found the pistol and placed it where I could easily reach it.

I felt I had only been on the floor for a few minutes when I was awakened by a great pressure against my body.

Sarbast's voice came to me as through a hazy fog. 'Joanna, move.'

It took me a few seconds to shake off my confusion.

Sarbast's foot got tangled in the quilt, accidentally spilling me on to the barren floor. I heard his heavy steps as he moved hastily from one corner of the room to the other.

'Sarbast, what are you doing? Shouldn't you rest?'

He didn't answer. Reluctantly, with an effort, I opened my sticky eyes.

Sarbast tugged the quilt off me. 'It will be clear to the east and north. That's the route we will take.'

I was in a world of my own. I rapidly batted both eyelids several times and held one unsteady hand in front of my eyes. I stared in relief. My sight had already improved. There's my Sarbast! Although what I could see was blurry, I could identify his familiar face and the outline of his muscular body.

I stood there, still uncertain. My feet probed the uneven floor for a secure spot.

'Sarbast, look at me.'

'Joanna, please.'

'Sarbast, I want you to look at me, now.'

His breath was loud, forced through his mouth and nose. He had become a mad dragon, I thought with amusement.

'What?' Holding a pair of shoes, he turned to stare at me with visible annoyance.

'Sarbast, I can see.' I paused, smiling. 'I can see a little.'

His look of exasperation slowly evolved into an expression of utter delight. 'You can? Really?'

'A little.'

He was suddenly close, looking intently into my eyes. Then he said, 'The whites of your eyes are bright pink.'

'Pink?' I smiled. 'My eyes are now my favourite colour?'

I was delighted that I still had eyeballs at all. I had been obsessing over the possibility of dried-up eyeballs, like Auntie Muneera's.

Sarbast added, 'And a milky glaze covers both eyes. Are you sure you can see?'

'Yes!' I said, more loudly than I intended.

'Time will bring it all back. It will,' he stated confidently.

'Yes?'

'Yes. Your sight will get better, day by day.'

'If I can only see this well, I will not complain,' I promised him, and myself.

Sarbast drew me to him, holding me tightly. I felt happy tears running down my cheeks. I wiped them against Sarbast's shirt.

Ignoring his soaked shirt, Sarbast held me at arm's length and started to laugh.

I drew away, looking at his face and smiling affectionately. 'My wild stallion,' I whispered. Despite the possible danger hovering over us, I felt an urge to run and shout my happiness. The hut was too small to contain my joy, so I rushed outside.

I felt beautiful and strong. My blurred but grateful eyes rested on the contours of the rugged terrain. I wanted to run to the top of the mountain. My happiness made me silly. I ran in tight circles on the small level section in front of the door, laughing, thinking, I am an untamed mare, a suitable match for my wild stallion.

Out of the corner of my eye, I saw that an amused Sarbast had followed me.

He held out his hand. 'Come. Come into the house.'

I went to him and he nuzzled my neck with his sexy moustache. My knees felt weak and I wanted only one thing, to feel as close to him as a man and woman in love can feel. I longed to tell him that I might be pregnant, but I held back.

Sarbast was looking over my shoulder. He whispered, 'I feel them out there, waiting. It may be today, or tomorrow, or next week, but they are there. We are in for the fight of our lives, Joanna.'

Almost as an omen we heard the distant crack of gunfire. Where did that come from?

We scurried into the house to gather our meagre belongings.

There was so much to do. We must leave Bergalou. I must get medical attention. Another location for the PUK radio station must be organized.

As I looked fondly at our little home, bidding a sad farewell in my mind, I reminded myself that I should not be disheartened, and that the most important thing was to survive, to live so that we could love, and fight, another day.

20

Escape to Merge

Bergalou to Merge
Autumn 1987

Quickly we made our way to the centre of Bergalou, where we found a small group of villagers. Dirty and exhausted, they looked haunted and numb.

With the chemicals, everything had changed.

I looked around, grimly nodding. I saw several people who were wearing all their clothes on top of each other. In any other setting, their balloon bodies would have been a cause for merriment. I wondered, however, if their awkward attire might make uphill climbing dangerous, although I reasoned that if they tumbled into a ravine, their puffed-up garb would protect their bones.

Only a few people had gathered. My heart thumped hard. Where was everyone else? Had Sarbast lied to keep me from worrying? Perhaps there were more dead than living.

When I asked, I was told that most of the fighters were remaining behind to defend Bergalou, at least until a new location for the radio station was established.

Looking around, I felt incredibly sad, thinking that the once-bonded unit of Bergalou inhabitants would soon be a broken necklace, scattered like loose pearls throughout Kurdistan.

It was then that I noticed that many fighters had been afflicted with the same small blisters. They served as a scary reminder that we had all been exposed to poisonous gases. I overheard someone say that the blisters would heal, over time. There was nothing to do but forget about them, although I couldn't stop fretting about my injured eyes, which still hurt. My sight was diminished and perhaps it would weaken even more. I was looking forward to getting out of Bergalou so that I could seek medical attention.

I had other worries. I touched my belly with my hand. I had to guard myself. I must not stumble and fall. I had walked over the mountains surrounding us more than once and knew that the terrain was treacherous, with serrated rocks so sharp that a touch could rip open the flesh, and unexpected drops that plunged more than a thousand feet.

My stomach gave a little lurch. I couldn't see Ashti and her family. Nor did I see Bahar, Kazal or Pakhshan with little Lasik. I wondered if the other women had already left Bergalou. When would I see them again?

I turned my attention back to Sarbast and saw a familiar face: Kamaran, Sarbast's cousin, who we had heard was set to complete his PUK military training. In a worried voice, he asked, 'Joanna, are you all right?'

'Kamaran!' I laughed. His friendly face felt like a tonic.

I had forgotten how much I liked Kamaran. I had seen him a number of times in Baghdad, for he and Sarbast were not only cousins but close friends. Many people teased him, saying he looked just like Tom Cruise. He was not only handsome but genuinely nice, with a warm personality. He was exceptionally intelligent as well, a graduate in economics. But like Sarbast, he had forsaken a comfortable career to risk his life as a *peshmerga*.

Kamaran told me, 'I was on my way to Bergalou when some fighters on the trail told me that Bergalou had been hit by chemicals. I came as quickly as possible.'

Sarbast interrupted. 'Kamaran will be coming with us to Merge.'

I was delighted to hear it.

Both men squatted on the ground, using their fingers to draw our escape route in the dusty earth. Although the PUK controlled a lot of Kurdish territory, there was no way of knowing the location of our enemy exactly. The safest route for us would be to the north-east. We would walk over the rugged spine of mountainous terrain. The journey would normally take a fit man a full day of ascending and descending. With my limited vision, I would slow our journey. I was ashamed that I had become a burden. I hated that feeling. I hated being vulnerable.

But in truth, every woman in Iraq was vulnerable. Papers had recently been uncovered that documented a sordid fact: Saddam's government had established the heinous position of 'government rapist', attached to Iraq's prison authority, whose only duty was to rape wives in front of their husbands, or daughters in front of their fathers. Every Iraqi husband and father seethed in fury at the revelation, and every woman recoiled at the dire possibility, as in our traditional society rape was considered the most dishonourable fate possible for a woman. It was an unbearable thought. But if I were ever to be captured as a PUK supporter, it could be my fate. It had happened to thousands of innocent Kurdish women and girls.

'Let's go, Sarbast,' I said.

Sarbast agreed. 'Yes. It's time.' As he stood up he told me, 'We're splitting into small groups. It will be just the three of us in our group. I'll be the head; you, Joanna, will be the body; and Kamaran will be our tail.'

I stepped forward, my sadness at leaving suddenly forgotten. Bergalou, and indeed the entire valley, suddenly felt nothing more than a place to die.

Sarbast had thought to bring along three empty water canteens, for we would surely find plenty of uncontaminated water in the mountain springs. Both he and Kamaran were weighed down with Kalashnikovs. I had concealed the pistol in my coat pocket. But Kamaran had no baggage of his own, as he had dropped his personal items on the path the moment he was told of the chemical attack and unselfishly ran to our rescue. So he accepted half of Sarbast's load and insisted on taking my satchel.

Kamaran explained with a smile, 'Let's not burden our head.'

The three of us left Bergalou, bidding a few solemn farewells to the fighters still making their plans.

A steep stony pathway took us out of Bergalou. My limited vision added a new dimension of stress, so we kept close to each other. I was comforted by the fact that I could reach forward or backward at any moment for assistance. I kept my eyes cast downwards, watching for the back of Sarbast's heels; but chiefly I concentrated on the path, which fortunately was worn smooth by many years of passing feet. I mechanically placed one foot before the other, counting off my miseries. My throat burned with thirst and my ears were strained by the anxious need to listen. I felt certain that at any moment I would hear the clamour of nearby enemy soldiers or the reverberations of their guns.

I looked upwards at the sky. The rising sun was glossing the stony mountain with its brightness. It was a cool morning shrouded in mist. I was thankful that I had thought to add a jacket over the traditional *peshmerga* man's trousers I was wearing.

As we slogged uphill, I spotted a few tufts of wild flowers. My throat grew even more parched and painful. Noting the flowers' dew-washed petals, I bent and picked several flower stalks while maintaining my stride, and lapped at the dew droplets with my tongue. The moist drops were delicious, cooling my tongue and throat slightly.

I heard Kamaran chuckle behind me.

I smiled too, because I felt better.

I was even more grateful as the trail wound through to concealed areas, for the stony path's open exposure was disquieting. If there were marksmen watching Bergalou, our three figures would be tempting.

Suddenly a rustle sounded from nearby bushes. I instinctively cried out.

A mountain goat leapt in front of Sarbast. I was annoyed at myself.

Sarbast turned to look at me, expressing surprise at my lapse. I knew that he was very proud of his freedom fighter wife, as he was always proudly introducing me to newcomers to Bergalou. I hated disappointing him.

Kamaran stepped forward and reassured me with his big smile. I knew then that I was in for a very long and demanding day.

After an hour, my calves throbbed from the path's never-ending upward slant, the pads of my feet sharply ached, and my throat and mouth burned with a maddening thirst. That thirst was growing so torturous that I truly feared I might be driven mad.

I managed to walk for a brisk three hours before I began to sway dangerously.

Kamaran whispered, 'Sarbast, five minutes' rest.'

Sarbast turned, surprised that the tough Kamaran needed even a single moment, but when his eyes flashed in my direction, he saw Kamaran's point.

I gratefully sagged down on the damp earth trail, breathing heavily.

In the quiet of our halt, there was a wonderful surprise. I heard the trickling noise of running water. The thought of clear sparkling water drew me out of my trance.

'Do you hear it? There.' Sarbast pointed. 'There's a running stream.'

'Where?' Kamaran looked.

I moved my swollen tongue around in my mouth. I was going to drink that water, whether or not Sarbast declared it safe from chemicals. I planned my strategy. I would leap into the spring before he could move to stop me. I could be quick on my feet when the occasion called for it.

'Wait.' Sarbast lowered the gear he was carrying and heaved his Kalashnikov and heavy supply of ammunition from his shoulder, carefully placing them against a bush. He unhooked the water canteens he had strung from a wire tied across his chest. To my relief, he said, 'Up this high the waters will have escaped contamination.'

Through a small gap in the foliage I could see a rivulet of water as it coursed over smooth rocks and into a small pool before it flowed downhill. I licked my lips. That pool of water was a beautiful sight.

Sarbast leaned over and tasted the water. He nodded and called out, 'Yes, I was right. It is clear.'

The discovery of that cold stream lifted all our spirits.

Kamaran reached for a filled canteen and passed it to me. 'Our pace is bound to improve now.' He smiled. 'We were becoming dehydrated.'

I could not stop my greedy gulping. Nothing had ever tasted as delicious as that spring water. It was fresh and cold. After drinking my fill, I took a tightly balled handkerchief from my trouser pocket, soaked half and dabbed it to my forehead and lips, before tending to my swollen eyes. Surprisingly the water stung my inflamed eyeballs, but I repeated the exercise, holding the cold cloth against them.

I drank the last drop before handing over my canteen so that Sarbast could slide down the slope again to refill it.

After taking our second fill of water, Sarbast suggested that we change clothes. Before leaving our house we had taken the clothes stored in plastic. We would change now and throw our contaminated clothing into a nearby ravine.

I was so eager to get out of my filthy clothes that I needed no urging. I leapt to my feet. The *peshmerga* trousers I had purchased in Sulaimaniya were old and growing uncomfortable, binding my waist tightly like a girdle. I stood impatiently, waiting for Sarbast to open the container, and then I plucked out a clean pair of trousers and a pink blouse made of polyester. I elbowed my way through the dense brush and hurriedly removed my tainted clothes, rolling them up and tossing them to Sarbast. 'Here.' I yanked the pink blouse over my head and smoothed it down with my fingers. I checked that my pistol was tucked in the pocket of my overcoat. I decided to keep on my soiled coat, for we might spend the night in the mountains, and no matter what time of year it was, nights were chilly at high altitudes. I kept the same shoes on, for they were the most comfortable for walking. My hair had tumbled loose from its elastic band. I shook it free before gathering it once more into a long ponytail.

Too soon I was back on my blistered feet, climbing the seemingly endless serpentine trail.

Were we not running for our lives, the journey would have been serene, so far away from a world troubled by wars and dictators. But there was no time to admire the tapestry of greens and browns channelling our path, or the gentle hollows in little open spots dappled by sunlight through the trees.

As I walked over the mountains, Kurdistan's past flowed over me like the pages of history. Primitive hunters had stalked wild animals here, and campfire-lit faces had sat in circles by local caves. Along the path where I was placing my feet, earliest man had spread out from Iraq – known then as Mesopotamia – to cover the earth. My beloved land was once the centre of the civilized world where writing was invented and the first laws were created. Thinking of our own desperate situation, I sadly mused on where it had all gone wrong. At what point did the region cease its civilization and revert to such lawlessness?

Sarbast called me out of my trance. We had come upon an area of the path snarled with stiff brushwood. Sarbast slowed, and then halted, deciding, 'Let's eat and rest before we go forward.'

I was saving what little energy I had left, so I didn't bother to reply, although I was grateful that we would finally eat something. I reminded myself that I must nourish my body for the sake of my baby, who was slowly evolving into a certainty in my mind. I crumpled to the ground, tucking my legs under my body. I opened my canteen and tried to wash the toxins from my eyes once again. The pain was relentless.

Sarbast knelt down in front of me. 'How are you, darling?'

I nodded, holding the handkerchief to my eyes. 'I am all right.'

Sarbast lightly caressed my shoulder before standing up to walk over to Kamaran. I heard their low muttering voices.

I uncurled my legs and leaned my head towards my lap. After a few moments of rest, it was with some surprise that I felt a cool, weighty object cross the lower part of my legs. I raised my head to see a long black snake twisting slowly across my outstretched limbs.

'*Snake!*' I cried out. I moved faster than I had ever moved in my life, leaping into the air. My quick movement hurled the snake into the air too and then it hit the ground with a heavy thud and slithered into the underbrush.

I stood panting, my hands at my throat.

Sarbast and Kamaran looked my way, puzzled by my scream.

'*A snake!*' I shouted again, pointing at the bushy area into which the snake had disappeared – a section I realized with dismay that we must soon pass through.

'Were you bitten?' Sarbast asked.

His voice was so calm that I felt a flash of anger. I stared at him. I had definitely seen the flickering tongue, and had even felt a delicate flick against my leg, but no, its barbed fangs had not exploded into my flesh.

'Well, he licked my leg with his tongue,' I replied huffily.

I leaned down and lifted my trouser leg, searching my bare skin for any sign of a bite. There were no marks on my flesh, thank God.

Both Sarbast and Kamaran laughed merrily. 'Well, then, be grateful you were only licked and not bitten,' Sarbast said easily, before turning back to Kamaran to resume their conversation.

I glared at my husband's back.

I rose to my tiptoes, keeping my contact with the ground as slight as possible, as my dimly-seeing eyes scanned the ground for the snake.

Sarbast and Kamaran opened a tin of peas, along with three tins of sardines. We would eat and get back on the trail as quickly as possible. Sarbast was pleased at our progress and began to tease me, slowly bringing me round to a better humour. He said we had covered so much ground that there was a good chance we would arrive in Merge by nightfall.

I felt a rush of relief at his news, for after my brush with the snake, I shuddered to think of spending the night on the ground in the forest. All Kurds know that snakes are drawn to the warmth of sleeping bodies. I had heard plenty of tales of *peshmerga* waking to discover a friendly snake coiled contentedly alongside them in their bedding.

Sarbast and Kamaran quickly ate the sardines. They insisted that I eat the peas.

'Supermen,' I said with a chuckle, certain that without me, the two of them could sprint from Bergalou to Merge without stopping, climbing the mountains of Kurdistan as nimbly as goats.

Just as I had swallowed the last of the peas, I heard a distinct rustle in the trees. I reached for my pistol while Sarbast and Kamaran seized their weapons. Sarbast motioned for me to take cover behind a large bush. Kamaran slipped behind a large tree.

Sarbast stood quietly, listening; then he left us to retrace our steps. The wait for his return felt endless.

I was uneasy when I heard the sounds of men's voices. Had Sarbast been captured? I listened for a few moments before deciding I must go and see for myself what was happening. I took a few steps, but Kamaran lightly cleared his throat and shook his head from side to side, mouthing no. It took all my resolve to do as he told me.

Sarbast suddenly reappeared. 'It was nothing – only another group of *peshmerga* travelling through the mountains.'

'What will we do if we run into enemy soldiers?' I asked, voicing for the first time my biggest fear.

Sarbast shrugged. 'We fight, until . . .' and he drew his finger across his throat in a chilling motion.

Kamaran gave a choked laugh. He could always see the funny side. He pushed back his heavy glasses with one hand and held up four fingers of the other hand. 'Joanna, don't worry, for there are four things I know will never come to pass. Number one: Saddam Hussein will not die peacefully in his bed.' He chuckled as he raised his water canteen to his mouth to drink, loudly smacking his lips as he declared, 'And, number two: the fresh water springs of Kurdistan will not change into fine champagne, as I wish. Number three: your dear cousin Kamaran will never reside in a palace, as I wish. And' – he paused for emphasis – 'number four: neither Sarbast nor I will ever allow our enemies to take us alive.'

Despite our dire circumstances, I smiled. Just being around him lifted my dwindling spirits, reminding me that, despite our homelessness, we still had much to be thankful for.

Even Sarbast was amused. 'Let's move on,' he snorted through his laughter.

I began to feel the safety of Merge pulling me on like a powerful magnet.

Merge! The very name sounded like magic to me. It would be wonderful to be back in that village where I had met up with Sarbast before our honeymoon. That meeting seemed to be in another lifetime.

Mercifully, the high hills soon passed behind us and we began to cross lower, rounded mounds. This terrain was easier to manoeuvre than the steeper rises behind us, but at the end of a long day of walking I barely noticed. Among the hills and trees, dusk came quickly, which slowed our pace.

Sarbast held up his right hand and halted.

I looked past his shoulder and saw a gravelled road threading through the valley. We could connect to that road at the base of the hill. Beyond the road was Merge.

Sarbast stood silently, surveying the area.

I gazed down from the hill, listening for the far-off sounds of life from the distant village. I heard nothing. I studied the valley below, which was green with fields of crops and vividly coloured wild flowers.

I had travelled up and down Iraq, and to my mind Kurdistan was its most beautiful asset. The lush highlands and emerald valleys were a terrestrial treasure chest overflowing with irreplaceable riches. Sadly the region was threatened by the effects of war, which I feared would empty it of all that was good.

Sarbast stepped back to speak quietly to Kamaran, but my ears were honed to his words. 'Who knows what's happening all over

Kurdistan, even this far north. We should split up. Meet us at Karim's house in an hour.'

Kamaran darted back into the tree line. He would wait for us to pull ahead.

My ears pricked up at Sarbast's warning. Did he believe that Ali Al-Majid's Fifth Army had dropped chemicals throughout Kurdistan? Would we find Merge abandoned?

An evil wind was blowing from Baghdad.

An ever-cautious Sarbast ordered me, 'Joanna, walk a few paces behind me, and say nothing.'

'OK,' I agreed easily, for I did not want my husband to observe me too closely. I was keeping a secret from him. My sight had worsened in one way, while improving in another. I was gaining clarity, but losing expanse. My eyesight's scope was being overtaken by shadows at its periphery, only a narrow tunnel remaining sharp. I felt as though I was peering into the sunlight through a slit.

I was frightened that I was going completely blind. I did not want to tell Sarbast. At least not yet, for there was nothing he could do but worry.

Sarbast walked rapidly ahead, though not so rapidly that I could not match his pace. When the hilly incline folded into the gravelled road, we hugged one side of the road. Normally the thoroughfare into Merge would be bristling with townspeople going about their routine activities, but the road was empty. The absence of travellers convinced me that Merge had been hit by chemicals as well, but when we rounded a bend I was relieved to see a sign of normal life. Four women were walking down the road towards us, all sauntering with an effortless willowy swing. They were wearing brightly coloured cotton dresses with matching scarves on their heads. Even with my limited vision, I could see that the heaviest of the women had rolled and twisted a white turban atop her head, where she balanced a large pot. Kurdish women are expert at maintaining their equilibrium and poise while they transport heavy loads on the flat of their heads – a useful skill I had never mastered, despite several hilarious attempts.

I studied the outlines of the pot. Perhaps it was filled with yogurt. I lightly touched my lips with my tongue. I would have loved some cool yogurt.

We passed the women and, not wishing to seem unfriendly, I exchanged with them a smile and a nod of greeting. But the smiles and nods did not lead to conversation, for in our uncertain times Kurds, fearful of *jahsh*, did not open dialogue with strangers.

We were suddenly overtaken from behind by two middle-aged men riding on donkeys. Their full Kurdish trousers hung wide around their waists and hips, tapering to their ankles. Both riders' legs swung out at the sides, while one of the men reached back to tap his donkey's backside with a small tapered stick.

We were soon on the stretch of the road that cut through the village, and more townspeople came into view. Strangely, none of the people passing looked at us with the slightest curiosity, although we were so dirty and dishevelled that I thought we would arouse suspicion.

My stomach churned with hunger when we passed a group of young men hawking Fanta orange drinks and walnuts.

An old woman was squatting on the ground, busily occupied making rudimentary gas masks. She was carefully covering small pieces of charcoal with cotton wool and cloth. I knew that her next step would be to stitch the pieces together into half-moons of gauze before sewing a small string of elastic to the edges, with which to secure the mask around the head.

I had seen such homemade devices before. I believed they were basically useless against a fully-fledged chemical attack, such as the one that had driven us from Bergalou. The crude screens were little more than a tool to ease the mind of victims who had no access to modern gas masks. To my mind it was terrible that not every person in Kurdistan possessed a gas mask. But Saddam had made it a crime for Kurds to own gas masks, and now I knew why. However, our PUK leaders had outsmarted him. Every *peshmerga* gas mask had been smuggled into Kurdistan on the back of a mule.

Without our masks, Sarbast and I both would be dead, along with many others living in the Jafati valley.

Sarbast turned right through a small alley and into another street. To my eyes, each house looked the same as the next. Modest and clean, most homes were decorated with pots of colourful flowers outside the door and perched on window ledges.

Finally we arrived at our destination, the home of Karim and his wife Sozan.

Sarbast knocked lightly.

I saw the glitter of Karim's intense eyes peering through the crack in the door.

'Sarbast,' he said as he opened the door, 'you're safe! We were worried!' He grabbed Sarbast by the shoulders. 'We heard just now that chemicals were dropped on all the villages in the valley.'

My heart thumped loudly, even as we were being welcomed into their humble home. Karim and Sozan were also a *peshmerga* couple; and despite having met them only briefly during our honeymoon, I felt their affection and returned it. They offered heartfelt, simple hospitality. They urged us to leave our shoes and belongings at the door, and to sit.

Sozan said what I most wanted to hear. 'You must be hungry. I will get refreshments. Later, after the children have returned from the neighbours, I will prepare a meal.'

'Tell us, what have you heard?' Sarbast asked in a worried voice.

'Baghdad is bragging,' Karim said in a frustrated tone, 'that Sergalou and Bergalou were both hit. According to the announcement, the PUK took heavy casualties.' He cast a worried look at Sarbast. 'Am I hearing the truth?'

Sarbast replied, 'Well, it is true we were hit with chemicals. But no one died. There were serious injuries, so there may be casualties to come. I have no information from Sergalou or the other villages in the valley. For sure they meant to kill us all. We are going to set up a new radio station in a safer area, further north, away from the front and from Saddam's armies.' With a satisfied grin, he said, 'We have our equipment.'

'Many people are fleeing from the Jafati valley,' I added.

I heard a sound of distress from the kitchen. I could only surmise that our hostess was expressing her fear that Merge might soon face the same threat. Sozan was a mother with children to protect. Her alarm was understandable. I patted my belly protectively.

'Praise Allah no one died, at least,' Karim muttered.

'We would have had many dead without our masks.'

'Ma'am Jalal?'

'He was not in Bergalou. But I assume he's safe. We would have heard, otherwise.'

Karim sighed heavily. 'That is good.'

Jalal Talabani, called Uncle Jalal by his devoted followers, had joined the Kurdish resistance when he was only fourteen years old, and was elected to the party's central committee four years later. Always serious, he studied to become a lawyer, graduating as a barrister in 1959. After clashing with the leaders of the Kurdish resistance over his belief that the freedom movement should be more democratic, Talabani formed the PUK in 1975. Over the years, he had earned not only the respect of Kurds but international admiration as well. He served his fighters well and was revered by them all. To lose Jalal Talabani would be a serious blow to the movement.

Karim probed further. 'Rumour is that they dropped a cocktail of toxic gases, consisting of—'

Sarbast finished Karim's sentence. 'Most likely sarin, and other nerve agents. I saw burns and blisters.'

I held up my fingers. 'See,' I said. 'Like this.'

Karim stared open-mouthed at my fingertips. Sozan rushed in from the kitchen to have a look. 'I will get some salve,' she declared.

Sarbast repeated, 'Without the gas masks, we would all have died during the attack.'

I examined Sarbast's fingers. They were blister-free. Other than a nagging cough, he was unaffected by the gas.

Since the beginning of the Iran–Iraq war, the *peshmerga* had more than held their own against Saddam's army, enjoying victory after victory, retaking much of Saddam-controlled Kurdistan and chasing his armies out of Kurdish lands. With Iran's help, we had envisaged victory within the year. With a strong Kurdish hand at the bargaining table, an acceptable peace could be brokered, and we Kurds would finally achieve meaningful autonomy. But now Saddam, though weakened by the war with Iran, was gaining in strength, for that war was winding down.

My mind raced. How could we fight back? Where could we run to seek refuge? All the neighbouring countries hated their own Kurdish populations. Turkey? How could we rush into the arms of a government that distrusted its Kurdish population even more than the Iraqi government? Syria? Syria's president, Hafez Assad, was as aggressively violent a man as Saddam. To hold power, Assad had already proved that he would extinguish entire communities, if necessary. The Syrian Kurdish population was as tightly controlled as their Iraqi brothers. Iran? Although the Iranian government was currently an ally of the Iraqi *peshmerga*, that was only because they were at war with the Iraqi government. At home they too repressed their own Kurdish population. Yet if Saddam kept up his chemical attacks, Iraqi Kurds would be pushed over Kandil mountain, the geographical barrier between Kurdistan and Iran.

I buried my head in my hands.

Would Kurds never be free?

Karim noticed me. 'Joanna? Are you unwell?'

Sarbast answered quickly. 'Joanna's eyes were damaged by the toxins. She was temporarily blinded, but her sight is slowly returning.'

I brushed away my tears and looked up, smiling. 'But we are alive, Karim. We are alive to fight another day. That is the victory.'

Sozan bustled into the room and handed me a tube of first-aid salve, which I began to smear over my blistered fingers.

She rushed back into the kitchen and then quickly returned, balancing a copper tray loaded with Kurdish specialities. There was a pot of sweet cardamom-scented tea, some raisins and walnuts, Kurdish pastries dripping with honey and four glasses of cold pomegranate juice. I could barely restrain myself, but I remembered my manners and waited for Sozan to pour the tea and present each guest with a small cup.

Just as I tasted the delicious scented tea on my tongue, a soft knock sounded on the door.

A questioning look flashed across Karim's face.

Sarbast explained, 'That must be Kamaran, my cousin. He travelled with us. We split up outside the village. He was to meet us here.'

Karim walked over to the door, carefully asking for the caller's identity before opening it.

Kamaran whispered his name and was quickly allowed entry.

The three men drank tea and munched the nuts and raisins, discussing their plan for a new radio and communication centre. I ate a pastry and listened as each fighter heatedly expressed his opinion as to what the PUK's next step should be. Their voices became a buzz of background noise. Fatigue and a full stomach created an exhaustion in me that brought on a deep sleep even as I sat rigidly upright on the sofa.

★

Hours later, I was bewildered to awake on a single bed in a small room that I did not recognize. Where was I? And where was Sarbast?

Recollections of the day before flickered in my mind. I soon remembered that I was in the home of Karim and Sozan in Merge. I was thirsty and hungry and reasoned that I had been put to bed by Sarbast.

I felt my swollen eyes with my fingers. I felt no more discharge, but they were still painful.

I examined my surroundings. The room was immaculate, though sparsely decorated. Apart from the bed I was on, there was nothing but a small round table covered with a fancy embroidered white cloth, and three pictures of Kurdish landmarks on the walls. I looked up to see a tiny barred window high up one of the walls, covered by a lacy white curtain. Light filtered in through the window. My vision was clearer. That cheered me up.

I stood up and stretched. My entire body felt raw and aching.

I hobbled out of the bedroom in my bare feet into a narrow hallway and then followed the passage into the living area, where Sozan was tending one of her children.

Sozan looked up as I entered and smiled. She had typical Kurdish colouring, with fair skin, dark eyes and black hair. Her features were not symmetrical, but her smile was so warm and sympathetic that I found myself wondering why I had not noticed her beauty before.

'Joanna! Did you sleep well?'

'Too well. I feel drugged,' I admitted with a yawn. 'Where is Sarbast?'

Sozan flashed a cheerful smile. 'You fell into such a deep sleep that none of us could wake you.' She teased me, 'You were in a coma. Sarbast brandished roast chicken under your nose, but even that delicious aroma didn't wake you.' Sozan laughed. 'Dear girl, there was nothing to do but for Sarbast to put you to bed. Then we ate dinner. Later we slept, too. You, darling Joanna, slept through the entire night. Sarbast asked that I let you sleep until you woke. He said you had been so brave and strong that you had earned a long rest.' Sozan's smile faded as she studied my face with concern.

I felt a little shiver of foreboding rush through me.

'Joanna, I must tell you that Sarbast and Kamaran left early this morning for Sandoulan.'

'No!'

'Joanna, listen. There are so many roadblocks between here and Sandoulan that they must avoid the main roads and take the mountain path.'

I was stunned into silence, but my mind was active. Sarbast had gone! Without me.

'How long ago did he leave?'

Sozan read my mind. 'You will never catch up with him. He left hours ago.' She stroked my arm. 'Listen, Joanna, we have heard that Iraqi checkpoint soldiers are very careful now. They will allow women and children to pass, but take the men who try to cross, even boys as young as twelve. Sarbast and Kamaran are clearly *peshmerga*. It would risk their lives to chance a checkpoint.' Sozan paused. 'We have information that the government has a new policy to automatically execute all fighters. The soldiers murder our men in the woods as soon as they stop them at the checkpoints.'

'But I should be with Sarbast!' I shouted. 'I can walk. See!' I marched around the room, twice.

Sozan slowly shook her head. 'You, dear child, have passed your physical limit. You must rest today, and you will be taken to Sandoulan by car.' She gestured at a small bundle of papers that rested on the kitchen table. 'Sarbast left your Iraqi identification papers here. As far as the government is concerned, Joanna, you are a pure Iraqi Arab, an Al-Askari. There is nothing in your official papers to bind you to Kurds. You have an excellent chance of passing the checkpoints without a hassle.' Sozan's voice lowered as she glanced at her small son, who was absorbed watching a cartoon on a black-and-white television set. 'You should leave soon, though. Planes have begun to fly overhead. We don't know what is about to happen.'

It was only then that I became aware of the enemy planes droning in the sky. After months of living as a target, I had come to recognize every reverberation of an aeroplane. I knew how a plane rumbled when it was only surveying an area and I recognized the special roar when a plane was approaching to drop bombs. I listened for a full minute before deciding we were in no immediate danger.

Not yet, anyhow.

Sozan placed her hands on my shoulders, confirming what I thought. 'We believe they are reconnaissance planes. They taunted us yesterday as well, circling over our heads for the entire morning.'

I was not upset about the plane, but I was offended by Sarbast's departure. From the first day of our marriage, I had never been a burden to my husband. Even yesterday, when I was impaired by weakened eyesight, I had matched every step that Sarbast and Kamaran had taken.

I became so agitated that I shook with anger.

Sarbast knew how stubborn and determined I could be, so he had purposely avoided a scene by leaving while I was asleep. I would never have let him leave without me had I been awake. I would have literally wrapped my body around his; I would have chased him through the neighbourhood – anything to avoid a separation at this, possibly the most dangerous time of our lives.

I paced around the small room, flapping my arms. I had never been so upset.

Then my stomach plunged at a new thought: perhaps I would never see Sarbast again. Sarbast might be dead, even as I stood safely in Sozan's kitchen.

I had no way of knowing where he was or what was happening to him. Unexplained disappearances were happening all over Kurdistan. How would I ever find him if he never turned up in Sandoulan? That thought made me shake in frustration and anger. I could have strangled him with my bare hands; however, I did not want anyone else to harm him.

Sozan took charge. Steering my body with her hands, she turned me around and pushed me into her small kitchen. 'Let me prepare you a nice breakfast. A boiled egg and some bread and jam and nice hot tea would be good, yes?'

If I was going to chase Sarbast over the mountains, I must be strong, I reasoned. I must eat.

Soon I was eating a delicious breakfast, but while eating, I caught an unpleasant whiff of my own body odour. 'I must have a bath, Sozan. Since the attack, I've only rinsed off the chemicals. I am so smelly and dirty that I cannot abide myself. What do you think? Is it safe?'

Sozan surveyed my unkempt appearance, and obviously caught my scent, for she said, 'Yes. A quick one then.' She added, 'Very early this morning I washed all your clothes. They are hanging out in the sun drying. I will get you some to wear now.'

I smiled in gratitude as she turned away to go outside.

As I finished my bread and jam, I watched Sozan through the small window. The washing was hanging almost directly over their family bomb shelter. Wonderful, I thought: it is good to know where the shelter is, in case those planes decide to attack. Sozan manoeuvred around the entrance to the shelter, fingering my garments to check for dampness and then selecting several pieces of the freshly laundered clothing.

Sozan was a genuine friend. I only hoped that I could help her in return should she ever need a safe haven.

She quickly returned with a dress and clean underwear, all deliciously fragrant and imbued with the sunny breezes of Kurdistan. Then she led me into the family's bathroom, walled with grey concrete blocks.

The tiny room was dark and nearly featureless. High up above was a small window no bigger than a man's two hands flattened.

I wedged myself close to the metal water barrel that had been placed carefully on top of a liquid gas heater. There was an ancient tap on the bottom of the barrel and a small metal bowl on the floor beneath. I decided I would first fill the bowl and pour water over my head and body, then soap up before finally rinsing.

Sozan returned to pass me a bar of soap, a small cup of shampoo, a flannel, and a frayed but clean terry towel.

'Be quick,' Sozan cautioned me as she left the room.

'I'll create a new bathing record,' I called after her.

I removed my clothing as quickly as possible. I poured the warm water over my hair and body — not once but many times, savouring the water as it streamed over me. I poured a small amount of shampoo into my palm and began rubbing it into the roots of my hair, scrubbing with my fingers as hard as possible.

It felt exquisite.

But life can change in only a moment.

Standing there covered in soap suds, I suddenly heard the unmistakable roar of an aeroplane engine, so near that when I placed my hands on the wall I felt it vibrate. But I did not panic. Having lived in Bergalou, and endured many close calls, I simply held my breath, waiting to see what happened. The plane lifted at the last minute without dropping its load.

I exhaled. Perhaps the danger had passed.

Before I had time to rinse off I heard the sound of the plane re-approaching. Soap suds trickled down my face and back, but there was no time for anything but to flee. I blindly clutched at my dress and heaved it over my head. If I was going to die, I would do so with my clothes on.

Just as I moved a leg to run out of the room, I heard the loudest roar of my life, a blast so thunderous that my eardrums buzzed with pain.

I threw back my head and opened my mouth, shrieking.

Explosions began to sound all around. I fell to the floor with my knees bent, protecting my face and head with both arms.

It really was the end. I was going to die.

I was overcome by rage at Sarbast. He did not even say goodbye. I was going to die alone.

I screamed his name, '*Sarbast!*' and as I did so a blast rattled the walls and shook the floor beneath me. In my last clear moment of thought, I remembered the baby and felt enormous sorrow. I felt my body lift into the air. Like a feather in a strong wind, I was flung into the unforgiving concrete wall of the grey bathroom.

Then darkness took me.

21

Bombed in Merge

In the Forbidden Zone, Merge, Kurdistan
Autumn 1987

I was most fortunate to have been bombed. The violence of the attack had thrust me straight into paradise.

Or so I first thought.

Through the tranquil haze of what I believed to be heaven came an unfamiliar voice, drawing my attention. That's when I saw my father.

I watched in bewilderment as his silhouette twisted round until he became clear to me. Then I heard my formerly deaf-mute father speak.

His handsome face strained with worry, he lightly scolded me, 'Joanna. What are you doing here? You should be at home with your mother.' His voice sounded exactly as I had always imagined it, gentle and self-assured. I was breathless. It was a moment I had fantasized about since I was a little girl, when I would whisper, 'Daddy, Daddy, please talk to me.'

As his familiar image began to recede, I heard an echo, a distant voice. Someone was calling my name. 'Joanna! Joanna! Are you alive? Joanna?'

I groaned. I struggled to piece my thoughts together, but my memories were uneven, unable to harmonize. Moving my arms with effort, I patted my head and face with the tips of my fingers and was puzzled to find that my head was slippery. Had I been swimming?

'Joanna?'

I twisted to uncurl my legs.

'Joanna, yell out if you can.'

My confusion mounted. I opened my eyes, shivering, and examined the dark space encircling me. Although the air was murky, I could see well enough to know that I was sprawled on a concrete floor.

Pieces of memory slowly began to fit together. I was in Merge, in Sozan's house. I had been bathing when enemy planes bombed the village.

I lightly stroked my head again, wondering how long I had been unconscious. It felt as if blood was gushing from my head on to my face and neck. I must have sustained serious head injuries. I groaned more loudly than before, fearing the worst, despite the fact I was free of pain.

Sarbast! Where was he?

'Joanna? Where are you?'

Desperate to make my location known, I attempted to call out, but I could only manage to gurgle weakly from the back of my throat. My mouth was blocked. Was my jaw broken?

I delicately explored my mouth with my fingers. It was obstructed with a mass that felt like hardened mud. Panicking, I used my fingertips to dislodge the mass. I had no idea where it had come from, or what it was. I spewed out the chunks I had loosened, gagging and spitting. My gashed tongue and torn lips tasted of blood.

It brought to mind one of my mother's favourite sayings, when she warned me to hold my tongue. 'Joanna, open your eyes, but not your mouth.' I supposed that, as usual, my mouth had been open wide at the wrong time. I managed a wry smile.

'Joanna! Come out! We are under attack!'

I produced a low growl. Why didn't someone come to me? Was I buried alive? Had the roof and walls of the house collapsed on top of me?

'Joanna!'

My mouth finally cleared of obstruction, I gave out a loud scream.

'You are alive! Praise God!'

I had been heard. I imagined the entire village of Merge frantically burrowing through the wreckage, risking their lives in the open air to free me. I would meet my rescuers halfway. I was still naive, even after my time in Bergalou.

Using all the strength I could muster, I pushed upwards with my hands. I could feel nothing penning me in. I began to grope about, trying to find my bearings.

Finding my way out was a challenge. There was debris everywhere. I crawled on hands and knees to the open area between the bathroom and the bedroom. I sat back to take stock, giving myself a few moments to adjust my vision. The house itself was still standing. The supporting concrete walls had withstood the blast.

I trembled with relief. How many times would I beat the odds? While unlucky to undergo such close calls with death, I had been lucky that I had lived to tell the tale.

I patted my head. It was still wet with blood. I remembered striking the concrete wall with my head. I hoped I didn't have concussion.

'Joanna?'

I croaked, 'I am here.'

'Can you come out?'

I tried to pull myself up but could not. My arms were too weak to support my body. My legs were shaking.

'I am here,' I repeated weakly, tears forming in my eyes.

That's when I heard the roar of an aeroplane. Our enemy was still about.

Hearing the promise of further disaster, I flung myself forward, crawling again on hands and knees. Shattered glass slashed the palms of my hands and the flesh of my knees through the fabric of my dress.

I made my way through any opening that I could find until finally I saw my rescuer. It was Karim. I looked about. There was no one with him. I was shocked that he had come alone. Had everyone else been killed?

He extended a helping hand. 'Come, Joanna. Come with me.'

I checked a second time to see if there were other rescuers.

Karim answered my questioning look. 'Everyone is in the shelter. This raid is too dangerous.'

'Oh,' I said, understanding that Karim had taken a huge risk by coming out into the open during the bombing raid to search for me.

He tugged on my hand, pulling me to my feet, asking, 'Can you walk?'

I nodded.

We could hear bombs exploding near by.

Karim quickened his pace. 'Come on. We must get to the shelter.'

He escorted me to the main Merge shelter near by, rather than the tiny earthen shelter next to the house. I was relieved. I had had enough of those narrow dens during my time in Bergalou.

The explosions grew louder just as we slipped into the shelter. We had barely made it.

Sozan called out, 'Praise God, Joanna is alive!'

Karim released my hand and I stumbled towards Sozan. She rushed to meet me, holding my arms and leading me to a small gathering of women and children. She said, 'I knew you were taking a chance in having that bath!'

The women gathered round me. Several shook out towels and began draping them over my head and shoulders, while others started examining my bleeding hands and fingers.

I choked out my fear. 'Am I going to die?'

'*Na!* You will live.'

'But my head?' I gingerly tapped the back of my head.

One woman jumped to her feet, saying, 'Let me see.' She stood over me, removed the towels and tenderly drew my hair left and right, examining my scalp underneath.

I held my breath.

She shrugged. 'You are fine. There are only a few scratches, in fact.'

I perked up. 'Really?'

The woman held my face between her hands. 'Your face is pitted from cement chips. Your lips are scratched raw.' She smiled. 'But you will live.'

A third woman reported, 'Your dress is ripped. Your knees are bleeding.' She looked closer. 'There is glass embedded in your knees.'

I nodded. But my knees would heal. I was most apprehensive about my head injuries. I looked at the first woman. 'But my head.' I cautiously touched the top of my scalp. 'What is the source of all that blood?'

'There is very little blood. You are feeling the shampoo in your hair.'

I drew my hands to my chest, giggling. I had forgotten that I had had no time to rinse. Enormous relief swept over me. But just when I was feeling respite from my worries, my lower belly gave a lurch, as if something had broken loose.

I gasped. Was my unborn child safe? I inhaled deeply, cupping my belly with my hands.

'Do you hurt there?' Sozan asked, her face twisted with worry.

I shook my head, not wanting to share my secret with anyone unless absolutely necessary. Besides, I was not even certain I was pregnant.

Sozan called out for her husband to bring the pail of water kept in the shelter for villagers to use. There were no glasses available so I was encouraged to drink straight from the pail, and I did. It was delicious fresh spring water.

Afterwards two of the women carefully picked the glass pieces from my knees.

Sozan rustled up a couple of blankets and a pillow, announcing, 'This raid is not going to end soon. You should rest.'

I curled up in a corner, and she spread a blanket over my body and gave me dry towels for my head, as there was no place in the shelter to rinse off the shampoo.

I slept through the remainder of the raid. I was finally roused by the sweet sound of Sarbast's voice.

'Joanna, wake up.'

Groggy, I turned my head to find him looking at me.

'Joanna?'

A happy moment! He was alive. 'Sarbast!' I sat up, unaware of the comic figure I was cutting until Sarbast burst into laughter.

'Did you know that you have towels on your head?'

'Sarbast! See what happened! You shouldn't have left me!' I spoke in an angry tone, but in reality I was overwhelmed with joy that he was alive, and that I was alive. We had been given a second chance, once again.

Sarbast was unable to stop laughing. He pulled on the towels still draped over my head and shoulders. 'What is this?'

'I was in the bath,' I retorted.

He leaned down and lifted me up. 'I think you need to finish that bath, darling. You have streaks of soap all over your face.'

'It's not soap. That's from pieces of cement,' I snapped, feeling a return of my earlier irritation that he had left me in the first place. 'Trying to protect me from the trail, you left me in worse danger. Had you not abandoned me, I would have been safe, with you.'

He lightly grasped my arm. 'Come. Let's go back to Karim's house. We'll discuss our plans.'

Tired and sore, and limping because of sharp pains in my knees, I stepped outside, where I looked around. The sunset was especially beautiful, pink with golden streaks, but the sun was setting on a village partially destroyed by our enemy. Nevertheless, we were alive, and at that moment nothing else mattered.

I felt another cramp, again in the lower part of my stomach. If I was indeed pregnant, our unborn child was in grave danger. But there was nothing I could do, for there was no medical care available in Merge other than the most basic first aid. The nearest medical facilities were in Sulaimaniya. It was impossible for me to travel there now. Besides, we had heard that the Iraqi government had ordered execution for anyone seeking medical treatment for injuries caused by chemicals. My eyes would quickly reveal that I was a survivor of Bergalou. They were still red, swollen and sticky with discharge.

But I was desperate to save my unborn child. I would walk slowly. I would sit quietly as much as possible. Perhaps the fetus would settle down. As far as my eyes were concerned, all I could do was administer more eyedrops and hope for the best.

I glanced at Sarbast's face, wondering if I should tell him of the possible pregnancy. One quick glance at his creased face told me that he was occupied with many other troubles. I would not add to his worries.

I had not known it at the time, but when Sarbast had departed without me, if I had hurried I could have caught up with him. Sarbast had warned Sozan of my determined character, so in order to give him and Kamaran ample time to get away, she had stretched the truth when telling me that he had departed hours before. In fact, I later discovered, when I was questioning Sozan he had left the house only moments before. That explained why he had returned to the shelter so quickly. He and Kamaran had been only thirty minutes into the trail when they heard the bombers. They could even see the enemy aeroplanes overhead. Kamaran later told me, 'Sarbast stood as stiff as a man frozen, watching those planes drop bombs on Merge. He called out your name before turning to sprint back, hurdling over large boulders and steep gullies.' Kamaran laughed. 'You are very dear to your husband, Joanna. Never doubt it.'

While Kamaran's words brought me a rush of happiness, I was more determined than ever that we not be parted. But it was not to be. It was too risky for Sarbast and Kamaran to travel by the main roads and they must cut through the forests. I had too many injuries to go with them. With my eyes still impaired, and my knees stiff and sore from cuts, it would be impossible for me to ascend hilly terrain. Because by then I felt certain I was pregnant, I thought it best to rest my body, and I shocked Sarbast when I meekly agreed that he would go one way and I would go another.

Sarbast and Kamaran would meet me in Sandoulan, a four-hour car drive away or a brisk ten- or twelve-hour hike. At the last word, Sandoulan was still held by the PUK, but the settlement was only a few kilometres from government-occupied areas, so it could fall into enemy hands at any time. From there we would work our way to Sangaser, a dangerous place for us, for the town was controlled by our enemies. Yet we had no choice, for we were to join a famous smuggler there who would take us over Kandil mountain. It was to be a very hazardous journey. We would be hunted like animals for the duration of the trip.

Sarbast touched a nerve when he asked if I would consider returning to Baghdad, saying that perhaps I could slip back into the city and avoid what was surely coming, and that he could not bear to see me die.

I stared at him in disbelief, hissing as I shoved against his hard chest with my balled fists. He had his answer. Our fate was bonded. We were one. We would burst out alive on the safe side and rebuild our lives, or we would die together. It was that simple. Whatever our destiny was, we would be together.

While I do not doubt that other wives have loved their husbands as much as I loved my Sarbast, I am certain that none have loved their husbands more.

After Sarbast and Kamaran left Merge for a second time, I finally completed my bath, dressed in fresh clothes and readied my two small bags.

A few hours later Karim, Sozan and their children bade me farewell. Karim was not a *peshmerga,* so they were hopeful that Saddam's men would not target them. I joined a group that was travelling to Sandoulan. Sarbast had arranged my transportation in a car with trusted acquaintances. We did not see any signs of our enemy because the main road from Merge to Sandoulan was still controlled by the PUK.

On the way I gaped from the car window at groups of harried Kurdish refugees hurrying along the road on foot, moving purpose-fully. All the men were armed with Kalashnikovs, the Kurdish weapon of choice, with cartridge belts draped across their chests. Women had babies wrapped to their bodies. Toddlers trailed behind their mothers while older children, apparently bewildered by the upheaval, pulled on cords looped to the necks of cows and donkeys. Chickens and ducks were caged in wooden crates lashed to the sides of donkeys. I felt devastated by their situation. Where would civilians find safety when there was danger all around us?

The drive itself would have been magnificent had it not been for the fact that we were running for our lives. It was late autumn and the frost had not yet touched the foliage of the forest trees. To my eyes the trees looked like mammoth bouquets of green, gold and orange towering over the pale brown of withered grasses. The rolling hills spread out to a distant mountain range. The snow had not arrived but it was cold enough to make me glad the sun was shining, bringing its warmth to the brisk autumn air.

I knew it would be colder still under the canopy of the thick tree cover. I stared hypnotized into those forests, knowing that my Sarbast was on foot somewhere out there.

When we arrived in Sandoulan, a tiny settlement of only a few houses, I was driven directly to a small dwelling where a couple by the name of Abdullah and Minich lived. They too were *peshmerga,* and in charge of an underground human railway of fighters fleeing from the Jafati valley.

I was crushed to learn that Sarbast and Kamaran had not yet arrived, although common sense said it would have been impossible unless they had miraculously sprouted wings.

The couple offering hospitality were undeniably handsome. Abdullah was nearly as good-looking as Sarbast and Minich was a dark exotic beauty. They were fearless, too, seemingly unconcerned that they and their three small children were certain to die hard deaths should their activities be discovered by the *jahsh*. No death was more brutal than that meted to those concealing Jafati PUK fighters.

Because of my injuries, everyone insisted that I rest, but I could not until I knew that Sarbast was safe. The kindly couple settled easily with me under a walnut tree, and we drank sweet tea and ate Kurdish bread and cheese while waiting for the forest travellers. I leaned my head against the trunk of the large tree, intermittently closing and opening my eyes. With every rustle of the autumn leaves I searched the trail.

After several hours muffled voices alerted us that someone was walking up the path and suddenly there they were, pallid from exhaustion yet smiling and waving as though walking for ten hours was a lark and we were embarking on a family holiday rather than another long race for survival.

I was ecstatically happy to see my husband again, but reading his intent face I could see that something was amiss. After saying a quick hello to everyone, Sarbast said that we must leave Sandoulan as soon as possible. He declared that he could sense danger coming. Our enemy was gaining on us, he said, and everyone in Sandoulan was in the gravest danger.

With his words, my hands felt clammy and the hair on my head stiffened. I had been with Sarbast long enough to grasp that he had a true talent for sensing real danger just before it struck. I, for one, did not want to dismiss his intuition.

I pulled myself up. I was ready to leave at a moment's notice. The sooner we started, the better.

After Sarbast and Kamaran had slurped a quick cup of tea, they set off again, eating for the first time in twelve hours as they went. Their aim was to rent a vehicle to transport us over the rocky dirt road to the dangerous *jahsh* town of Sangaser. I couldn't dispel a sinking feeling at the thought of the challenges ahead, but we had no choice but to travel into the midst of the enemy forces who had cleverly planted themselves, like poisonous serpents, around the base of Kandil mountain, the main escape route.

Luckily Sarbast and Kamaran found an available vehicle capable of crossing the rough terrain, and the following morning we bid farewell to the hospitable and courageous Abdullah and Minich. Had I known what lay ahead, I would have pleaded with them to accompany us, for the handsome and affable Abdullah's destiny was bleak. He would soon be killed in a heated battle with our enemy and Minich and their children would be running for their lives.

But we were as yet unaware of the scope of the tragedy about to overtake all of Kurdistan.

Four days after leaving Merge, we reached Sangaser.

Entering Sangaser was relatively simple, for the *jahsh* living there would never believe that any *peshmerga* would be so foolish, reckless or even courageous as to voluntarily enter their armed camp; indeed, most *peshmerga* avoided the town by travelling through the woods. We could not climb Kandil mountain without a guide, which was why we were to join a famous Kurdish smuggler, known as Crazy Hassan for the chances he took, a man celebrated for his daring as well as his knowledge of every footpath criss-crossing Kurdistan.

We drove directly to Hassan's door. The man looked the part, a true mountain man. He was only a few years older than Sarbast, tall, wiry, with bushy hair and a large moustache.

Hassan told us to sit and gave us tea. 'You've come at the worst time,' he solemnly announced. Making a clicking noise with his tongue, he added, 'My brother is a *jahsh*, and he tells me that over a thousand *jahsh* have congregated here, and more are coming.'

With a quick jerk of my head I looked at Sarbast. Our smuggler was the brother of a *jahsh*! Sarbast's face was a mask, revealing nothing. I exchanged a grim glance with Kamaran.

Hassan reported, 'They have their orders. The PUK camps in the Jafati valley are the first priority. Baghdad means to shut down the radio station for ever. The *jahsh* role is to harass and kill retreating fighters. That means you. They will inflict punishment on any civilians who assist the *peshmerga*. That means me. From now on, they will be flushing villagers out of their homes, killing the men and boys, and sending the women and children to the south, to refugee camps. They mean to empty Kurdistan.'

My heart raced.

Sarbast's response was cold and calculating. 'If this is true, we must leave now.'

'It is too dangerous,' Hassan replied.

Sarbast sneered, 'I thought you were a real smuggler.'

Crazy Hassan did look crazy then, crazy with rage at Sarbast's insult.

Sarbast leaned back lazily, as though he didn't have a care in the world, yet I saw his muscular arms tensing.

Any moment now I knew there would be an altercation. Sarbast had always been more daring than most, but he was pushing his luck now, I feared. Both Sarbast and Crazy Hassan were powerful men, but we were in Crazy Hassan's territory. What would keep this man from calling for the *jahsh* to come and capture us?

Crazy Hassan's eyes narrowed. 'I will see.'

'Yes or no,' Sarbast said quietly. 'If you don't have the skills to get us up Kandil mountain, I will find someone else.'

Crazy Hassan took up the challenge. 'I will do it. But you will do what I say.'

Sarbast's eyes were glittering. 'When do we leave?'

'Not today. I will talk to my brother now. He will give me the information I need.'

Sarbast got up. 'We will go with you.'

Kamaran stood beside Sarbast. Both men adjusted their weapons.

Crazy Hassan looked over at me. 'She will stay here, with the women.'

'Yes,' Sarbast agreed. He nodded at me, his eyes conveying a message that I should remain calm.

I was paralysed with fear as I watched the three men march out of the house. Why on earth was Sarbast willingly entering the house of a *jahsh*? Had he gone crazy, too? If he made it back safely, I decided that I would nickname him Crazy Sarbast. I couldn't believe the dangerous turn our journey had taken. Would Sarbast be killed? If so, would I be turned over to our enemies?

Just then Crazy Hassan's wife and several other women collected me from the sitting room, chatting easily as though all our lives were not in the balance. I found the courage to ask Crazy Hassan's wife, 'And your brother-in-law is a *jahsh*? How does that work?'

She appeared to be a coarse-mannered woman with a pitted and prematurely wrinkled face that hinted of many years of hard work, but she proved to be kindly-natured. She laughed at my question. 'Oh, he is not really a *jahsh*. He takes the government's money but he is harmless. He protects his brother, my husband.'

I hoped what she was saying was true, because my husband's fate depended on her husband and his brother.

Her tale was believable, for the history of the *jahsh* was complicated. In the past, most Kurds would die rather than accept one dinar from the Iraqi government to spy on their friends and neighbours. *Jahsh* were so despised that they were known by the derogatory term 'donkey foal'. But some Kurds changed their attitude during the long war with Iran. That war changed the life of all Iraqis, including the Kurds in the north. Every Iraqi man was expected to go to the trenches and defend the Baghdad government. If a Kurd refused to fight, his family members were imprisoned, their homes levelled and young men killed. And then there was the embargo. The government tried to starve the Kurds by launching an austere food embargo. With families starving, a few Kurds began accepting the government stipend, pretending to be informers to avoid having to fight.

Greed became a factor, for the *jahsh* were well paid. There were even bounties placed on the heads of certain *peshmerga*, such as Sarbast, who became famous by writing and broadcasting. With so much money at stake, *jahsh* numbers swelled to several hundred thousand.

We now found ourselves in the thick of *jahsh* territory, uncertain whom we might trust. Nobody, was my guess.

My worst fears were kindled when Crazy Hassan returned without Sarbast and Kamaran. Perhaps he had traded my husband's life for a new car. I became wild with rage, set to claw his eyes from his skull.

Sarbast had obviously predicted my reaction. He soon sprinted in, reassuring me that all was well and saying that it was too dangerous for the three of us to be together at Crazy Hassan's home. I would be safe there with the women, and unnoticed when the *jahsh* started searching homes, which they did nightly. Crazy Hassan's brother's house was less likely to be searched, because he was a known *jahsh*, so Sarbast and Kamaran were going to spend the night there. Sarbast trusted both men, the smuggler and the *jahsh*. I trusted neither.

That night was the longest night of my life.

The following morning Sarbast and Kamaran returned. While Kamaran looked rested, Sarbast appeared gaunt, his eyes hollow and ringed by wide black circles. During a moment of privacy he confessed to me that he had not slept for a moment. While Kamaran slept, Sarbast had sat in the hallway, guarding the house. Nothing had happened, fortunately, but Sarbast was an exhausted man on edge.

Crazy Hassan protested that it was still too dangerous to leave Sangaser, but Sarbast argued against him, until finally Crazy Hassan agreed to make an attempt.

He led the way on his mule, while we followed on foot. But shortly after leaving the town we spotted a roadblock ahead. *Jahsh* were swarming like angry bees all over the area.

We quickly turned round for a second sleepless night.

The following evening we made a second attempt to flee from the town.

We ran into another roadblock and returned once again to Sangaser.

By this time Sarbast was a man crazed. For the first time in my life I began biting my fingernails. Only Kamaran kept his cool.

On the third evening Sarbast confronted Crazy Hassan again, telling him, 'We are leaving tonight, Hassan.'

When Hassan demurred, saying he would wait and see, Sarbast shouted, '*Even if Saddam Hussein himself is standing guard at the roadblock, we are going through!*'

We finally had some luck. On the third attempt to leave Sangaser, we managed to creep past the roadblocks without being noticed while the *jahsh* guards were busy interrogating other unfortunate travellers.

Success was sweet but I could not forget that the journey ahead would be even more treacherous. We knew that the *jahsh* would menace us until we reached the top of Kandil mountain.

As we followed Crazy Hassan and his large grey mule, I gazed into the distance. I could already see the white veil of snow covering the peaks of Kandil mountain. It would be a beautiful sight in any other circumstances, yet I declined to enjoy it for I knew that I had to climb the mountain. My heart gave a lurch. If we did not perish along the way, and lived to find ourselves at the base, how would I ever manage to ascend that towering peak?

God would have to intervene on this one, I decided.

Once again, I soldiered on.

22

Climbing Kandil Mountain

In the Forbidden Zone in Kurdistan near the Iranian Border
late October 1987

Up until that journey, I had given little thought to mules. But after only a few moments of desperate clinging to Crazy Hassan's pack mule, that mule became my entire world. I became acutely aware of its every move, from the positioning of its enormous ears to the placing of its hooves. My only goal in life was to hang on tight, and to avoid tumbling out of the saddle and falling on to the hard ground. My arms clung to the animal's neck and my backside stuck up in the air. It was obviously an incorrect position for a rider, for the mule appeared as uncomfortable with me as I was with him.

I was as terrified as I had ever been.

As soon as we were safely out of town, Sarbast and Crazy Hassan had joined forces to insist that I ride on the mule. I was walking too slowly, they claimed, although I felt confident that I was keeping up. Sarbast gave other reasons for their decision. The journey to the Kandil mountain range would take two or three days of hard walking. My injuries were not yet healed. I would slow us down.

I reacted indignantly. While I had ridden a small donkey on occasion, donkeys are quite low to the ground, and my long legs would very nearly brush the hilly grasses. If I tired of riding I would simply stand up, allowing the donkey to trot off under me. But Crazy

Hassan's mule was a different story. I have always had a fear of heights, and Crazy Hassan's mule was massive, much taller than many horses. Undoubtedly it was considered a magnificent specimen, with its beautiful light grey colouring, broad chest and large expressive ears. Crazy Hassan was very proud of it. I had reason to believe that our guide loved his mule nearly as much as he loved his children. But for me the mule was terrifyingly tall.

I resisted until Sarbast made a desperate plea. 'Please get on the mule, Joanna! There is no time to waste. You are going to get us killed.'

I stared up at the mule. It was already loaded with my two sacks of belongings, hanging like saddlebags on either side. My pink bedding, which had caused disagreements with Sarbast all along the way, was thrown across its back, giving the mule additional height that it did not need.

The three men were watching me. I took several deep breaths, deciding that since my knees were throbbing perhaps I should give mule riding a chance.

'OK, I will try,' I said meekly.

I had no idea how to mount the mule. I circled it warily, looking for a good spot to make my climb. Its eyes opened wide, alert to my every move. The mule obviously believed me unworthy of a ride because when I stepped towards it, he stepped back.

With a harsh sigh Sarbast finally handed his Kalashnikov to Kamaran and, in one quick move, lifted me in his arms and settled me on the mule's back. I remembered Sarbast's sister teasing me about my *peshmerga* trousers and realized that she had been correct: I could accomplish daring feats in them.

Kamaran, who was full of quips, made a joke I did not hear, prompting chuckles from Sarbast. I would have shot both men a filthy look but I was too unnerved to make any sudden moves. Nothing was amusing about sitting on that mule. I was so high above the ground that I felt dizzy.

Gesturing with his hands, Crazy Hassan instructed, 'Rock your weight from side to side. Let the mule get a feel for you.'

I gaped at him. He was certainly crazy if he thought I was going to rock. Instead, I bent low and hugged the mule's neck.

Crazy Hassan wiggled his head in disgust and, with his thick moustache twitching, he lifted one of the reins and gave me the other. Then he led the mule down the trail.

While I hung on awkwardly, the mule plodded on mechanically, surefooted even in the dark, its large graceful ears moving in perfect rhythm with his rolling gait. I decided to privately name it Beauty, for its owner was justifiably proud of his appearance. I soon discovered it was best not to touch Beauty unnecessarily when I accidentally brushed the back of his head with my face and he suddenly stretched his neck out so far that my upper body was stretched along with him, and I nearly fell off. No, Beauty was not happy with his reluctant passenger.

I was barely breathing I was so anxious. But the mule finally relaxed and its pace lengthened.

Sarbast asked, 'How are you, darling?' and I grunted without further explanation. I didn't want to upset Beauty with aimless chatter.

I found the strangeness of mule riding the greatest misery, with every moment exhausting me. Every nerve felt alive, throbbing and tingling, and I expected to be tossed to the ground at any time.

Crazy Hassan was a long-time smuggler for the *peshmerga*. For years he had been in the risky business of supplying the *peshmerga* in the area of Kurdistan Baghdad labelled the Forbidden Zone. He and his mule were experts at supplying the *peshmerga* with medicine, food, weapons and ammunition. Baghdad intended to starve out the *peshmerga*, but smugglers such as Crazy Hassan thwarted that strategy. To decrease the danger, some smugglers even trained teams of mules to cross the mountains unaccompanied from the Iranian villages that were main supply depots for Iraqi Kurdish *peshmerga* to the smuggler, who would be waiting on the Iraqi side of the border to unload the goods. After a rest and feeding, the mules would be sent back to Iran. The situation often turned tragic for the poor mule. If a mule was packed carelessly, and the load shifted while it was on the trail, the mule would lose its footing and tumble to the ground, unable to rise. Unless discovered by a sympathetic traveller, it would lie there until attacked and eaten by wild animals, or until it died from starvation. Kurdistan could be a cruel place, for man or beast.

Crazy Hassan was appalled that any smuggler would risk sending his mules on those solitary runs. 'I would never risk my beauty,' he professed, looking at his mule with such affection that I thought for a moment that he might kiss it on its large loose lips.

I had to admire his courage. The smuggler's life was perilous. None of us could ever forget that the *peshmerga* would not have lasted a month without the help of smugglers.

Within a few hours, a terrifying incident occurred.

Crazy Hassan abruptly halted, and began shouting at the top of his voice. 'This is Crazy Hassan! This is Crazy Hassan! Who is there? I'm crazy! Get away or show yourself! This is Crazy Hassan!'

Sarbast and Kamaran raced to stand beside me. I watched with a sort of horrified fascination as they raised their weapons.

Who was following us? The *jahsh*? Saddam's foot soldiers?

When Beauty's entire body quivered I decided it would be wise to leap off his back before he bolted. But then I looked at the ground and changed my mind. If I were pregnant, such a dive to hard ground so far away would surely cause a miscarriage. Deciding not to risk it, I tucked my head as low as possible, for I knew that Beauty and I were a tempting target.

Hassan continued screeching his threats that he was a crazy man and the intruders would be even crazier to cause us problems. Crazy Hassan was clearly proud of his nickname.

Just then we heard a voice from the night respond. Crazy Hassan obviously recognized it and calmed down. He walked over to where the voice was to sort out any misunderstanding.

When he returned he told us that it was one of a gang of four smugglers who often preyed on travellers in the area. They were opportunists, not murderers. Without Crazy Hassan we would have been robbed. I snorted, thinking how disappointed they would have been had they robbed the three of us. We were the poorest of the poor.

The night seemed to have no end. Perched miserably on the back of the mule, I only half-listened to the men's muted conversations. I fretted about the child I believed I was carrying. A physical mishap might cause new problems. I became so weary that I began to see visions of Baghdad, longing for my old bed, desperate for a real meal. For the first time since I had married I wondered what I was doing in dangerous Kurdistan in the middle of the night, sitting on a mule that did not even like me.

Just when I thought I was going to drop off the mule like a stone, Crazy Hassan called a halt beside a small stream, saying, 'We have passed a danger point. We can rest here for a while and then leave before dawn.'

His words were the sweetest I had ever heard. While Crazy Hassan petted Beauty, whispering sweet nothings, Sarbast helped me to the ground.

It was not a night that encouraged aimless chatter. We gathered in a silent circle to share our simple fare. Crazy Hassan had packed fruit and nuts and Sarbast had bagged some Kurdish bread, which after being baked hardens like a cracker, but when sprinkled with water becomes soft and edible. Kamaran took the bread to the stream and prepared it for us.

I ate very little, and then walked over to the stream to slurp cold water from a small puddle beside it. While I was drinking, Crazy Hassan and Beauty came up beside me to share the puddle. I stared for a startled moment at Beauty's open mouth and large teeth. Then I sighed. Suddenly I was beyond caring. I scooped up another hand-ful and drank greedily.

Sarbast guarded me while I squatted behind a small bush because Crazy Hassan had cautioned that we were in an area frequented by wild animals, mainly wolves and bears. After I told Sarbast that I was worried more about snakes and scorpions than bears, he watched for ground movement. Then he tenderly bundled me in my pink bed-ding, whispering that his brave Baghdad bride had made him proud.

I was too tired to respond, but before I closed my eyes to sleep, I saw that he was sitting guard over me, watching for bears, I assumed. Only in Kurdistan could we have found such a lonely place. I fell asleep with flickering visions of Sarbast wrestling with a wild bear in our little camp.

Hours later a loud noise woke me. Birds were singing and muffled human voices were humming. I sat up in a hurry and warily looked around. I was stunned to see that our campsite was crowded with a mass of humans and a large group of pack mules.

My mouth went dry. I looked at Sarbast in alarm but he was smiling. 'It is all right,' he assured me. 'This is a smugglers' haunt. They all know about this place. It is a popular stopping point for them.'

Although none of the smugglers did anything to cause the slightest concern, I was the only woman in the camp, so I was in a rush to leave. We ate our bread and fruit, and after witnessing several mules slurping from the stream, I postponed quenching my thirst. Water springs were abundant in Kurdistan and shortly after departing we would stumble upon another stream, I thought. I would relieve myself later, as well, I decided, as the bushes in the area were too small for complete privacy.

Sarbast reluctantly agreed that I could walk for a short distance before returning to Beauty's back.

Delay marred the day's journey, as Crazy Hassan constantly gestured for us to stop so he could listen for any unusual noise. We were still in the area controlled by the *jahsh* and government troops, and only he knew exactly where the government checkpoints were located. There were moments when we were not even allowed to whisper for fear we would be heard, and if Hassan had had his way we would have ceased breathing altogether.

It was a miracle that we were not discovered. Crazy Hassan didn't make us feel any better when he shared a few hair-raising tales about previous travellers who had been caught by the *jahsh*. These poor families had been separated, the men taken off to be executed and the women sent to jail to endure horrors that Crazy Hassan refused to describe. However, we were reassured when he bragged that he had never been caught by his enemies; his missions were always success-ful. But we were soon crouching in the grass again after hearing enemy voices through the thicket. Even Beauty sensed the danger. The mule seemed in perfect harmony with its owner, stepping softly whenever Crazy Hassan became fixated on noises around us. Beauty gave every indication of being a very intelligent mule.

Soon there was reason to feel sorry for Beauty. Obviously he had eaten something that had created terrific intestinal problems. Sarbast was conferring with Crazy Hassan, and Kamaran and I were speak-ing quietly, when we were startled by the explosive passing of mule gas. I blinked, silenced by the sound and the smell, and too embarrassed to acknowledge what I had heard. But Kamaran, who was born a prankster, could not resist making a few jokes. We fell further behind Beauty, keeping a safe distance, for he continued to expel gas loudly. The situation worsened. With each step Beauty made, more gas blasted, the explosive sounds becoming louder and longer. Unable to restrain himself, Kamaran began imitating the mule by making revolting noises with his mouth.

Although at first I did not find Beauty's misery funny, Kamaran was making the most of our joyless situation by finding something to laugh about. He carried on until I was infected by his mirth.

Hearing our peals of laughter, Crazy Hassan took offence. He walked back to us, scowling. 'Are you mocking my mule?'

Crazy Hassan's reaction fired Kamaran's enthusiasm. His forehead wrinkled and his bright eyes glittered as he laughed boisterously. Unable to restrain my merriment, I cupped my hands over my mouth.

Sarbast was displeased as well. His face grim, he sternly ordered, 'Stop it. This is not a game.'

With the greatest effort, Kamaran and I restrained ourselves.

That poor mule found no relief. Because of his predicament, I convinced Sarbast that I should walk for a few hours more, until finally he and Crazy Hassan ruled that my walking pace was holding us up and that I must ride again.

And so I did. In fact, I was beginning to feel some affection for Beauty, admiring his tirelessness in twisting in and out along the trail. I began to feel relaxed enough to look around me at the land-scape. I was soon hypnotized by the sight of the magnificent Kandil mountain range slowly coming into full view.

While the daytime journey was not as frightening as the night-time experience, there were still many reasons for discomfort. The sun was surprisingly strong for the time of year. Then I reminded myself of our high altitude and realized that the sun would remain intense from that point on. The rays were so dazzling that I bent my head to my chest to guard my eyes from the glow. I was thankful that the snows had not yet come, however. Snowstorms would have added extra danger to an already perilous journey.

Our travel routine was simple. We moved forward. We stopped and listened. We moved forward again. We halted to listen. Only rarely did we stop for a rest. Our biggest concern was that checkpoint locations had changed since Crazy Hassan's last trip through the area. A number of times we could actually hear the voices of our enemies through the thick foliage. Those moments were the worst of all. If discovered, we would be executed. We would almost certainly be tortured prior to execution.

On one such stop, while Crazy Hassan was energetically working a large toothpick in his mouth even as his eyes swept the landscape, searching for danger, Sarbast pledged that he would not allow us to be taken. 'Better to die in a gun battle than in the armpit of your enemy,' he swore. He looked into my face. 'Do not worry. I will kill you myself, rather than see enemy hands on you.'

I was unsure whether to be relieved or terrified. Certainly, I knew that my husband possessed an iron core. If it was necessary, he would find the strength to honour his pledge, even if it meant looking into my eyes for a final farewell while pumping a bullet into my brain. I shivered at the prospect. I knew that if such a tragic moment was our destiny, Sarbast's sorrow would be more agonizing than my own.

Only Kamaran seemed relaxed in the face of threats, amazing me with his ready smile and quick wit. Of our group, I decided, he would be the greatest loss. He was young and unmarried and had not yet experienced the love of a woman.

Perched high on the mule, on a journey that did not encourage pointless prattle, I decided I would take responsibility for watching the horizon for any sign of our enemy. Thankfully, I saw none. But the countryside was increasingly interesting. Scrub grass was everywhere but the land was growing ever more hilly, a promise of what was coming. My stomach lurched and I became sombre, aware that I was nearing the biggest challenge of my life. Even Beauty sensed the gravity of the situation, becoming even more strained and tense. The famous Kandil mountain range loomed higher and larger until finally we arrived at its base.

I was awed into silence, staring upwards until my neck muscles began to throb. I could not even see the top. Sunbeams were dancing on the polished rock. I had anticipated climbing a mountain covered with trees with dirt paths winding like ribbons to the top. But Kandil was not the mountain of my dreams. Dread settled in my stomach as I realized that I was expected to scale bare granite. I could not believe that Sarbast truly believed me capable of climbing it.

And how would a mule find its footing on that glossy rock? Were we going to leave Beauty behind? Surely not, for Crazy Hassan openly loved his mule. And Beauty was carrying our goods, as well.

For the first time since we had started the trip, even Kamaran was silent.

That was when Sarbast gave me the worst news. 'You will not be walking, darling. You will be on the mule for the entire ascent.'

Mouth open, I stared at him. He was asking the impossible of me.

The next news was even more grim. Crazy Hassan announced, 'It is too dangerous to start the climb now. We will be spotted from below, tempting enemy fire. We will wait over there' – he pointed at a bushy area – 'until dusk.'

I looked once more at Sarbast. So he planned for me to sit on a mule and trust that mule to climb the steepest mountain in Kurdistan, in the dark of night? He had lost all good sense.

While we waited for the sun to go down, I sat rigid, staring at the mountain. From what I could see, Kandil had steep cliffs and drops of thousands of feet. As I sat high on the mule I would be flanked on one side by serrated rock and on the other by ravines so deep that if Beauty suffered one tiny misstep, we would both plunge off the mountain to certain death.

I had never been more miserable. For the first time in my life, I had been presented with a test that I couldn't hope to pass.

Sarbast attempted to cheer me. He sat by my side, encouraging me to eat the last of our fruit, patting my hands and even stroking my shoulder, a sign of intimacy rarely shown in public in our Kurdish world. He was leading up to something ominous, I felt certain.

Finally he said in an offhand way, 'The mule can climb that mountain blindfolded.'

I gasped loudly. So now I knew. That was how they coaxed mules over such high mountains. That was how they kept fidgety mules from leaping off mountains. I jerked my hand back from Sarbast, my words coming in a rush. 'No! It is settled then: I will go back to Baghdad.'

'What are you talking about, Joanna? There is no going back to Baghdad from here. Tehran, perhaps, but not Baghdad,' he added with a chuckle.

I glared at him. 'Listen to me, Sarbast. I am not going to sit on a blindfolded mule who is being coaxed over a mountain over ten thousand feet high!'

Sarbast's expression was baffled for a moment. Then a tentative smile twitched, and slowly he began to laugh. Once he had started, he could not stop, laughing with such intensity that tears began to roll down his face.

Well, I thought, Sarbast has finally gone mad. I had been expecting it. No man could live under the extreme stress Kurdish fighters endured, day after day, year after year, without paying a mental price.

At that moment Kamaran popped out of the bushes to find out the cause of the merriment. Even Crazy Hassan and Beauty looked our way with interest.

Sarbast wiggled his head back and forth, still laughing. 'Oh, Joanna, that is funny.' He laughed again. 'That is really funny.'

I was shaking with anger, suddenly realizing that I had misunderstood. He had not been speaking literally. The mule would not be blindfolded.

Of course, Sarbast made merry over my confusion. Crazy Hassan thought it a good joke that I had even considered the possibility he would blindfold Beauty for a dangerous mountain climb. On the contrary, he said, 'My mule is so intelligent that sometimes I let him select the best route.'

The news that our path might be selected by the mule failed to reassure me. Yet the prospect of crossing the mountain on Beauty's back was suddenly less frightening. I had discovered that any situation could be even worse.

Our little caravan was soon on the move again. By now the sun had dipped below the horizon, but a glow of pink light remained. My nervousness returned when Crazy Hassan walked ahead to coax Beauty to start the climb. My weight shifted as the mule's head, neck, shoulders and barrel rose higher than his rump.

Detecting my gathering alarm, Crazy Hassan warned me, 'Sit lightly. If a mule feels that the weight is shifting incorrectly, or if the load is too heavy, it will leap off the mountain.'

I'm certain I looked like a wild woman. 'Sarbast! Overloaded mules will fling themselves off mountains. Here,' and I nudged one of the two bags with my knee, 'take this bag,' I pleaded. 'Kamaran, take the second bag.'

I overheard my husband and his cousin chuckling. At that moment I wanted to slap both their faces.

It was then that I knew my fate depended on the good graces of

Beauty, the mule. Regrets haunted me. How I wished I had fed Beauty my fruit, and petted his nose and kissed him. I should have cupped water in my palms for him to drink. But I had missed my opportunity to bond with Beauty.

That was the beginning of a nightmarish night. As Beauty's hooves clattered on the granite, his neck and shoulders strained and his veins popped. Perspiration broke out all over his body. I trembled in fear when I heard pieces of rock break off under Beauty's hooves and, gathering small stones, crash down the mountain. For the first time I understood the wisdom of the PUK in choosing the Kandil mountain range for their new hideaway. No regular army could fight its way up to the top of such a mountain. The new radio station would certainly be safe.

Within an hour of starting the climb, Hassan, ever alert, sensed we were being watched. He quickly guided us to some wide crevices between the rocks that offered protection, gesturing that we must hide. He subsequently returned with the news that there were enemy soldiers lingering at a new checkpoint almost directly below us, and that they had a clear sight line to our position. He must find another route. He left to explore.

We waited for an interminable time. I was too edgy to rest, but Sarbast and Kamaran, being true warriors, used the time to grab a few moments of sleep. My vision was not yet perfect, but improving, and it was helped by a slight light from the moon. My eyes were drawn to the outline of my husband. I speculated on the times he had spent in similar situations, hiding from his enemy. All the while I had been back in Baghdad, I had been unaware of the reality of the *peshmerga* life. I had always thought of the fighter's life as one of constant action and adventure, not realizing that the truth was much less exciting. For every moment of action, there were many more moments of endless delay, which fighters spent trapped out in the open, tormented by hunger.

Determined not to be the weak link that I knew the men considered me to be, I vowed that I would be as strong and brave as the other *peshmerga* women I had met, and that I would not cause further problems for Sarbast.

Finally Crazy Hassan returned, gesturing for us to follow him.

Adrenalin was high as we inched up to yet another mountain

passage. After an hour of climbing, Crazy Hassan seemed satisfied that we had escaped the eyes of our enemy, focused on the mountain face.

The evening was a series of close calls. When we were not seeking refuge from prying eyes, we were climbing on rock crags so narrow that I could not bring myself to look down. For some bizarre reason Beauty was more comfortable walking on the very edge of a precipice. Even if there was ample space for him to hug the mountain wall, he seemed to take perverse pleasure in living life literally on the edge. Once or twice the mule overstepped, teetering inches away from plunging over the cliff. Each time Crazy Hassan managed at the last minute to pull him back. The continuous plunging and straining as we manoeuvred along narrow paths made me rigid, locking up my muscles and causing my entire body to throb.

After four hours of terror, Crazy Hassan said we would stop for six hours. Beauty, he said, had reached his limit.

Sarbast lifted my trembling body off the mule and I stood flexing my legs and arms, every muscle coiled with tension. I couldn't believe that I had survived.

When Sarbast mentioned that we had not yet reached the most difficult part of the climb, my heart sank. I stared at him in disbelief.

We ate a snack while Crazy Hassan fed, watered and wiped down the sweaty Beauty. After eating, we silently arranged our sleeping quarters. It was cold on the mountain, but we spread all our clothes over us. I was lucky to have my pink bedding as well. But I could not relax on that stony ground. And, despite my exhaustion, I was unable to sleep. When I looked around, I saw that both Kamaran and Sarbast were draped easily on the hard rock surface. Even in the cold mountain air, they were sleeping with complete abandon, as contented as lizards in the sun.

Crazy Hassan took the first watch; Sarbast took the next, then Kamaran. I offered to take a turn as well, but Sarbast refused, saying that I was using all my energy just getting up the mountain, and that was the most important thing of all.

Despite the dangers, it was beautiful at the high altitude. The dark of night was slightly lit by a crescent moon and twinkling stars that appeared so close that I felt I might pick one out of the sky. Staring reflectively up at the heavens, I placed my hands on my belly, feeling secure in the knowledge that my child was anchored safely inside me and resting. For the first time I enjoyed fully the idea that I might be pregnant. As soon as we were out of danger, I would tell Sarbast. I imagined the unrestrained joy he would feel, and how he would twirl me round with happiness. Later we would cuddle and plan our child's future together.

'Child of my heart,' I whispered. I hoped our baby would look just like Sarbast, even if a girl.

Thinking about how I so desperately wanted my child, for the first time in my life I allowed myself to wonder how my mother could have ever considered harming me when I was in her womb. I would have sacrificed my own life to protect my unborn child.

I fell asleep staring at the stars, sleeping splendidly, enjoying a full five hours of unbroken sleep. When Sarbast woke me the following morning, the sky was pale with the fleeting dawn.

I was filled with anticipation. In only a few hours we would reach our destination of Dohlakoga, the site of the new radio station. We were all eager to get the final dangerous leg of the journey behind us.

Our day was filled with challenges. I experienced moments of sheer terror combined with grim satisfaction. The path deteriorated, the trail becoming so narrow that there was barely space for Beauty to walk. He appeared to be struggling, wincing with hooves tender from the sharp ridges of the mountain rock. I was faring little better. Once when I accidentally glanced down I saw trees and bushes so far below that they appeared no larger than matchsticks, and I swayed dangerously. It didn't help the situation when the morning sun became a torment, hammering against my head and face. The journey must end, I thought. Another hour will break me.

Enduring the glare of the blazing rays, I stared upwards to see that we could not climb much further. The massive rock was running out. My excitement escalated. For the first time, victory over the mountain seemed possible. I then glanced below, into the distance. Our enemy was down there, owning only the ground where they stood. They would never conquer Kurdistan. Never! We Kurds were too focused on victory, willing to sacrifice everything for freedom.

A short distance from the very top of the mountain, we arrived at a wide plateau. We were at Dohlakoga. We had arrived. With Beauty's last step I felt as if I had been presented with a priceless gift.

Sarbast lifted me from Beauty's back one final time. I stroked Beauty's forehead, knowing that I owed the mule my life. Beauty opened his lips, showed his teeth and brayed, 'Whinee . . . aw . . . ah . . . aw.' I laughed with pleasure, petting Beauty a second time.

I looked around the plateau. We were not alone. Forty or fifty fighters were there to greet us, including two women, one of them Ashti from Bergalou. I was delighted to see little Hema, with his full cheeks and his cute budding mouth. He appeared to be thriving, despite the harsh environment, and had not suffered any long-term ill effects from the poisonous gases. Ashti's husband Rebwar was the radio station engineer, so he was most important for the success of the new radio station.

There were few buildings at Dohlakoga, and they were not built in any particular order. Most of the fighters were living in tents, although more permanent construction was ongoing. Simple dwellings were rising up, including a bomb shelter, simple one-room homes, and even a communal bath and toilet, which sounded good to me. I was in desperate need of a bath, but would have to wash from a basin for the time being.

Taking off my soiled clothes, I gratefully washed, my skin refreshed by the feel of cool water. Just at the moment when I believed that our worst troubles were behind us, pain flared in my belly like a burning fire.

That was when I lost my already much loved baby.

I cried bitterly.

23

Searching for Auntie Aisha

Saqqez, Iran
Summer 1988

Saddam's army was on the move, bringing death from the south to the north, its soldiers bearing bullets, its airmen dropping gas canisters. The only question remaining for most Kurds was: when would we be struck by a bullet or inhale poisonous gas? I no longer expected to survive. How could I be hopeful of life when so many others were dead or dying?

Since we had fled from Bergalou, Kurdistan had erupted in chaos as Saddam's troops swept in. The mountains and valleys swarmed with Kurds literally running for their lives. The threat escalated when Ali Al-Majid unleashed his chemical weapons not only against the *peshmerga* but against all Kurdistan, including the civilian population. Thousands of terrified Kurds perished during the gas onslaught. I had believed us unlucky to be making our journey at a time of high tension between Baghdad and Kurdistan. But I was wrong. We were lucky to be among the first Kurds climbing Kandil. The real rush was then yet to come. As the situation deteriorated into crisis and a virtual Kurdish holocaust, Kurds were forced from their homeland and fled on foot. Thousands of men, women and children perished on Kandil mountain. Mothers and fathers were driven to such panic that they lost babies and left toddlers behind to die alone on mountain passes.

We Kurds believed that once the rest of the world learned of the chemical attacks, civilized people would demand that the Baathists cease their barbaric actions. To our surprise, no one seemed to notice. The world's disinterest made the Baathists even bolder, so they began using chemical weapons in an even more brutal manner.

And so the Kurdish genocide gained momentum.

Sarbast and I had not had a home since we had fled from Bergalou. When we reached Dohlakoga it became obvious that it would be impractical for us to spend the coming winter months there. The radio station was not yet operational and therefore Sarbast's skills as a writer and radio broadcaster were not yet needed. Housing was scarce. As winter approached, many fighters were still living in tents. There were three *peshmerga* wives in Dohlakoga, but no special exceptions were made for women. Sarbast and I lived in a small shed used to store tools. But winter would bring heavy snows, and flimsy buildings would not offer protection from high-altitude winter storms.

As we had witnessed, Dohlakoga was challenging to reach even when the weather was perfect. During the harshest winter months travel would become impossible. Snowdrifts were often twenty or thirty feet deep, making delivery of supplies extremely difficult. These circumstances meant that the number of fighters must be trimmed to the minimum during the winter months. All unnecessary fighters were asked to leave.

Our trek to Dohlakoga had been so dangerous that we were keenly disappointed. But once our frustration ebbed, we felt a flicker of relief. Dohlakoga was a harsh environment for someone with ailing health. My eyes, although much improved, remained trouble-some. There were many days when my vision inexplicably blurred. Although the cuts and bruises I had suffered during the Merge bombing had completely healed, I was experiencing various problems arising from the loss of my unborn child. I needed medical attention.

Sarbast and I must leave and travel on to Iran, at least temporarily. Kamaran was told to remain in Dohlakoga. The three of us had become a team, so the split was painful. But Sarbast and I stoically said our goodbyes and prepared for the difficult journey down the mountain. Crazy Hassan and Beauty had left Dohlakoga shortly after we arrived, so we had to hire another mule for the trip.

The trip down the mountain proved easier than the trip up. Most helpfully, there were no enemy soldiers looking to shoot at us on the Iranian side of the mountain. Despite the more favourable conditions, however, I was within mere inches of falling from a cliff several times. Thankfully, we survived our downward trek.

Our destination, the Iranian border town of Al-Wattan, was only seven or eight hours' travel from Dohlakoga. We hoped to find temporary housing there until Sarbast received orders for his next assignment.

I was looking forward to having a rest there but my heart skipped a few beats when Al-Wattan came into view. 'It's very remote,' I said. 'And it looks as primitive as Dohlakoga.' Everywhere I looked I saw crude dwellings and poorly dressed residents. 'It's cold here, too.' I took a deep breath. 'I hate the cold.'

Sarbast grew impatient with my complaints. 'Of course it is cold, Joanna. We are still very high up.' He looked at me reproachfully. 'Be thankful you won't be living in a tent.'

He had a point. We were fortunate in that regard. As *peshmerga*, Sarbast and I would be allowed the privilege of settling in an ordinary Iranian village, unlike the Kurdish civilians fleeing the chemical attacks who were kept confined in refugee camps. We had heard that the camps were bleak and the refugees living in them unbearably miserable. With the proper documents, which Sarbast had obtained, we were free to come and go across the border as we pleased.

When we arrived in Al-Wattan, I was struck by the number of Iraqi Kurdish *peshmerga* already in the village. It was an ill omen. We soon learned that all rooms were taken. We were told, 'The town is full of Iraqis.'

After following rental leads for the remainder of the day, we still had nowhere to stay. I grew tense, knowing that even though it was still summer, the nights at high altitudes were very cold. When the light began to fade, a desperate Sarbast began to approach strangers on the street.

A tent was beginning to sound desirable.

Every villager turned us away. We had very little money, for *peshmerga* were poorly paid. The only gold we owned was the wedding bands on our fingers, and we were determined not to barter those.

Soon I began to feel weak. I became quite ill, limply hanging on to the mule.

Finally an Iranian man took pity on me.

He told Sarbast, 'My rooms are all rented.' But, with a quick glance at me, he offered, 'I do have a stable. You are welcome to sleep with my animals.'

Sarbast shocked him by accepting. 'Yes, that will do, temporarily.'

The man's words were like music to our ears. We were so exhausted that sleeping in his stable with the animals sounded like a grand idea. We meekly followed him home.

Ravenously hungry, I had visions of a hot meal. I was naive. Despite the fact that we were *peshmerga* and we had been fighting with the Iranians against Saddam, the eight-year war had festered in the hearts of the Iranians, for the war had proved a bloodbath for their men, and the reception the man's family gave us was as frigid as the mountain snow.

Thankfully I had thought to stuff a few pieces of bread and a chunk of cheese into the wide pockets of my *peshmerga* trousers before leaving Dohlakoga. At least we had something to eat before sleeping.

The stable was a small room attached to the house. The moment we stepped into it, the door to the cosy house was firmly closed. Sarbast and I stared at each other, and then at our sleeping quarters. We saw a very tight space between the stable entrance and the house. The floor was dusty earth. Mercifully, there was a knee-high barrier containing the farm animals within their designated area.

There were mules, cows, chickens, ducks and rabbits. We were serenaded throughout the night by a chorus of animal noises. The sounds and odours of large animals passing urine were nauseating. The room was infested with fleas, and during the night I felt them scampering about in my hair.

The misery of it all!

Sarbast and I cohabited with the farm animals for a week.

Throughout it all, Sarbast was an angel, maintaining a positive attitude and constantly saying that our situation could be worse. 'Joanna, we could be in the refugee camps.' I knew he was right, and that our living conditions could be even more ghastly. Other *peshmerga* had verified our earlier information: the refugee camps were horror camps.

I understood the Iranian government's position. Iran was still embroiled in a lengthy and bitter war with Iraq. It was understandably wary of the flood of Kurdish refugees from Iraq and suspicious that spies were mixed with those seeking refuge. Iraqi Kurdish refugees had been rebellious in their own country. Once settled in Iran, would they link up with Iran's own defiant Kurdish minority? Quite simply, the Iranian government did not know what to do with the Iraqi Kurds, so it shut them away in refugee camps, hoping for a military victory over Saddam so that they could be sent back to Iraq.

On that point our wishes were the same.

I would also never forget that although the refugee camps were deplorable, at least the Iranians were not intent on eliminating the Iraqi Kurds. In truth, the Iranian government was more humane to Iraqi Kurds than was our own government from Baghdad.

Sarbast and I continued our search for a room. With the rising of the morning sun we would hose off with cold water, trying to discourage the fleas, and then leave our dreadful quarters to walk about in the village, meeting up with various *peshmerga* acquaintances.

After seven days we met a *peshmerga* friend who invited us to move into a house he had rented for his wife and two small children.

I was in heaven! Despite the fact that there was no electricity, no running water and no toilets. Residents walked up the mountainside to use the springs as a toilet, which was inconvenient and unsanitary. Sarbast solved the situation for us when he and his *peshmerga* friend bought water hoses, connected them to a nearby spring, and rigged up a welcome water supply for the household.

Six months later Sarbast received orders from PUK officials to travel further into Iran, to a larger village named Saqqez. The PUK had gained permission to erect a new radio station there. Wishing to avoid a second winter in Al-Wattan, we were delighted.

Upon arriving in Saqqez, once again we found it impossible to find suitable living quarters. Our luck changed when another *peshmerga* alerted us to a vacancy in a home owned by an Iranian woman by the name of Shamsa. She was reserved when agreeing to the deal, coldly examining the two of us with her wide-set brown eyes. Her attitude expressed distrust of Iraqis, even Kurdish Iraqis. But Sarbast and I were very grateful for our little room in a decent home, and we took every opportunity to show our appreciation and to be good tenants.

After a few weeks Shamsa became less formal. She even advised me, 'You should return home to your mother, child. You are too young and innocent to live the life of a *peshmerga*.'

My heart fluttered with hope. Perhaps in time Shamsa and I could become friends, in spite of the suspicion that Iranians and Iraqis felt for each other.

But it seemed that it was not my destiny to anchor in any one place. Sarbast received orders to leave Saqqez to travel to a mountainous area near Halabja, south-east of Bergalou and Sulaimaniya. Once more the Iranian government and the PUK *peshmerga* had liberated the area from Saddam's army, and the PUK planned to set up another radio station there.

Sarbast was fiercely opposed to my going back into Kurdistan with him, but I refused to stay behind. 'I'm going with you,' I vowed.

For our last three months in Al-Wattan, Sarbast had been forced to leave me behind while he travelled back and forth across the border to join raids attacking Saddam's forces. During his absences I was frantic with worry, certain that each farewell was our last, for *peshmerga* were dying in large numbers. For me, the only advantage of the obligatory physical rest was the restoration of my health. Even my injured eyes had finally healed. For long months I had feared that my eyes were permanently damaged and that perhaps I would lose my vision altogether. To my relief, over time my eyes returned to normal. I felt incredibly lucky.

Before we left Iran, we had an important task to accomplish. While in Al-Wattan I had managed to contact my family, telling them that we were still alive, although exiled in Iran. During that call I learned that Auntie Aisha was missing: she had been out of touch since the chemical attack on Halabja on 16 March 1988. Her son Sabah and his three sisters feared that their mother had died during the attack. I convinced myself that she had taken refuge in Iran, in one of the many refugee camps. Sarbast and I decided to search for her.

There was one particular refugee camp in the border area that seemed most likely to be where she was because it specifically housed refugees from Halabja. I only hoped that Auntie Aisha was one of those displaced. If so, we would take her back to Sulaimaniya to be with her children.

Soon we were on our way there.

I could smell the refugee camp long before I could see it. I stared in the direction of the stench until I saw a soft cloud of dust tinting the skyline. As we drew closer, a gigantic city of white tents slowly appeared on the horizon. Mesmerized by the repetitive tent tops, I paid little heed to where I placed my feet, stumbling over rocks hidden by tufts of grass.

After I had stumbled two or three times, a concerned Sarbast asked, 'Are your eyes bothering you?'

'No. No.' All I could think about was our mission to find Auntie Aisha.

Sarbast gently held my elbow, guiding me through the field.

As we drew near, I spotted a meandering line of colour in the midst of the white, a bewildering sight until I identified it as colourfully dressed Kurdish women. I assumed that the women were queuing for bread or water.

I shivered, even in the heat of a summer day, remembering what Halabja had once been. Now its citizens were living in tents. Before the attack, Halabja had been a busy town of approximately fifty thousand Kurds. Situated only a few kilometres from the Iranian border, the bustling town was a magnet for trade, and the location of a shrine to Al-Sheikh Ali Ababaili, a revered Muslim sheikh who was buried there. That shrine was the reason Auntie Aisha had moved from Sulaimaniya to Halabja in the first place. Always a pious Muslim, after raising her children she drew even nearer to her faith and expressed a desire to live close to the shrine as she aged. She bought a small house in Halabja and spent many pleasurable days joyfully worshipping at the shrine.

The chemical strike on Halabja had become well known because the Iranian government had had the foresight to transport photographers to the scene to authenticate the death and destruction. They and foreign journalists documented the deaths of five thousand innocent men, women and children. Numerous other victims died over the coming days.

I only hoped that Auntie Aisha was not suffering from painful injuries. She was of an age when it would be more difficult to overcome poor health. A strong sense of resolve flashed through me: I must find her. She was nearly as dear to me as my own mother. She had never failed us when we were in need, whether at the time of the unexpected death of my father or during one of our many financial crises.

I had another very important reason to find her. I had never shared with anyone, not even Sarbast, her mysterious spiritual appearance to me during the Bergalou chemical attack. I had been moments from death when her appearance inspired me to live. I had a strong desire to describe that puzzling scene to Auntie Aisha, to ask her if she had been at prayer during that time or if I had been on her mind.

I briefly closed my eyes and muttered a prayer, asking that when I opened my eyes Auntie Aisha would appear from inside that refugee camp and grasp me in a heartfelt hug.

I opened my eyes expectantly. Sadly, my prayer had not been answered.

'We will find her,' I said to Sarbast with an emotional catch in my voice.

The camp confining the Halabja refugees was the most populous refugee camp on the border, since Halabja had been the largest of the Kurdish cities emptied by the chemical attacks.

There was a reason the Iraqi government had targeted Halabja. Prior to the attacks, the PUK and Iranian forces had liberated Halabja from Saddam's forces. This had reportedly caused Saddam to fly into a rage. He ordered the Iraqi army to use all measures to retake the town, regardless of loss of life.

When the Iraqi army attacked Halabja, the town's population of fifty thousand people had swelled to seventy thousand from the influx of refugees from neighbouring villages which were also under attack. Our enemies first pounded Halabja with mortars and rockets. Then on 16 March Halabja was bombarded with a cocktail of mustard gas, sarin and tabun. Many residents remained in their shelters, wrongly believing that they were in the safest place. Because toxic chemicals concentrate at lowest levels, entire families died in low-lying shelters. Those who caught a whiff of the chemicals and realized the horrifying truth of the weapons being used against them ran outside to escape. But without gas masks, there was no time for many to reach high ground before succumbing to the poisonous gas. Many of those exposed suffered a host of painful symptoms before dying on the streets. Witnesses reported seeing victims dying while hysterically laughing or vomiting green bile until they died.

During and after the attack, Halabja emptied.

Was the bustling city of Halabja I remembered from my youth now a ghost town? We would soon know, because Sarbast and I had plans to travel to the area. A lump of dread gathered in my throat. What might we discover there? But for now, I put my mind to the problem at hand: finding Auntie Aisha.

After Sarbast had presented our identity papers to an unsmiling Iranian revolutionary guard, we were allowed entry into the heavily guarded and fenced camp.

Silently, we walked side by side into the enormous refugee camp. I saw members of the Iranian Red Crescent, in charge of distributing food rations.

With its flapping flimsy tents and garbage strewn everywhere, the camp was dismal. Displaced Kurds were standing or sitting all around us, staring at us with curiosity. After taking a few steps, we hesitated, pondering where we should begin our search. Forked pathways were packed with clusters of people. We had heard that during the past six months over a hundred thousand Kurds had sought refuge in Iran. From the looks of that crowded camp, I believed that most of them were staring directly at me.

How would we ever find Auntie Aisha in that mass of humanity?

'Which way?' I asked my husband, raising my hands palms up at the enormity of it all.

Sarbast lifted his shoulders in a shrug. 'What difference will it make which path we take?'

I sighed deeply. The large number of refugees was disorientating. 'Maybe you will see someone you know and they will help us,' I said hopefully. Other than the few years Sarbast had spent at university in Baghdad, he had lived his entire life in Kurdistan. During his years of being a PUK *peshmerga*, he had travelled the entire region, often staying in Kurdish villages for a meal or for a night's rest. Perhaps he would recognize one of the refugees.

'I will search the faces on the left and you search the faces on the right,' I finally proposed.

When Sarbast did not respond, I glanced at him. His face had grown pale. To hear descriptions of the refugee camps was depressing, but to see the catastrophe with one's own eyes was the most painful thing possible. I understood his horror. My husband had sacrificed his entire adult life for freedom for the Kurds, forgoing a career and postponing marriage and children. At the age of thirty, when most men have settled in a career, he was a poor man, without a home and without a job, each meal possibly his last. The tent city represented total failure of all his efforts and those of the other *peshmerga* and the PUK.

Our despair deepened when we heard the saddest sound of all, the haunting cries of ill babies. Remembering my own recent loss, and convinced that the combination of the chemical attack, the bombing and the climb up Kandil had cost me my precious child, I felt full of sorrow. It was at that moment that I realized we Kurds had lost everything. All our hopes and dreams were smashed.

Nothing would ever be the same.

A terrible new world had replaced our familiar world. Kurds accustomed to living in the scenic beauty of bountiful valleys and mountains, tilling their fields, tending their thriving livestock and raising their sons to inherit the land, had lost it all. Their dreams dissipated along with the brown puffs of smoke unleashed by the chemicals. Kurds were now scattering all over the earth, forced to adjust to new lives inferior to those they had known before.

It was the bitterest loss.

Sarbast and I walked on, cautiously, in silence. As we moved about in the camp, the ring of my sorrow widened with the refugees pressing in all around me. Each refugee was trapped in a crowd, yet seemed very much alone. The forlorn faces of the camp children drew me like a magnet, their sad eyes reminding me of flickering candles, half-burned out, their little shoulders hunched down into their chests.

One small boy only four or five years of age wandered aimlessly past me, unaware of the world around him, his dreadfully blistered face tucked low. What horror had that child lived through? What tragedy had befallen his community, his family? I trembled for his lost life, imagining that one moment he had been a child at play and the next he was running behind his parents, screaming in agony at the invisible fire falling upon his face. Where were his parents? Had he been left a lonely orphan?

My hands bunched into fists. I want answers, God! What will happen to the children?

Everywhere I looked I saw children of sorrow. I closed my eyes, wanting to escape those haunted stares, longing for the power to lift the children up and whisk them out of the camp. But I could do nothing. I didn't even have the money to buy them sweets.

My thoughts were interrupted by exclamations of welcome from a group of refugees sprawled around one of the many tents.

'Come, come!'

'Sit! Sit!'

Sarbast gave me a perceptive look. We must accept their hospitality.

We entered the refugees' circle, sitting cross-legged on the ground to talk. A crowd began to form and raised voices were eager to know what we were doing there, impatient to learn the latest news from outside. They wanted the violence to end so that they could go home.

Sarbast and I exchanged another meaningful look. I read my husband's mind. We were not to tell these poor people the bitter truth: that their homes no longer existed. Sarbast and I had recently learned that as the Iraqi army emptied the towns and villages of Kurds, it had become common procedure for crews of army engineers to blow up all buildings. Bulldozers followed to level the rubble. Flourishing communities of Kurdish homes, businesses, schools and mosques had been turned into piles of concrete. Wells were poisoned. Livestock were exterminated.

Wicked Saddam authorized that wilful destruction with the intention that the Kurds would have nothing to return to.

But the refugees did not know what had happened after they ran from their homeland. News of the outside world was kept from the camp refugees. Perhaps there are times when ignorance is for the best.

To turn their minds to other matters, Sarbast and I began asking about Auntie Aisha. 'My aunt is Aisha Hassoon Aziz. She moved from Sulaimaniya a few years ago, to be close to the shrine. Her grand-daughter Rezan was living with her shortly before the attack. Rezan was away on the day the chemicals were dropped. She was spared the assault.'

I was not surprised to learn that Auntie Aisha was popular and well-known in Halabja. Nearly everyone claimed to have heard of her. She was quite famous, in fact, a virtuous Halabja resident, making such an impression that word had spread through the community of her goodness.

When Sarbast gravitated towards the men, I turned to talk to the women, telling them about Auntie Aisha and hoping for some firm news of her whereabouts.

One woman named Jamila, who was elderly and so skinny that her face was virtually concave, said loudly, 'Aisha Hassoon Aziz's reputation was as pure as the saints she revered. Her acts of goodness were numberless.' Her brow wrinkled. 'I believe that she was chosen to read the Koran at the gathering of the women during the Eid Al-Mawlid Al-Nabawi.'

I nodded eagerly, familiar with the annual celebration of the Prophet's birth. I even remembered a time when Auntie Aisha had led the females in our family during the ceremony. I was only a young girl, but I had been mesmerized by the magic of the evening. Auntie Aisha had sat with her back to the wall, chanting songs praising the Prophet. As she chanted, she lightly shook a leather tambourine. Afterwards, a feast was served. The dishes were spread out on a colourful carpet laid out on the floor and I distinctly recalled a whole lamb stuffed with rice, lots of vegetables, delicious minced meats and every kind of fruit.

Jamila continued, 'She took care of the poor, your aunt.' She glanced around, a glint of excitement in her dark expressive eyes. 'You say that Aisha Hassoon Aziz is in this camp?'

'I hope so,' I replied. 'She did not go to Sulaimaniya, where we would have expected her to flee. Now her son and daughters can't find her.'

By this time more refugees had gathered round us, for news that PUK *peshmerga* were in the camp had gone round rapidly. The PUK was much admired in Halabja. The conversation rapidly swung from Auntie Aisha to the mass murder of Kurds and the flight of the refugees, and then back again to Auntie Aisha and again to the dark tragedy they were living.

'How can Saddam kill women and children?' muttered one young woman who was cuddling a tiny baby. Someone whispered to me that the baby had been born early during the shock of the exodus. Without medical care, it was not expected to live.

The aged Jamila snorted, slapping her hands together. 'When a cat wants to eat her kittens, she says they look like mice!'

Three or four cute teenage girls jostled each other, smiling at the old woman's witty remark.

My eyes could not avoid the suffering of the children. Almost every woman was holding a child. They all bore visible wounds.

A fussy toddler continually rubbed her eyes, which were oozing thick mucus.

A waif-like little boy complained, 'My feet, Mummy.' His mother held them high so that I could see his wounds. The soles of his little feet bore inflamed cuts. She explained, 'There was broken glass on the roads. There were so many little feet freely bleeding that when we got to the mountain snow, it turned pink.'

Another small face was furrowed with infected blisters.

The smallest of the children wheezed and struggled for breath. Her lungs had been affected by the poisonous gas.

A mother with thin black hair robotically reported, 'My husband died last month during a raid. When the chemical attack came I had to leave three of my five children. I only had two arms. I could only carry one child in each arm. The other three could not keep up. I will never forget their screams as they pleaded with me not to leave them behind.'

One particularly sad-faced woman said dreamily, 'I left my baby on the mountain. He was dying from the gases. I had to save my other children. When I laid him on a flat stone, he opened his little eyes and stared at me as though he knew his fate.' Her brown eyes were dulled and her long fingers fluttered around her head. When she began sobbing loudly, two of the teenage girls led her away.

Every refugee had a tragic story to tell. Faces and stories began to merge. I was robbed of any idea of a response. What could I say? There were no words. What could I do? I had no resources, no way of helping those helpless women. When I brushed away my tears, the old woman, Jamila, patted my stomach and announced, 'Kurdish wombs will have to make up the loss.'

I was jolted by her insight, her remark prompting memories of Auntie Aisha, who always knew what was in my mind and in my heart.

Sarbast, unaware of the solemn turn the women's conversation had taken, tapped me on my arm. 'Joanna, you need to hear this. Come.'

I nodded to the women and edged away to listen to a man with thick features and a moustache framing thin lips. He was describing a sight he had seen. 'After the gases in Halabja had cleared, and before the army bulldozers came, I slipped back to my neighbourhood to find my wife and three daughters. I found them. They were all dead in the house. Praise Allah, I had taken my two sons with me for the day, so they were spared. After burying my wife and daughters I took the time to check houses in our neighbourhood. Aisha Hassoon Aziz lived near by. I called out her name. Like this,' and he cupped his hands around his mouth and opened it so wide that he exposed his stained and broken teeth. 'Lady Aisha Hassoon Aziz!' I then called out her granddaughter's name. No one answered. The house was unlocked, so I walked through the rooms. When I stepped out of the back door I saw her. She had been praying in the back garden and she had collapsed on her prayer rug.'

'No!' I cried. 'No!'

Startled by my outburst, the man looked at Sarbast for guidance on whether he should continue.

'Go ahead,' Sarbast said, patting me on the back.

I hunched forward. 'Tell me only this: was she alive?'

The man answered quickly and decisively. 'No. She had been dead for a day or more by then.'

I could not absorb the words I was hearing. Perhaps the man was mistaken. Why would she go into the garden to pray during a gas attack? But with a sudden flash of insight, I knew that the man was exactly describing Auntie Aisha's reaction to the chaos. Of course she would have turned to prayer at the moment of greatest danger. While everyone else was rushing to survive, she instinctively turned to God.

I was struck with a sorrowful certainty that he was telling the truth: that indeed the woman he was describing was Auntie Aisha.

I had a flash of joy that Rezan had not been at home. She was alive and well, thank God.

'I wanted to bury her, but I was afraid to wait much longer. I covered her up with two or three prayer rugs I found inside her house. When I returned several days later, I saw that someone else had buried your aunt in her garden. At the time there were groups going around the city, burying the dead before the enemy soldiers had a chance to desecrate the bodies.' He repeated, 'She was buried in her garden. I am certain of it. There was a new grave next to where I had left her.'

There was nothing else for the man to say.

I sat. Numbness crept through my body. Auntie Aisha was dead.

And I knew who had murdered her. Ali Al-Majid, fulfilling the wishes of his cousin Saddam Hussein, was the man responsible for the deaths of many thousands of innocent people, one of whom was my saintly Auntie Aisha.

Sarbast and I made our way from the camp back to Saqqez. I fretted endlessly about how I would notify Auntie Aisha's four children of her demise. Making telephone calls was expensive and difficult. A letter would be too cold and impersonal. What about Mother? She would be stricken by the news. Finally I got a call through to my brother Ra'ad. He was the one who shared the bitter news.

My only comfort was knowing that Auntie Aisha went to God doing what she loved best, praising and honouring Him. As for her appearance in Bergalou, it was a mystery that I would never solve.

In the weeks following I could not get out of bed. At first my lethargic state was blamed on depression brought on by the loss of Auntie Aisha, but I felt so ill that Sarbast and I finally concluded that I had food poisoning. Nothing I ate would stay down. Knowing that we were set to leave Saqqez soon and understanding that Sarbast was looking for any excuse to leave me behind, I went to a doctor to request medicine to ease my violent nausea.

That's when I discovered the news that threw our life plans into a tangle. I was pregnant. The lady doctor said that there was no doubt. I was going to have a child. In less than eight months Sarbast and I would be parents.

Suddenly I remembered the old woman in the camp and her penetrating look into the future: 'Kurdish wombs will have to make up the loss.'

I wept with joy.

24

Kosha, Child of My Heart

Saqqez, Iran
8 May 1989

I was sleeping soundly when I was stirred by abdominal pains so sharp that I found myself hunched over in the middle of our small bedroom, incapable of recalling how I got there. My breath was shallow and fitful as I waited to see what would happen next. To my misery, the pain soon struck a second time. I gasped loudly, cupping my hands over my protruding belly.

I looked at Sarbast. He was snoring.

I had spent most of my pregnancy alone in Saqqez. Sarbast was off fighting our enemy in Kurdistan, but he had made arrangements to be with me as my pregnancy progressed. We were uncertain of my exact due date. I had only seen a doctor once, the lady doctor who had told me of my pregnancy. Since that visit, I had studied the calendar on my own, guessing when our child might be born. Kurdish refugees, even pregnant *peshmerga* refugees, were not provided with Iranian medical care. Without money to spend on medical services, I could only hope and pray that our child would be born without complications.

For the third time pain radiated from my back and lower abdomen throughout my body. Something was dreadfully wrong. I stumbled to Sarbast, pulling on his shoulder. 'Sarbast, wake up.'

Sarbast's warrior reflexes were sudden and sure. His eyes shot open and he automatically reached for his weapon on the floor, his full attention directed to the only entrance to the room. When he saw there were no intruders, he looked at me. 'What? What?'

'Sarbast, I am very sick. I am having terrible pains.'

'It was the milk,' Sarbast replied with quick certainty. 'You didn't boil it long enough. You have milk poisoning again.'

I considered what he was saying. Believing that I needed a lot of milk, I had been drinking large quantities of Iranian milk lately. It had to be boiled before drinking. On several occasions I had miscalculated the length of time necessary to make the milk safe, and I had become violently ill.

Actually, I had been sick for most of my pregnancy, unable to keep down most foods and liquids. Even the smell of food made me gag. Often the odour of food prepared on the hotplate in our one room would drive me outside. To help keep it down, I was forced to eat my meal on the porch. I could eat only small amounts and although pregnant I was very skinny. A small bump was the only proof that our family was about to increase. Few people believed that I was nearly nine months into my pregnancy.

After discovering my condition, and remembering the serious consequences of the journey from Merge to Dohlakoga, I had agreed with Sarbast that it was too risky for me to accompany him into Kurdistan. I must keep our unborn child safe. My landlady, the wonderful Shamsa, had become a friend and, because Sarbast was away much of the time, proved a marvellous support. No longer aloof, she had grown to love me, and she expressed her affection by preparing special soups and Iranian rice and vegetable dishes, encouraging me to eat.

Although no one could ever replace my mother, Shamsa had become a very good substitute.

Sarbast was staring at me.

'Sarbast? I am having severe stomach pains. What should I do?'

'Come back to bed. It is only the milk. You will feel better in the morning.'

I turned on the light and looked at my watch. It was four in the morning. Everyone would be asleep. He was right. I would be better in the morning. I dragged myself to the bed.

Sarbast pulled the cover up to my chin. 'You will be OK, darling. Go back to sleep.' He turned away, his voice muffled. 'Wake me again if you need me.'

Sarbast, who after ten years of the fighter's life was accustomed to sleeping on hard ground, quickly fell into a deep sleep on our cotton mattress.

The pains failed to cease. In fact, they increased in intensity and frequency. I knew nothing of what to expect in a pregnancy, but something was starting to tell me that my pains had nothing to do with milk poisoning.

The pains increased in severity until I could no longer remain in bed. I got up and began to pace. Sarbast did not hear me. Two hours later I became frightened and decided to go to Shamsa. She would know what to do.

There were two floors to Shamsa's small home. She rented out the downstairs and lived on the upper floor. Her husband had died years before, leaving her with five children. Two of her daughters were married and her two sons lived at home while attending university. Her youngest child, a daughter who was seventeen years old; was still at school.

I knocked on her door and stumbled into the room at her command.

Before I could speak, Shamsa gave me a single glance and declared, 'You are having the baby.'

'No. No. I have milk poisoning.'

'No, my daughter, you are having the baby.'

I stood frozen to the spot, suddenly terrified. I knew nothing of babies. What had I done? I should have guarded more carefully against pregnancy, at least until I could be with my mother.

Shamsa was all business, giving instructions to her children before grasping my arm and leading me downstairs. 'Where is Sarbast?'

'He is asleep.'

'Wake him. Tell him that we need to go to the hospital, now. While I get ready, you take a quick bath.'

I nodded numbly. I had never been more frightened in my life. I was ill prepared in every way. I had nothing ready for the baby. Although Shamsa and I had been knitting some tiny clothes, nothing was finished. It had all seemed a game, a preparation for a doll, but suddenly the truth dawned: soon a helpless baby would be living with us. I rushed about, confusion mounting. I called out, 'Sarbast! Get up! Get up! I'm having the baby.'

The cover was over his head. A muffled voice came from underneath. 'It's the milk.'

'No, Sarbast! Shamsa says the baby is coming.'

Sarbast sprang to his feet. He scrambled to find a clean shirt and trousers while I took a cold bath. There was no hot water in Shamsa's home. Iranian homes were not equipped for bathing, but there was a huge marble Turkish bath in the city centre. There were rooms for families, rooms for women and rooms for men. Sarbast and I had often used the family bath, enjoying the luxury of the plentiful hot water and the luxurious accommodation. The one thing I had enjoyed about living in Iran was that Turkish bathhouse. But there was no time for a hot bath that morning.

We left in a rush, taking nothing with us. The hospital was an agonizing thirty-minute walk from Shamsa's home and despite being in the middle of labour I was going to have to walk every step. The unrelenting birth pains were so agonizing that I felt a primitive urge to lie down on the pavement and let nature take its course. But I knew I could not. I must get to the hospital to make certain my baby was safely delivered.

And so, once again in my life, I found that there was nothing else to do but soldier on.

I knew nothing of the torment awaiting me.

The pains were so intense that I had to stop walking during every contraction. I stopped, held my breath and braced myself against the buildings on the street. Trying to stifle fully-fledged screams that might bring the police, I groaned instead. Sarbast and Shamsa were helpless bystanders and our odd trio received many stares.

We finally arrived at the local hospital. It was no surprise to discover that I was not welcome there. Although Shamsa said to the admissions clerk, 'My daughter is having a baby,' they soon discovered that I was a refugee, and by that time the Iranians had wearied of Iraqi refugees. We refugees were enemies in their minds, people who were using up medical services needed for their own people.

Nevertheless, a nurse was called to guide us to the delivery wards. I received a shock when she told Sarbast that he could not accompany me. 'No,' she said. 'Men are not allowed in the maternity ward.'

I looked anxiously at Sarbast. It was the most pivotal event of our lives and I wanted us to share it. Besides, I was frightened. I did not want to be alone.

When Sarbast saw my look of despair, he became forceful. 'I must be with her. This is our first child. My wife needs me.'

The nurse's face became a mask of fury. With a heavy neck and a powerful frame, she was a frightening opponent, ready to do battle against any Iraqi *peshmerga*. She glared at me, and then at Sarbast. 'No, it is the rules. Go and stand behind that mesh.' She gestured behind us.

Sarbast and I both turned to look. Heavy wire mesh from ceiling to floor divided the large room and behind it was a waiting area. Were husbands in waiting considered wild animals in that hospital?

Helpless in the face of such an overpowering personality, I said to Sarbast, 'Wait there. It's all right. Shamsa will be with me.'

The nurse then turned to Shamsa, gruffly demanding, 'Where are her things?'

'I have nothing,' I stammered.

The nurse ordered Shamsa, 'Go and get her a gown and clothing for the baby. We do not supply those items.'

With tears in my eyes, I watched as Sarbast dutifully went away to stand behind the mesh. Shamsa followed him.

Terrified, I trailed behind the inhospitable nurse, making the loneliest walk of my life. I doubt I would have been more miserable if I had been told I was being led to my grave.

I was admitted to a ward where other women were waiting to have their babies. I was informed that there was no doctor available to deliver my baby, but I would be provided with a midwife or a nurse, according to the difficulty of the labour. Without a comforting word, I was put to bed and told that I would be taken into the delivery room when the time came.

Everything was wrong. Never had I felt so vulnerable. The pain was unrelenting. I was the youngest child in our family and had foolishly paid no attention to the business of childbirth. I was the most uninformed woman in the world about what was coming. My ignorance made me frightened.

I was on my own at a time when I needed my mother or my sisters. Tears of fear and loneliness rolled down my face.

I wanted my mother! I turned my head and faced the wall, sobbing, 'Mother.'

A voice near by responded. 'Child, what are you doing here alone?'

I opened my eyes to see a friendly face, a middle-aged Iranian Kurdish woman. 'You are such a sad little thing. This is a happy occasion.' She glanced around the room. 'Where are your sisters? Where is your mother?'

'I am a refugee,' I confessed tearfully. 'I am alone.'

That kindly woman was overweight in a cuddly sort of way. I smiled through my tears as she leaned towards me. 'Hug me, child. Pretend I am your mother.'

And I did.

That lovely lady spent the next few hours darting between my bed and her daughter's.

Around ten in the morning, a grim-faced midwife came to take me away, saying, 'It is time.'

Along with my fear of what was about to happen, I felt a rush of doubt. How could she know it was time? No one had come to examine me.

My sweet companion hugged me goodbye, whispering, 'It will be over soon. And when they place your little son or daughter in your arms, that baby will become your whole heart.'

The next stop was a chamber of horrors. I was told to climb on to a wooden birthing table. It was so narrow that I was in danger of falling off on to the concrete floor. I could not lose myself in contractions for fear I would lose my balance.

Every moment of the birth was a nightmare. I was in a delirium of pain, but I was given nothing to relieve it. There was no attempt to calm me. There was no sympathy, no care. With brusque incompetence, someone roughly pulled my child from my body before he was ready to appear. I was screaming and so was my child.

I heard my child!

Then, just when I was sinking to a murky place I feared I might never leave, I heard Shamsa's voice. Oh, the joy! She had been allowed into the delivery room. She clasped my hands and spoke soothingly. 'It is over. You have a son, Joanna. You have a son.'

I was too shattered to understand the significance of what had happened.

While a nurse cleaned my son and wrapped him in a blanket, the midwife stitched my torn body. Claiming 'There is no topical anaesthesia available for Iraqis,' she stitched mercilessly, suturing as if stabbing me, with a sort of angry joy. When I cried out, she jabbed harder. I whimpered, pleading for her to be gentle, but she ignored my pleas.

The torture seemed endless, but finally it was over.

And then I saw my son.

He was so beautiful. I could not stop staring at his tiny oval face. His adorable eyes were large and dark. His slender nose and full lips reminded me of Sarbast. His dark hair lay smooth as if it had been combed.

Shamsa held him close to my face and I breathed in his baby smell. My eyes clouded.

I looked at Shamsa and said with delight, 'I am a mother.'

Several hours later I insisted on showing Sarbast our son. I could not wait until the following day for him to see the little miracle that had come into our lives. Gloomy Sarbast was still behind the wire mesh, Shamsa told me with a little chuckle. There were no wheelchairs for Iraqi refugees, so I limped stiffly down the long corridor while Shamsa cradled my son in her capable arms.

Sarbast slowly came into view, his fingers clutching the wire. His eyes were on me.

I stepped as close as the wire would allow. My voice was breathless. 'Look, Sarbast. Look at your son.'

Sarbast's glittering eyes fixed on his son. His face broke into a smile. 'Kosha,' he said.

For the past few months Sarbast and I had searched for the perfect name. We had decided that if our child was a son, we would name him Kosha, which means 'struggler' in our Kurdish language.

'Kosha,' Sarbast repeated.

I stared at our little struggler, our little Kosha, who already had my whole heart.

But Kosha seemed to resent our absolute adoration. He opened his mouth and produced a cry of protest.

We laughed with complete happiness. Our son was perfect.

Sarbast turned back to me, smiling with pride and joy. 'You've done it. You've done it, Joanna.'

'Yes,' I replied, 'we have done it in the end. We triumphed.'

And we had. We had been hunted like animals, but we had fought to survive. Although Kurdistan was in disarray, and Kurds by the thousands had died while we lived, we would regroup, and we would return. The Kurdish dream would live on.

Kurdish wombs had already started making up for the loss of life.

Epilogue

Freedom

20 July 1989

At immigration control at Heathrow airport, Sarbast turned to face me, a small smile of triumph on his face. His eyes met mine as he gave a quick nod of his head. Without saying anything, he began to stoop and gather up our few belongings.

My knees were as weak as my nerves. I felt my legs trembling beneath the folds of my skirt. I could barely stand.

Sarbast was the most persuasive man in the world. To my amazement, his words had prevailed with the sombre-faced immigration officer. We would not be turned away and placed on the next flight to Damascus, where we had arrived from. We would not be arrested and put in prison. We had been accepted as refugees, seeking asylum in the UK. Sarbast and I, with our baby son Kosha, could enter England freely, and would be given help and support while we applied for legal residency.

We really were safe, removed for ever from the chemical weapons of Saddam Hussein, free from the gloomy refugee life in Iran and far away from bullying Syrian officials. We were in England. In England we could create a new beginning. In England we could live safely. In England we could raise our precious son.

I looked into Kosha's little face and tightened my hold. The enormity of the moment caused me to weep. I sobbed in happiness.

We were the lucky ones.

My darling Sarbast looked so worn and weary. During nearly three years of married life, we had lived through more troubles than most couples married for fifty or sixty years do. Yet those trials and tribulations had made us so close that I knew that even if I lived for another hundred years Sarbast was the only person in the world who would perfectly understand my every thought and my every emotion. He had shared my every grief, and even at that moment I knew he was missing the same people I missed, and, like me, was still dreaming of our beautiful Kurdistan.

I was amazed by the kindness shown by the immigration officials at Heathrow. They rallied round, arranging accommodation and food, providing us with money and even offering legal assistance to help us attain legal status. After years of dealing with Iraqi government officials who routinely harassed us, even if they didn't want to murder us, I simply couldn't believe the compassion of those strangers.

My thoughts drifted back to one of the happiest days of my life, the day when I had travelled from Qalat Diza to Merge to greet my new husband. How could I have known then the tears in the making inside me, the countless tears that were still to be wept? I was so young and in love that I had truly believed that dreams come true, that our battles would be won and that our sacrifices would produce the greatest victory: freedom for Kurds.

But Kurdistan was not free, and so many who had loved Kurdistan's mountain ranges were now dead or living as unwelcome refugees in foreign lands.

I had finally come to realize that even if Saddam succeeded in massacring every living Kurd, the world was never going to take notice. Saddam was the darling of the Reagan administration and his genocide of nearly a hundred thousand Kurds had been virtually ignored.

Like Sarbast, I could have endured the refugee life for ever, but motherhood changes everything for a woman. After bringing Kosha into our world, my husband and I finally agreed that we should leave the area and seek a new life in a country where we could raise our children safely.

My brother Ra'ad helped us. He sent money for us to pay for our passports and bribe officials in Iran and later in Syria. Without him, Sarbast, Kosha and I would have ended up refugees in a tent city, like those we had visited in the camp for Halabja survivors, for with the nearly total defeat of the PUK, there was nowhere in the area left to run. After the war between Iran and Iraq had ended, Iraqi Kurdish refugees became a festering sore for Iran and were no longer welcome there. Nor was it possible to return to Iraq to live: it was more than likely that Sarbast would have been executed and I would have been imprisoned. Our new-born son would not have survived.

In a world so corrupt, money can solve most official problems. With Ra'ad's generous help, Sarbast had managed to arrange some papers, and we left Saqqez and travelled to Tehran, taking the first flight we could get out of Iran. From there our plan was to work our way to any country that was accepting Kurdish refugees. I had to fight hysteria when I discovered that we were heading for Syria, yet another Baathist country. Although Sarbast stoically assured me that we could handle the situation, I could think of nothing but the dour Baathist faces I knew we would face upon arrival.

To my despair, I was right to worry. The Syrian officials who met us at the airport were furious to see Iraqi Kurds. Suspicious eyes lingered over our documents and passports, and we were abruptly pulled from the immigration line and refused entry into Syria. We were put into isolation in a primitive shelter under the airport terminal. If we didn't like it, we could go to jail. There were other Kurdish travellers locked up with us, but I was in such a fog of worry that to this day every traveller's face sharing our bleak plight remains blank, every conversation heard forgotten.

I was worried, too, about the lack of water and food. Our bags were confiscated, and I had only two spare nappies for my son. Too soon those nappies were both dirty. My two bottles of milk for Kosha were soon gone too. He screamed with hunger. After twenty-four hours we were taken away in a police car to a police station in Damascus, where we were to be interrogated. There was an under-lying threat that we would be turned over to the Iraqi government and sent back to certain death.

When I requested milk for my hungry son and was given water instead, the act seemed so callous it triggered a wild rage that burst from me in a mighty roar. Everyone around was startled by my outburst. Sarbast urged me to control myself, but I could not, feeling wild and strong and capable of slaying them all. As I was screaming insults, I suddenly realized that my outrage had changed the officials' attitude. Suddenly we were welcome guests, and we were taken from the police station to an apartment in Damascus and given assistance.

For two weeks I refused to leave that apartment. I saw nothing of the ancient city, wanting only to flee from a world where Baathists ruled. While I guarded my son, Sarbast set about obtaining forged papers and tickets, and arranged a direct flight to England. My new passport claimed that I was a citizen of the United Arab Emirates. Unable to organize British visas, we decided to leave Syria anyhow and to throw ourselves on the mercy of the British immigration officials.

Feeling like criminals, we were so nervous as we boarded the flight from Damascus to London that we could barely speak. I was certain that at any moment we would be pulled from the plane and forced on to the next flight to Baghdad.

I was so paranoid that when the aeroplane made an unscheduled stop in Cyprus, I convinced myself that our illegal status was the cause. After disembarking, all passengers were told that we would be there for ten hours. We were encouraged to leave the airport and visit the pretty little island. But I refused to budge from the terminal. I would do nothing that required exit and entry through yet another immigration office.

This time my worry was unjustified. We boarded without mishap, and the plane took off. When we finally entered the customs area at Heathrow airport, my heart was in my throat as I watched Sarbast step forward to the desk. He explained our predicament, confessed that we had fake documents and asked for political asylum on the grounds that we would certainly be murdered if we were forced to return to face Saddam and his Baathists in Iraq.

I remember little of that first night in England. Sarbast and I were both so exhausted from our long journey to freedom that we barely spoke. Our only concern was for the comfort of Kosha, who was understandably crying and fussy.

The following morning I woke early. I stared up at the dingy ceiling of the hotel room generously provided by the immigration officials until we could find an apartment. I was looking forward to having a place of my own, something better than a single room and without a ceiling stained brown by years of smoke and grime. The ceiling was symbolic of my own life, I decided. I, too, was once young, fresh and beautiful, but the past few years had aged me and toughened me. But we had been reprieved. We found ourselves suddenly free in a country where you weren't in danger of being taken away to be shot for the crime of being born Kurd.

I quietly turned my head and stared at the face of the man I loved more than my own life. My heart tightened with sadness. Sarbast's face was so weary-looking, even in deep slumber, but at least for the first time since we started our journey he seemed not to be enduring nightmares. There would, I hoped, be many restful nights to come. A warrior since he was a young man, perhaps Sarbast could finally heal in England.

Through the thin door I heard the muted sounds of laughing children running along the hotel corridor, fortunate children who had never known the fright caused by crashing bombs or booming artillery, or the horror of having to run away from one's home in the dark of night. I turned to stare at the cot beside our bed and watched the sweet face of little Kosha, out of physical danger for the first time in his life.

I quietly eased myself from the bed, lightly touching Sarbast's cheek, and walked over to kiss and then cover little Kosha's tiny pink feet. Then I went to the window and peered out from behind the heavy curtain. I took a few quiet moments to gaze into the distance, seeing the diminutive gardens of several English homes.

Would Sarbast and I one day have such a garden? How difficult would it be to leave behind the chaos of our life as freedom fighters and live a normal life? For years we had lived as beautiful butterflies, our wings pulsing with Kurdish passion. Could we really become a settled, refined English couple?

After taking a heartfelt sigh, I walked to a small desk wedged against the wall and settled into a wooden chair. I took a cheap piece of hotel stationery and stared at the blank page for many long moments.

Then I wrote down words that were too good to be true: 'Sarbast, Joanna and Kosha Hussain are free.'

We are free!

Appendix I: Glossary of Names and Places

Abu Ghraib prison: notorious prison complex in Iraq that was built by the British in the early 1960s and became known as the place where Saddam Hussein's government tortured and executed dissidents. Joanna's brother was imprisoned there. The prison gained worldwide notoriety when it became the site used by the American forces to torture Iraqis.

Ahvaz: Iranian city on the banks of the Karun River. It was the site of some of the most vicious battles during the Iran–Iraq war. Joanna's brother fought in the Iraqi trenches outside Ahvaz for many months and was nearly killed there.

Al-Anfal campaign: meaning 'the Spoils', this is the name of the eighth *sura* of the Koran. It is also the name given by the Iraqi government to the anti-Kurdish military campaign that lasted from 23 February to 6 September 1988. Ali Hassan Al-Majid, Saddam Hussein's cousin, was the overlord of this Kurdish genocide.

Al-Askari, Jafar Pasha (1895–1936): Joanna's paternal great-uncle. From a prominent Baghdad family, during the First World War he served with Prince Faisal and Lawrence of Arabia in command of the Hijaz regular troops. After the First World War he served in many government posts, including those of Minister to Great Britain, Minister of Defence and Prime Minister. He arranged for Joanna's father to be educated in France, and was assassinated in 1936.

Al-Bakir, Ahmed Hassan (1914–82): Baathist President of Iraq from 1968 to 1979 and a cousin of Saddam Hussein, who succeeded him in 1979.

Al-Dawa party: formed in Iraq in the late 1950s by a group of Shiite leaders to combat Baathist socialism, secularism and communism. It became more prominent in the 1970s and waged armed combat against the Baathist government.

Al-Majid, Ali Hassan (1941–): first cousin of Saddam Hussein. He led the violent repression against the Shiite and Kurdish rebellions and was given the name Chemical Ali for his role in the Al-Anfal campaign against the Iraqi Kurds. At the time of writing this book he was being tried for his role in that campaign and for other war crimes he is accused of committing.

Ayatollah Ruhollah Khomeini (1900–89): religious leader of the Shiite Muslim sect who was instrumental in overthrowing the Shah of Iran in 1979. He led Iran during the eight-year Iran–Iraq war.

Baath: the Arab Baath Socialist Resurrection party was formed on 7 April 1947 by Michel Aflaq and Salah ad-Din Al-Bitar, two Syrian university students. The Baath party still rules in Syria. The Baath party in Iraq was toppled in 2003 when coalition forces overthrew Saddam Hussein's government.

Baath Socialist party, Iraq: secretly founded in 1950. Its followers overthrew the Iraqi government in 1963. Out of power only nine months later, the Baathist party came back in 1968 and remained in power in Iraq until 2003.

Baghdad: capital city of Iraq, situated by the Tigris River. Baghdad was once considered the heart of the Arab empire and was second only to Constantinople during the city's golden age from 638 to 1100 CE, when Baghdad flourished as a centre of learning, philosophy and commerce.

Barzani, Mullah Mustafa (1903–79): Kurdish nationalist leader and President of the Kurdistan Democratic party.

Barzinji, Sheikh Mahmud (d. 1956): revered Kurdish leader who opposed the British, declaring himself King of Kurdistan.

Faisal I (1885–1933): third son of the first King of Hijaz (modern-day Saudi Arabia). Faisal fought against the Ottoman empire with T. E. Lawrence (Lawrence of Arabia). He became King of Syria and King of Iraq after the First World War and the defeat of the Ottomans, and was succeeded by his son Ghazi.

Faisal II (1935–58): the only son of Ghazi I, he was four years old when his father died in a car accident. He was assassinated on 14 July 1958 in the rebellion that caused the destruction of the furniture factory owned by Joanna's father.

Halabja: Kurdish town in the northern province of Sulaimaniya near the Iranian border. It became famous after the 16 March 1988 chemical attack, the largest-scale chemical weapons attack against a civilian population in modern times, which caused the deaths of five thousand men, women and children. The town was later destroyed by Saddam Hussein's forces, but has since been rebuilt.

Hussein, Saddam (1937–): son of a landless peasant who died before his birth, Saddam was raised by his uncle, rose to power through the Baathist party and became the President of Iraq in 1979. At the time of writing this book, Saddam was on trial in Baghdad, charged with atrocities including the Kurdish massacres of 1988. An Iraqi special tribunal convicted Saddam of crimes against humanity for the execution of 148 men and boys from the Shiite town of Dujail, thirty-five miles north of Baghdad.

Iraq, Republic of: Middle Eastern country that shares borders with Turkey to the north, Iran to the east, Syria to the north-west, Jordan to the west, and Kuwait and Saudi Arabia to the south. Modern-day Iraq was created in 1923 at a European Convention led by the British and French.

Iran: Islamic Republic of Iran, formerly known as Persia.

Jafati valley: mountainous region in north-east Iraq where the PUK located its command centre.

jahsh: Kurdish informers working for the Iraqi authorities.

Kandil mountain: highest mountain in Iraq.

Kurdistan ('the land of the Kurds'): an area of northern Iraq, southern Turkey, western Iran and north-east Syria. After the First World War, the Western powers promised the Kurds an independent state. This failed to materialize, and since that time Kurds have continued to seek independence, but their cries for freedom have been rejected time and again. At the time of writing, after the overthrow of Saddam Hussein, the Kurds of Iraq enjoy almost complete autonomy and the Kurdish region of Iraq is prospering.

Kurdistan Democratic Party (KDP): formed in 1946 and led by Massoud Barzani. It is a military tribal group. In the 1970s a member of the KDP, Jalal Talabani, broke off and formed a rival party, the Patriotic Union of Kurdistan (PUK).

Kurds: a distinct group from the Arabs, Turks and Persians, the Kurds are estimated to number thirty million and inhabit areas in Syria, Iran, Turkey and Iraq.

Mesopotamia: Greek term meaning 'the land between the rivers', including the area between the Euphrates and Tigris Rivers. Early civilization emerged in this area, which is known today as Iraq.

Patriotic Union of Kurdistan (PUK): founded in 1975, a break-away from the KDP, by Jalal Talabani who, in 2006, is the President of Iraq.

*peshmerga***:** literally meaning 'one who faces death', the term describes the Kurdish resistance fighters. As of January 2005, it is estimated that there were 80,000 Iraqi *peshmerga* in northern Iraq, the only militia not prohibited by the present Iraqi government.

Shatt Al-Arab: waterway created by the joining of the Rivers Euphrates and Tigris. It flows into the Persian Gulf.

Shiite: Islamic sect at odds with the Sunni Islamic sect over the successor to the Prophet Muhammad. In Iraq, the Shiite are in the majority.

Sulaimaniya: Kurdish city in northern Iraq, birthplace of Joanna's mother.

Sunni: worldwide, the leading Islamic sect in terms of numbers. In Iraq, however, the Sunni are in the minority. Joanna's family were Sunni Muslims.

Talabani, Jalal (1933–), President of Iraq: Born in Kelkan, Iraqi Kurdistan, and a graduate of Baghdad University law school, he is a secularist politician who has sought democracy and equality for women. He founded the PUK in 1975. In 1988, when Saddam Hussein's government used chemical weapons against the Kurds, he and his PUK fighters were forced to seek safety in Iran. After the 1991 Gulf War the PUK's influence was restored and in 2003, when Saddam was ousted, Talabani's progressive politics and affable personality gained him the presidency.

Tigris: one of two main rivers in Iraq, it flows through Baghdad.

Appendix II: A Chronology of Key Events Affecting Modern-day Iraqi Kurds

1918: The Ottoman Empire is defeated. British forces occupy Iraq, bringing Kurdish populated areas under British control. When the Kurds rebel, Winston Churchill orders the Royal Air Force to drop chemicals.

1919: Kurdish areas are added to the new Iraqi state, which comes under a British mandate.

1920: The Treaty of Sèvres provides for a Kurdish state, subject to the agreement of the League of Nations.

1921: Faisal is crowned King of Iraq, including Kurdish areas.

1923: Sheikh Mahmud Barzinji rebels against the new Iraqi government and declares a Kurdish kingdom.

1923: The Treaty of Sèvres fails to be ratified by the Turkish parliament.

1924: In rebellion against the new Iraqi government backed by the British, Sulaimaniya falls.

1932: Another Kurdish rebellion. Kurdish demands for autonomy are refused.

1943: Another Kurdish rebellion. This one is more successful, with the Kurdish fighters gaining large areas of territory.

1946: Barzani forms the Kurdistan Democratic Party (KDP), a tribally based Kurdish political party.

1946: The British RAF bombs Kurdish forces. Kurdish fighters flee into Iran, seeking exile.

1946: Barzani has to flee to Iran over a dispute with Iranian forces. He seeks exile in the Soviet Union.

1951: Barzani is elected President of the KDP, even though he is still in exile.

1958: Barzani returns from exile after the Iraqi monarchy is overthrown. The new Iraqi government recognizes Kurdish national rights.

1961: Jalal Talabani (b. 1933) becomes the face of Kurdish revolt after leading a Kurdish rebellion. The Iraqi government dissolves the KDP.

1963: Baathist coup succeeds but is overthrown nine months later.

1968: Baathists return to power with Saddam Hussein second-in-command.

1970: The Iraqi government and the Kurdish political parties agree to a peace accord which grants the Kurds autonomy.

1971: Peace between the Iraqi government and the KDP becomes strained.

1974: Barzani calls for a new rebellion after rejecting the autonomy agreement.

1975: Talabani organizes a new Kurdish political party, the Patriotic Union of Kurdistan (PUK). The Algiers Accord between Iran and Iraq ends Iranian support for the Iraqi Kurds.

1978: Talabani's PUK and Barzani's KDP clash, leaving many Kurdish fighters dead.

1979: Barzani dies. His son, Massoud Barzani, assumes leadership of the KDP and rules to this day.

1979: Saddam Hussein replaces al-Bakir as President of Iraq.

1980: Iraq attacks Iran. War breaks out.

1983: The PUK agrees to a ceasefire with the Iraqi government. Talks on Kurdish autonomy begin.

1985: The Iraqi government becomes increasingly repressive to Kurds. Talks break down. Iraqi government militia murder the brother and two nieces of Talabani.

1986: Kurdish fighters from the KDP and PUK join forces with the Iranian government against the Iraqi government.

1987: The Iraqi military uses chemical weapons against Kurdish fighters.

1988: The Iraqi military launches the Al-Anfal campaign against the Kurds. Tens of thousands of Kurdish civilians and fighters are killed, and hundreds of thousands are forced into exile in Iran, Turkey and Syria. The town of Halabja becomes the most recognized symbol of the heinous attacks.

1991: After Iraq is expelled from Kuwait, there is a Kurdish uprising. The Iraqi military wages war against the Kurds. Many thousands are killed and over a million are forced into exile, many forced to seek refuge in the mountains.

1991: A no-fly zone is established in northern Iraq to protect the Kurds from Saddam Hussein.

1994: Clashes between the PUK and the KDP turn into civil war.

1996: KDP leader Barzani appeals to Saddam Hussein for help in defeating the PUK.

1996: PUK forces retake Sulaimaniya.

1998: A peace agreement is reached between the PUK and KDP.

2003: Saddam Hussein's government is overthrown by coalition forces. Iraq's Kurdish people are free from government oppression for the first time since Iraq was formed after the First World War. Talabani is appointed a member of the Interim Iraq Governing Council.

2005: PUK leader Jalal Talabani is elected President of Iraq, the first Kurd in history to hold such an important post – a dream come true for all Iraqi Kurds.

Acknowledgements

I would like to thank Ra'ad, Hady, Ranj and Eric for their invaluable assistance.

Ranj, you made enormous efforts to help your Aunt Joanna, and me.

I would also like to thank my nephew, Greg, for always being there and patiently listening to me during many telephone calls during the difficult time of writing. The same goes for my dear friend Danny. And Jack is always there for me.

I would like to thank my Aunt Margaret, and Alece and Anita for their enthusiasm to read everything I write. You'll never know how much your comments spur me on.

This book would have been impossible without the valuable input of my literary agent, Liza Dawson.

I was so exhausted by the end of this process that I really could not have carried on to the finishing line without my British editor, Marianne Velmans, and my American editor, Hana Lane. You are both greatly appreciated.

I thank you all.

Index